IT Consulting Essentials

A Professional Handbook

Dave Faulise

ISBN 978-0-692-81520-5

Table of Contents

Part 1 – Starting and Stopping

Chapter 1 – Critical Thinking

Chapter 2 – Fundamentals

Chapter 3 – Letting Go

Chapter 1 – Critical Thinking

> "To know what you prefer instead of humbly saying 'Amen' to what the world tells you you ought to prefer, is to have kept your soul alive."
> -- Robert Louis Stevenson

It's remarkable how many books there are about consulting. A recent search of the Amazon web site produced over 18,000 titles. Wow! This clearly must be a topic about which more has been written than could possibly be known. While scanning some of the more popular consulting books Amazon carries, I found a fair amount of good information that's consistent with my own experiences as a consultant. I also found many "how to" consulting books that are long on theory but frustratingly short on specifics. There seems to be a real void that needs to be filled. I asked myself what should a book about consulting contain that would be more immediately usable than the material I saw in many of those other books. The answer came from another question: What is most useful when searching for solutions to client problems? What I find most valuable are stories and examples of work products from similar situations.

And that's what I have assembled here: stories and examples. This book contains several of the more useful work products that I've developed, refined, re-used myself, and shared with other consultants to help them help their clients. Seeing an example has always helped me to visualize the target result before I start working toward it. This book also contains accompanying client stories that describe how I created and used many of the examples. As John R, one of my favorite clients would describe it, this book is the "See Spot Run" version of how to create and run a small consulting practice.

As I began assembling material for this book, I asked myself, "Why would you, the reader, want to read this book and use it as a reference source?" As you've already discovered in just a few paragraphs, this is not exciting entertainment. There's no espionage, no murders, and no romance. So what drove you to this particular moment in time when you placed your eyeballs in front of this page?

The obvious assumption is that you're interested in the consulting profession. Either that or you're a friend of mine who feels obligated and is already beginning to regret the commitment to review this work. But if you're not a reluctant friend, and you have a genuine interest, I can make further assumptions about your background. You are probably already a consultant or you are seriously considering getting into the business, and your interest in this book is likely a result of wanting to know more about consulting. Further, I'm going to assume you are:

- Part of (or about to join) a large consulting organization, or
- Starting up your own consulting business, or
- Been at it for a while and curious about another person's experiences.

Structure

Let's save you time in finding information that may be of interest to you. I don't intend for you to read this book from beginning to end, like a novel. Depending on your professional experience and your specific interests, some chapters of the book will be more valuable to you than others. I've structured the material so you can navigate to those more valuable chapters by referring to the Table of Contents and by using the following guiding paragraphs. Here's a summary of the book's organization structure:

- Part 1 - Starting and Stopping: This part contains three chapters that address the thinking behind setting up your own consulting business. There is discussion in this first chapter about the thinking process itself and about how to apply that process to organize and establish a consulting business. There's also a chapter on the inevitable end of your consulting career. Chapters in this part are appropriate if you are considering starting your own business.

- Part 2 - Administration and Finance: This part is about establishing those operational functions that every business must have but that don't add directly to the bottom line, the necessary evils. These include payroll, insurance, legal, tax returns and financial statements. And for those who are eventually successful, there's also a chapter about investing your profits. The three chapters in this part are appropriate if you want to minimize the overhead required to run your own business. Read this part if you want a better understanding of how a professional services firm operates.
- Part 3 - Sales and Marketing: This part talks about how to obtain new business and, more importantly, about how to obtain additional work with existing clients. There is a chapter that addresses contracts and another chapter that talks about the right way to end an engagement. The four chapters in this part are appropriate if you are or plan to be a consultant in a professional services business.
- Part 4 – Execution: This part includes eight chapters that address some of the specific types of consulting engagements I've done. The material includes process guidance, and more importantly, examples of various work products and client deliverables. One or more chapters in this part are appropriate if you want to know how I delivered a particular type of consulting service and you want to see some useful results. I encourage you to resist the temptation to copy the example deliverables I've included, but rather use them as a starting point. Your client organization deserves to have results tailored to fit their unique needs.

Questions

Let's return to an earlier question: "Why are you reading this book?" Don't focus on the answer, but think about the question itself. The question inevitably leads to more questions. What's your background? What issues are you addressing that may be helped by what you find in this book? Are you facing a specific project or problem and searching for possible solutions? Are you looking at longer-term career choices? Why are you considering a consulting career? Why are you working at all? How can you extract some real value from this book that you can use today?

The layering process of questions leading to more questions is intended to result in discovery of fundamental evidence and facts. Most people are familiar with the idea of layered questioning as part of the discipline known as "critical thinking." Critical thinking relies first and foremost on the observation of facts. Accepting facts as they are is fundamental to the consulting profession. Interpretation and analysis of fact-based evidence allow objective explanations and conclusions, which in turn are necessary to form rational client recommendations and to initiate appropriate action. Fact-based analysis may sound easy, but I've observed other consultants who discarded selected facts that did not support their pre-conceived conclusions. To guard against inadvertently falling into this trap of selective blindness, my partners and I have used each other to play devil's advocate when evaluating particularly tricky situations.

My observation is that most business people do in fact use critical thinking, although they might call it by another name or possibly not name it anything at all. A few of my clients like to use the term "drill down" to describe a team's process of looking more deeply into a problem or expanding the details of a solution. This deeper investigation typically leads to the design of concrete solutions that can eventually be implemented as part of an automated system. One client who was considering replacing a number of core technology applications with a single decision management software product, asked me to lead their RFP (Request For Proposal) effort. We decided early in the project to "drill down" deeper into the one-page list of requirements they had assembled before hiring me. The result of our "drill down" exercise was a 22-page requirements definition document that formed the core of the RFP we issued. Our deeper understanding of requirements allowed us to quickly eliminate most of the vendors my client's team had been previously considering and to work more intelligently with the three remaining vendors until we eventually selected the right one.

I've also seen the idea of critical thinking in situations when a team wants to consider more broadly the impacts of a proposal. For example, the marketing department of a financial services company proposed to change how customer buying patterns were analyzed to better predict which products could be more successfully marketed to existing customers. The proposed change would require a restructuring of the customer database; however, the architect and designer of that particular database had long ago left the company, and there was no one in the organization with detail knowledge of the data structures. The operational "opportunity" to damage a technology that had not been touched or changed for half a dozen years clearly outweighed the value of improved customer buying predictability. The team's broader consideration of the proposed change led them to reject it and to recommend instead a re-write of the customer database system as part of the next year's development plan and budget.

I've been fortunate to work with several professionals whom I admire for their critical thinking and perspective. My list includes clients such as Dan B, Steve K, Kari A, John R, Shannon B, Alan C, Kathryn F, Rick G, Jim C, and John H, as well as other consultants such as Henry G, Dick T, Diane N, Bruce O, Dave J and my partners Frank and Mark. For example, John H, the Minneapolis managing partner at Price Waterhouse I worked for in the late 1970's, was an ethical and wise critical thinker who taught me that doing the right thing is different from just being right. John also taught me that ultimately we must do the right thing for the shareholders, not just for the executives, of our client organizations. He was spot on, particularly from his perspective as a CPA and an auditor. However, over the next several years I learned to take a longer view, and I realized that always doing only what's right for shareholders could eventually be harmful to an organization. A consultant should also consider what's right for customers and employees. Aspirations such as honesty with customers and loyalty to and from employees are unfortunately becoming more rare. These may be viewed by some as naïve and altruistic, but my observations are that they may, in fact, be essential to long-term survival for many businesses.

Thinking more deeply or more broadly about issues is something most business teams have experienced. What many teams don't consider though is the opportunity to think at a higher level. "Why" questions are particularly useful to get to those higher levels of investigation. This seems simplistic, but I'm constantly surprised by the lack of application and downright resistance to higher level questioning in some organizations. They like to go deep and wide, but not up.

Let's return once again to my earlier question: "Why are you reading this book?" This time, let's assume part of the answer is that you are considering starting your own consulting business. Now let's layer our thinking upward and ask, "Why are you working?" A short-term answer is to earn money that you need to pay bills. What about a long-term answer?

Answers

While you're considering your own answer, let me describe how my business partner, Frank Docherty and I addressed this same question of "Why are we working?" when we first formed our consulting business in 1991. We applied the same critical thinking skills to our situation that we had used to solve client problems. We knew we had to work for the immediate needs of paying bills and of surviving financially. But we also wanted a long-term answer to the question. Although Frank has a degree in computer science and I have a math degree, we had both taken required liberal arts classes during college, including psychology. We discussed Maslow's needs hierarchy and the idea of self-actualization, and we laughingly agreed it was a bunch of crap. We wanted a more practical answer that we could reference as an every-day guidepost or compass. Frank eventually came to the simple and brilliant conclusion that our primary reason for working long-term was so "we wouldn't have to work."

Notice the wording of that phrase. Specifically, note the "have to" part. Frank and I didn't say we wanted to stop working, but that we wanted to be in a position where work would be a choice, instead of a necessity.

As we applied more critical thinking, we asked the obvious next question: How do we get to the position of not having to work? The answer was that we needed to accumulate sufficient retirement funds. We then asked ourselves how could we do that, and how much is "sufficient?" We quickly determined that, for us, the answer to the "how" part of the question depended to a large extent on the answer to the "how much" part of the question. So we temporarily put aside "how." The answer to "how much" depended on what standard of living we wanted to maintain, the amount of debt we would be supporting and other related issues. We decided to simplify our calculations by eliminating many of the variables. What this meant from a practical perspective was that we would take debt out of the equations. In other words, part of our answer to "How do we get to a position of not having to work?" was to pay off all debt. This meant no mortgage, no car loans, and no credit card debt over 30 days. We then each looked at what it cost us per month in 1991 dollars to maintain our standard of living, excluding debt service. Our individual numbers were close to each other, and we decided to go with a single monthly amount that would apply to either of us. Rather than provide the actual number and divulging our personal finances, I'm turning hypothetical here by presenting an example.

Let's use $4,000 per month or $48,000 per year to maintain a hypothetical standard of living. We apply a composite 30% federal plus state tax liability, which increases the annual amount needed. We reduce the result by an estimated amount of social security. Then we apply an 8% average annual return for the retirement funds and a 3% annual inflation adjustment for a net real gain of 5%. To further simplify the math, we use another assumption that we will not reduce the retirement fund base when we retire, but would instead use only the 5% average real gain for our annual spending. To demonstrate the math, following is a restatement in a more organized fashion using as a starting point the $4,000 per month needed to maintain a hypothetical standard of living:

- Amount needed per year in after tax dollars = $4,000 x 12 = $48,000
- Plus $20,000 per year (30% composite rate) to pay Federal and State taxes = $68,000
- Less $18,000 estimated annual Social Security benefits = $50,000
- Anticipated annual investment gain of 8%, less inflation factor of 3% = 5%
- Base amount needed in retirement portfolio ($50,000 divided by 5%) = $1,000,000

Getting past the mathematics, this example target retirement fund calculation results in each partner needing $1,000,000. Obviously I've "gamed" the calculations here so the example results in a nice, round number. The plan also assumes, as previously stated, that we will have zero debt. We also wanted to get there by age 55. In summary, the overall work goals for this example can be simplified into a three-part numerical mantra of "1-0-55," which translates into one million dollars in retirement funds with zero debt by age 55.

Getting There

Once Frank and I had a handle on "how much," we could address the "how" part of the question that we had temporarily put aside. How do we get to the position of not having to work? Frank and I conceptualized four aspects of a solution as to how we could get there:

- Business Type. We concluded that we were going to continue to be in the consulting business because consulting was what we collectively knew best, and we already had more experience doing consulting than anything else. We did talk briefly about other types of businesses we could build, but no other options held the potential of getting us to our goal.
- Business Structure. We wanted to structure our consulting business to achieve the greatest income possible for the longest period of time possible within the operational boundaries we set. We considered the pros and cons of leveraged and non-leveraged models. Given our collective prior experiences and being brutally honest about our working styles and preferences, we decided to stick to a non-leveraged structure. See Chapter 2 for more discussion of this decision.
- Revenue Supplement. It didn't take a stroke of genius to determine that earnings alone would not get us to our goal. We had chosen a non-leveraged model, and that effectively limited our maximum annual revenue to the number of hours we could each work per year times the billing rate we could charge. After allowing for taxes, business expenses and personal living expenses, there just wasn't going to be enough left over each year to accumulate the target retirement funds over the number of

years we wanted to work. In other words, we couldn't "earn" our way to our goal. We concluded we had to supplement our earnings with investment gains, and we decided to invest our retirement funds using an approach that closed the gap between earnings and our retirement target. Chapter 6 describes of our investment strategy.

- Budgets. Starting with our first year, Frank and I contributed the maximum allowable to our tax deferred retirement funds, and we saved additional money in non-qualified retirement accounts. In effect, retirement savings became sacred and came off the top of our revenue. We determined how much we had for living expenses by first subtracting taxes, retirement contributions and business expenses from our top-line revenue. We were determined to live within the confines of what was left, our personal budgets. In fact, this discipline turned out to not be as hard as we initially thought it would be. We didn't have to live Spartan lives. We simply didn't increase our standard of living as our incomes increased. We didn't buy the next bigger car or house or boat. We refused to compromise our "retirement dollars first" principle.

By the way, we did get there. It took me two years longer than I planned, but I made it. Frank achieved his target retirement fund at the same time I hit mine, but since he's two years younger than me (and better looking in his opinion), he reached the target on schedule. Frank is so competitive, and he never misses an opportunity to remind me that he achieved the goal by age 55 while I didn't. Show off.

Summary

Critical thinking skills are essential to be a successful consultant. It is thinking that is disciplined, logical and informed by factual evidence. It requires unemotional observation, interpretation, analysis, and understanding. These skills are not only needed to solve client problems, but they are also necessary to determine the basic structure and operations of the consulting practice itself.

When Frank and I started our consulting practice, we identified:

- Our starting position, which was that we had to work to survive.
- Our desired end state, which was that work would be a choice.
- How we would get there, which is described in more detail in Chapters 2 and 6.

In 1996, Mark Janda, a colleague who had previously worked with us at KPMG, joined Frank and me as the third partner in our firm. Before joining us, Mark reviewed our prior thinking and our business decisions as I've described them in this chapter. In spite of his serious misgivings, Mark really needed a job. I'm joking. Mark's agreement with and enthusiasm for the direction Frank and I had created made us even more confident in our business model and plan. The three of us have enjoyed our journey together for more than 20 years because we periodically reinforced for each other that consulting was what we most wanted to do.

Our story isn't a formula for anyone else's success. But the critical thinking process we used can provide useful guidance. If you are serious about being in the consulting profession, I recommend you ask yourself fundamental questions and use critical thinking to determine what you want to do, why you want to do it, and how you'll get it done. Look clearly and objectively at your situation, believe in yourself, and stretch your abilities. Everyone is unqualified the first time they try something new. We each were when we first got into the consulting profession.

Chapter 1 – Critical Thinking

Chapter 2 – Fundamentals

"I am still learning."
-- Michelangelo's lifelong motto

The structure of the consulting business that Frank Docherty and I created was driven by three fundamental decisions that we summarized into a single question: "What products and services will we deliver to what clients using what resources?" Steven Brandt addresses this question in depth in his 1981 book, "Strategic Planning in Emerging Companies." The remainder of this chapter looks at each of the three parts of the question and describes how Frank and I made the decisions we did to create answers appropriate for our business.

Products and Services

Specializing in the right set of services was key to creating our "brand." We wanted to convey an image of being professional, competent and worthy of being hired. Having a broad range of services would provide us with more areas of opportunity; however, if too broadly defined, it would possibly convey an image of being competent with many skills but not necessarily outstanding in any of them, "a Jack of all trades, but a master of none." A narrow range of specialized services conveys expertise, but if too narrow, could exclude us from consideration for other work that we could competently do. Also, being too specialized would run the risk that our area of specialization could become obsolete.

To help us address this question, we looked back at how some of our prior employers had dealt with the issue. We had experienced a broad range of services at KPMG, and there were a lot of talented people with many skills, but our consulting clients appeared to be confused at times by the firm's attempts to market the consulting division as having experts in almost every business topic. Periodically a national Consulting PIC (partner in charge) would be named for a newly conceived service, and this PIC would bombard us and our clients with marketing materials claiming the new service would cure many business problems for almost every client. We had various PICs representing functional "solutions" that cut across every industry, and we had PICs for industry "solutions" that cut across all functions. Many of these new services disappeared after a few months only to be replaced by newer and more wonderful "cure-all" services led by different PICs. Several years after I left KPMG, the firm spun off the consulting practice, and eventually it disappeared. A broad range of service offerings didn't cause the demise of KPMG's consulting practice, but it clearly didn't help it survive either.

An example of firms specializing in "too narrow" a range of services happened with Y2K engagements in the late 1990's. For those who (because of youth or serious self-prescribed medication) don't remember the 20th century, Y2K is an acronym that meant "year 2000" which was used to describe a large array of technology projects that were made necessary by the transition into the 21st century. Many computer application systems built prior to 1990 used date fields that only included 2-digit years. After all, it was silly to waste two whole characters of storage when all dates would naturally start with "19." In the early 1990's someone looked ahead and proclaimed that most computer applications would crash in January 2000. For example, if a customer were late in making a payment on their credit card and paid in January 2000 rather than December 1999, the late payment penalty calculation, based on a 2-digit year, would result in negative 99 years and 11 months of interest, which would cause the bank's computer system to credit the customer for almost 100 years of interest. Yikes! The problem was believed to be ubiquitous and created mass technology paranoia. It affected banks, insurance companies, nuclear power plants, national defense systems, hospitals, etc.

Every piece of code became suspect, and an entire Y2K industry was born that did nothing but research, update and test computer programs and files for potential date problems. My perspective at the time was that the vast majority of the Y2K code problems were in fact benign and could be easily fixed by using a more reactive approach to correct them individually as they were each discovered after January 1, 2000. However, paranoia was rampant within most organizations, and finding all the errors was treated as a "life and death" priority. After all, an incorrect date in your company's fixed assets records might cause a nuclear meltdown. Really? You're a clothing retailer and don't own a nuclear reactor. Regardless of logic to the contrary, Y2K paranoia was rampant. Y2K "experts" were in huge demand and were charging premium rates. Entire consulting businesses specialized in Y2K. Mark conducted a Y2K planning engagement for one of our clients, and after that project, Frank, Mark and I made a conscious decision to decline any additional Y2K opportunities. We knew we were sacrificing higher billing rates, but by the summer of 2000 when the Y2K panic was over, the three of us were still billing every hour we could work at our standard rates while many of our consulting colleagues who became Y2K experts couldn't find work at any billing rate. They had become specialists in an obsolete skill, while we had not.

Back in 1991 Frank and I decided that we would market ourselves as "project managers" because almost all the projects we had previously done had some flavor of project management associated with them. Branding ourselves as project managers had the advantage of giving our clients a simple way to classify and remember us, and it was not overly limiting because many of our consulting skills could be included under the project management umbrella. Knowing what services we would offer and how we would brand ourselves gave us the first of our three fundamental decisions.

Clients

The next decision was the most difficult of the three. To whom would we offer our services? The answer of "everyone" was deceptively easy, but intuitively we knew it was wrong. We had neither the funding nor the expertise to mount a broad marketing and advertising campaign to reach "everyone." Also, our experience with KPMG, as described earlier in this chapter, taught us that even with sufficient funding and a lot of marketing, there is no guarantee of success when taking a broad approach.

Realizing that it would likely be self-defeating to target a broad market, we applied some critical thinking to the problem by asking ourselves more questions. Who had hired us in our prior consulting jobs at KPMG, Price Waterhouse, Consumer Systems and Cap UK? Instead of company names, we listed names of specific individuals who had hired us, and we looked for common traits among those people. Our conclusions were that in most situations, the people who had hired Frank already knew and trusted Frank and, likewise, the people who had hired me already knew and trusted me. The occasional exception came as a result of a strong referral from a person (who knew one of us) to his/her colleague who trusted that person's judgment.

Our list of prior client individuals who knew and trusted one or both of us became our initial target client list. We temporarily eliminated most of the people because of the non-compete agreements we had signed when we each left KPMG. The list of remaining clients became our answer to the question of, "To what clients would we initially offer our services?" This was the second of our three fundamental decisions.

One advantage of targeting a small list of prior clients with whom we had existing personal relationships was that we didn't need to be sophisticated marketers. We were rarely in danger of being called sophisticated at most activities, especially marketing. We were fairly good at closing sales, but not at finding opportunities.

Once in the door, we were proficient in presenting our proposal, asking for the business and shutting our mouths so the client could agree to hire us. I say more about the selling process in Chapter 8.

Resources

Deciding to have a finite client list eliminated (or at minimum postponed) the possibility of growing our consulting practice into a large company, and it dictated our resource model. I spoke about choosing a non-leveraged model in Chapter 1. Additionally, Frank and I both had experience as "workers" as well as "administrators" in our prior consulting lives, and we agreed that we clearly preferred doing rather than administrating. We were also conscious of the risks associated with a leveraged model:

- If we hired the right people and trained them well, they could easily hang out their own shingles as competitors.
- If even a single staff person got sick or became unbillable for other reasons, that consultant would become a serious drain on a small company's finances.
- If a staff person's performance or deliverables caused us to get sued, we could lose our entire business.

Knowing that we could not possibly offer all related consulting services, we relied on a "stable" of trusted colleagues who could offer those related services, such as system development, technical writing, training, testing, etc. I talk more about this topic in the Referral section of Chapter 8. Note that although we didn't leverage these referral resources from a financial perspective, they were candidate resources for project execution.

In summary, a larger firm creates leverage, but it takes time and is risky. A small firm of one to three practitioners is clearly less risky, but there's a financial ceiling created by the maximum number of hours we can bill each year. Because we knew ourselves and our preferred working styles, we chose the low risk, financially limiting, non-leveraged resource model. This was the final of our three fundamental decisions.

When Mark Janda joined Frank and me in 1996, we looked again at our resource model and reaffirmed our prior decision to limit risk by staying small. This decision isn't necessarily right or wrong for anyone else. We believed, and still believe it is right for us, and the key point to make here is that we made the decision consciously rather than allowing events to take us there.

A few years ago, my son Mike also created a technology consulting practice with two partners. They have successfully pursued a leveraged model, and as of this writing they have well over 100 people in their organization, tapQA. The Minneapolis Star Tribune ranked tapQA as one of Minnesota's top work places in 2013. I'm proud of Mike's accomplishments, and I mention his company's success to demonstrate that there are multiple right answers to the resource model question. I believe that the resource decision is significantly driven by the other two fundamental decisions about products and clients.

Revisiting Decisions

Clearly, it is important to consider fundamental issues when first establishing a business. Re-considering them periodically is healthy, and many organizations perform an annual planning exercise to re-think their strategies. My observations of these annual planning events is that most of them are not particularly useful because they become mechanical repetitions of prior planning events and the participants don't really question basic premises. Instead they jump immediately to discussions of how to expand the customer base or how to acquire a new product or how to reduce costs. These are important tactical conversations; however, I believe an annual planning exercise should also include re-consideration of fundamental strategic questions as posed in this chapter.

We didn't conduct formal annual exercises, but every couple of years, Frank, Mark and I would ask ourselves, "What should we be doing, who should we do it for and how should we do it?" Our answer each time was similar and ran along the lines of, "Project Management consulting is what we do best; we're still having fun; our old clients are still hiring us; and we don't want to change our delivery model. Let's go have a beer and call our strategic plan done for another year." Although we joked about it, the discipline of periodically having the discussion was healthy. On a few occasions we briefly considered the possibility of making fundamental changes, and we then consciously rejected those changes and re-committed ourselves to our existing business model.

A sole proprietor should also indulge in this re-thinking process once in awhile. Even if you never change your business model, it is comforting to periodically re-affirm that what you are doing makes you happy and that doing something else would likely make you less happy.

Frank, Mark and I try to maintain a balanced perspective by not allowing our chosen profession to become overly important relative to other dimensions of our lives. We regularly remind each other why we chose to be consultants, and our experiences with our client organizations periodically confirm why consulting is the right business for us. For example, I was helping a client organization transform their IT (Information Technology) operations from a mainframe architecture to web-based and client/server capabilities. Our team had a logical approach and good people, and we steadily achieved each of our milestones; however, the VP responsible for IT periodically suggested we try different tactics. He was a voracious reader, and whenever he read an article about a new technology, he naturally wanted to try it. We labeled his style as "management by magazine article." Each week I spent long, painful hours with him discussing his latest silver bullet idea and why it was a solution in search of a problem the company didn't have. I called Frank a few times during this project and whined to him about Mr. Magazine. Frank would then calmly remind me that the project would inevitably end, and I would have the luxury of going to my next client and not worrying any more about Mr. Magazine. Consulting is clearly the right profession for me, especially with two supportive partners who maintain perspective.

Working as part of a small, non-leveraged organization fits best with my personality. I worked for two of the largest and most highly leveraged professional service companies in the world at the time, Price Waterhouse and KPMG. I loved the work but disliked the administration and the politics. Although I was in the right profession, and those were both excellent and prestigious companies, they had the wrong organization structures for me personally.

Summary

The fundamental issues that Frank, Mark and I revisit periodically are contained in our three-part question: What products and services will we deliver to what clients using what resources? Each time we've asked ourselves this question, we've arrived at the same consistent answers:

- IT Project Management Consulting is what we do best.
- Our Current and Prior Clients are our best candidates to be future clients.
- Frank, Mark and Dave are the only resources we need.

Thinking about fundamentals is clearly necessary when forming a new business, and periodically revisiting those same issues is a healthy exercise. Although there are no universally right or wrong decisions, building a business without conscious decisions about the fundamentals just seems foolish to me. As Rule 8 of the "Ten Pretty Good Rules" states, "If you don't know where you're going, any road will get you there."

I reference items from the "Ten Pretty Good Rules" frequently throughout this book, and the list is worth repeating in its entirety here:

1. Never wrestle with a pig; you both get dirty and the pig likes it.
2. Never argue with an idiot; people watching may not be able to tell the difference.
3. Observe everything; admire nothing.
4. It's easier to obtain forgiveness than it is permission.
5. Rarely resist the opportunity to keep your mouth shut.
6. Don't ask the question if you can't live with the answer.
7. If you want a new idea, read an old book.
8. If you don't know where you're going, any road will get you there.
9. Never have a philosophy which supports lack of courage.
10. Never look back unless you intend to go that way.

Our small, three-person consulting practice worked well for us for more than 20 years, and we balanced some of the limitations of our small firm by developing and nurturing our referral network. The keys to success for us were thinking about the fundamentals and consciously sticking with our decisions.

Suggested Reading and References

Brandt, Steven C. *Strategic Planning in Emerging Companies.* Addison-Wesley, 1981

Fellows of the Strategic Studies Group, Naval War College, Newport, Rhode Island, *Ten Pretty Good Rules*, 1982-83

Chapter 3 – Letting Go

> "Where there is no strife there is decay.
> The mixture that is not shaken decomposes."
> -- Heraclitus

I had a difficult time near the end of my consulting career accepting what should have been obvious: Change is inevitable. I had a hard time accepting this fact when I worked as someone else's employee as well as after I started my own business. When I finally arrived at the age when I had planned to retire, I continued to accept new consulting engagements, and therefore I acted as if I were going to be a consultant for the rest of my life. Perhaps I had come to define too much of myself by my job and career. Regardless of the underlying cause though, ending my consulting career turned out to be surprisingly more difficult for me than I had imagined.

Based on candid confessions from some of my colleagues, I was not alone in my reluctance to accept retirement. But afraid to face reality or not, one way or another, change will eventually happen for everyone. Each of us will either transfer to another part of the organization, or be promoted, or leave the company, or retire, or die, or something else. Regardless of the reason though, a change in my job status was inevitable.

I was extremely fortunate to be in a position where I could retire and could do so by my own choice. I knew I was lucky, but it still felt unnatural to me.

Self-Delusions

My experience at KPMG is one example of my self-delusion about keeping a job forever. I was recruited into KPMG after having spent six years in the management consulting profession with a competitor, Price Waterhouse. KPMG brought me in as a senior manager, and after four years of giving almost every waking hour to the Firm, I was admitted to the partnership. I was 35 years old, I was on top of the world, and I assumed that I would be a partner at KPMG forever. The Firm had other ideas. When I reached my sixth year as a partner, almost one-fourth of the partners, including me, were forced to leave. The partnership had grown too large to be supported financially by the then current level of fee income, so the senior partners decided it was time to "thin the herd." I was confronted with the reality that having permanent job security as a partner and part owner of a large firm was really a delusion.

After I left KPMG, Frank Docherty and I started our consulting business. We established 55 as our target retirement age, and when Mark Janda joined us, we re-confirmed the age 55 target. There was no magic to that age. It just seemed like a good number at the time, and because we were in our early 40's, it was far enough into the future that it wasn't particularly scary. I turned 55 in 2004, and as I got close to that birthday, I decided that my retirement funds hadn't grown to where I wanted them. So I continued working for another two years to allow my retirement accounts to reach my target value. In the summer of 2006 I "retired," and the client I was working for at the time surprised me by hosting a retirement luncheon for me. A few months later though, I started saying yes when former clients would call asking me if I were available, and I found myself consulting again, but taking a month or two off between projects. Frank initially retired at the same time I did, and eventually he also started doing occasional projects when old clients called him, although he made sure he never worked during the summer months. Like Frank, I also tried to avoid working during the summer in order to take advantage of our short but beautiful summer in Minnesota.

When those new client opportunities would materialize, I discussed them with my wife who was oddly enthusiastic and urged me to accept each one. Hmmm. I suspect she wanted to get me out from under foot so she could have the house to herself more often.

When I accepted the first few projects after "retiring," I rationalized that I was bored when I wasn't working. That went on for over two years, and then the great recession started, and in 2009 my retirement nest egg lost about 30% of its value similar to what happened to the rest of the financial world at that time. I felt as if working had become a necessity again rather than an option. Four years later, my retirement funds were back on track, although the politicians in Washington seemed determined to create another economic train wreck through government shutdowns and by not raising the debt ceiling. The continuing cycles of political turmoil created uncertainty, causing the stock market and my retirement investments to fluctuate, which in turn gave me more excuses to continue taking on new consulting projects.

Theoretically, I would never run out of excuses to continue working because the world will always have some turmoil or craziness going on. If it's not politics and the economy, it's new wars or natural disasters or climate changes or terrorism or some other problem. Something will always happen to create economic uncertainty, and the markets will react negatively causing another temporary hit to my retirement funds and thus providing me with yet another excuse to avoid retirement.

Another way I rationalized continuing to work was thinking that if I found it easy to walk away from my career, then perhaps I didn't enjoy the work as much as being retired. But for me, I knew I really liked consulting. I got an adrenaline rush whenever I had a new opportunity to pursue. My ego was boosted when I delivered results to my client that I knew no one else could have done better. I woke up each day energized and eager to get to my client's offices so I could help tackle their problems. Sure, I've had a few crappy clients as I discuss in Chapter 10, but most of my engagements have been energizing, enjoyable and financially rewarding.

Looking at myself honestly, I had to admit that my excuses were less financial than they were emotional. Like many people, I had part of my identity defined by my job and career. I couldn't let go of working. I decided I needed to do something to allow me to accept the idea of retirement. At one point, I thought that writing a book could be the triggering event that might allow me to give myself permission to close the "consulting chapter" of my life. That also didn't work.

Another Perspective

As you may remember from Chapter 1, when Frank and I first formed our business, we determined that our company objective was to get to a state where, "Work would be a choice, instead of a necessity." I thought about this in the fall of 2013, and I decided that work had been a choice for a few years. I expanded on this concept and determined that not working can also be a choice. In other words, retirement doesn't have to be an "all or nothing" proposition. That perspective helped free me from feeling obligated to retire. I could retire, or not, without feeling as if I should or shouldn't.

Consciously giving myself a choice made the process more comfortable for me. I choose to be retired today. Tomorrow will take care of itself when it gets here. I don't need to define myself by my profession because I have other roles that are equally or more important, like being a father and a grandfather. There are additional things I can learn, and I want time to explore other interests, like traveling.

I don't need to work, but I can if I want. I can do volunteer work, like delivering meals on wheels, and I can spend more time with my grandchildren.

Summary

My initial difficulty retiring is an indication that I genuinely enjoyed my consulting career and that it was the right profession for me.

It took a small bit of courage to say no to myself and to stop being a consultant. Stopping wasn't an event. It was more of an elongated process of recognizing my own self-delusions, listening to my instincts, and applying some critical thinking to the concept of retiring. For me, retirement isn't an all or nothing situation. It's a daily choice, and I'm happy being retired. I feel extremely blessed to be in my position.

Chapter 3 – Letting Go

Part 2 – Administration and Finance

Chapter 4 – Administrivia

Chapter 5 – Finance

Chapter 6 – Investments

Chapter 4 – Administrivia

"The easiest way for me to grow as a person is to surround myself with people smarter than I am."
-- Andy Rooney

Administrative functions are necessary evils, thus the unaffectionate term "administrivia." They are necessary in order to avoid getting into complicated problems with banks, insurance companies, taxing authorities and various other government entities. They are evil because they consume the precious commodity of time and they don't generate a penny of revenue. My partners and I have continuously tried to minimize and simplify all of our company's administration. The sections of this chapter explain how we've dealt with the more significant and unavoidable administrative functions.

We had no income when we first started, so we were reluctant to spend money on services not considered essential. We retained an attorney and an accountant, established a banking relationship and obtained insurance. Those were not luxuries.

Legal

When we first started our business, there was no such thing as an LLC (Limited Liability Corporation), and we likely would have chosen to incorporate as an LLC had that option been available. Our choices were to form a partnership or to incorporate using one of the two forms available at the time. Although we refer to each other as "partners," we did not want to create a legal partnership because we wanted to protect ourselves individually from possible liabilities arising from the business. It's one thing to risk the assets of our company, but it's quite another to additionally risk our homes, cars and other personal assets as well. So we decided to incorporate. We created an "S-Corporation" rather than a "C-Corporation" because the S-Corporation offered simpler filing requirements and it helped avoid the "opportunity" to be taxed twice on company profits.

We engaged "ML," an attorney I had used previously for personal matters, and he filed articles of incorporation for us with the State of Minnesota. We've called "ML" two or three times since then with questions. His advice has saved us a lot more than the few hundred dollars we've paid him over the years. Trustworthy legal counsel is essential.

After we had been in business for about four years, it occurred to us that we needed to protect ourselves if one of the owners died or became unable to work. We did not want to get into a legal battle over company ownership with heirs or other family members. We therefore created a Stock Restriction Agreement stipulating ownership units and how a payout would be handled under various scenarios. Following, except for the signature page, is our Stock Restriction Agreement as amended in 2005. Note that it's less than two pages long. We like brevity.

****

Stock Restriction Agreement

This agreement was originally made on (date) by Faulise & Docherty, also known as Faulise, Janda & Docherty, a Minnesota corporation having its principal office at (location). It was amended on (date) by the corporation and all its shareholders. It was further amended on (date) by Faulise, Janda & Docherty and all shareholders of the corporation. All prior versions of this agreement are terminated as of the date of this amended agreement. Any and all buy-out provisions and/or stock restrictions not specified within this document are unenforceable as of the date of this amended agreement.

All shareholders have been provided sufficient opportunity to consider the provisions of, and amendments to, this agreement and to obtain legal, accounting and other advice as each deems appropriate. Each Shareholder has initialed each page of this agreement and has signed the final page, which indicates the number of shares owned by each shareholder.

The purposes of this agreement are to define the settlement process for a terminating employee and to impose restrictions on the transfer of the shares of Common Stock of Faulise, Janda & Docherty.

Terms and Conditions

1. The terms of this paragraph apply to shareholders who are also employees of Faulise, Janda & Docherty. The accounting records of the corporation include sub-accounts unique to each shareholder, and the shareholder's sub-accounts record all income and expenses specific to the shareholder. In the event of death, disability or any other situation involving a voluntary or involuntary termination of employment in the corporation, then the terminating shareholder (or his estate or heirs) shall be entitled to the net value (cash plus accounts receivable plus other income, less all expenses) of that terminating shareholder's sub-accounts. Settlement and payment shall be completed as soon as possible after all receivables are collected and a final expense statement is submitted by the terminating shareholder, but no later than 91 days following the termination effective date. Any receivables not collected by the 90th day following the termination effective date shall be written down to a zero (0) value for settlement purposes. Any expenses not submitted by the 90th day following the termination effective date shall be disallowed and assigned a zero (0) value for settlement purposes.

2. In the event of the death of a shareholder, then the Corporation or its surviving shareholders must purchase and the estate or heirs of the deceased shareholder must sell all of the deceased shareholder's shares. The purchase must be completed within

90 days after the shareholder's death. The price of the shares and payment terms are determined by the provisions of paragraph 5, following.

3. In the event of the disability of a shareholder for at least 365 consecutive days, then the Corporation or its remaining shareholders must purchase and the disabled shareholder must sell all of the disabled shareholder's shares. The purchase must be completed within 90 days after the 365 consecutive days of disability. The price of the shares and payment terms are determined by the provisions of paragraph 5, following.

4. In the event of any other situation involving a voluntary or involuntary transfer of part or all of any shareholder's shares of Common Stock, then the Corporation and the other shareholders, in that order, shall have successive options (rights of first refusal) to purchase the shares of Common Stock that are the subject of the proposed voluntary or involuntary transfer. The price of the shares and payment terms are determined by the provisions of paragraph 5, following.

5. For purposes of this agreement and as of the date of amendment of this agreement, the price of each share of Common Stock is agreed to be $1.00. This price will be periodically reviewed and adjusted by unanimous decision of the shareholders as they determine appropriate. These adjustments, if any, will be recorded in writing and signed by all shareholders as amendments to this agreement. Payment terms for any purchase of Common Stock covered by this agreement will be a lump sum unless otherwise agreed in writing by all parties.

The above 5 paragraphs constitute all of the terms and conditions of this agreement. In witness whereof, the undersigned have executed this amended agreement as of (date).

****

The above stock restriction agreement is short, but comprehensive. Many attorneys would be aghast at the brevity and would likely insist on dozens of pages of additional language. However, it suits us, and represents our collective thinking about how any of the owners who might leave the firm would be compensated. Fortunately, none of us has died, and when Frank and I retired, the company paid us for our stock shares according to the agreement. Simple, clean, and it worked just fine.

Banking

Our company's banking relationship is extremely simple. We have a checking account. Period.

We do not have a company savings account, a credit account, a line of credit or any other banking product. Although our company contributes to our IRAs, those IRA accounts are owned by each of us individually, not by the company. We refuse to have credit of any kind because we believe that "debt is evil." If the company needs to borrow money, one of the owners lends to the company what's required on a non-interest-bearing basis, and the company repays the loan within 30 days.

We receive two or three solicitations each month from banks and other financial institutions encouraging our company to get a credit card or to establish a line of credit. No, thank you. All of these mailings are shredded unceremoniously. Approximately a third of our consulting work over the past two decades has been done for financial institutions, and we therefore have learned a great deal about how banks make money, which may be why we are so cynical about incurring debt for ourselves.

Payroll is another administrative function that we decided to not do ourselves. We concluded that our time would be better spent doing billable consulting work. Also, the potential cost and lost time resulting from making a single payroll mistake would far exceed the annual costs of hiring a payroll service. We used ADP for the first several years, and then we switched to the payroll service offered by our bank because of convenience and the simplicity of doing direct deposits. Both firms charged us approximately $70 per monthly payroll plus about $50 for each quarterly and annual filing. We are satisfied with both firms, and we've not had any problems with the service either has provided. Note that each month we vary the payroll amount for each of us depending on how much cash is in the bank account. This is easily done with a quick phone call to our payroll service provider. We keep a minimal amount of cash on hand in our company bank account so we can each continuously get the maximum amount of cash out for personal use.

Compensation

From the day we first started our company until we weren't all working full-time, we paid ourselves basically equal salaries and bonuses irrespective of actual fees earned each year. This arrangement was based on two assumptions:

1. Regardless of what methods we might use to determine how much each of us should earn, things would even out over time. Based on informal tracking of who sold what projects during the first few years, this assumption proved to be valid.
2. We did not want to squabble over relatively small amounts of money. This point may seem minor, but to us it is huge. The foundation of our business relationship is trust, and we are each confident that all three of us are working equally hard to make the business succeed. Many partnerships flounder because of arguments over money, and we refused to fall into that trap.

When Frank and I started working part-time, we revised our compensation formula from a "divide by three" calculation to an "eat what you kill" approach, with each of us contributing equally to support common company expenses, like insurance, payroll fees, etc.

Insurance

Insurance is another of those necessary evils. Our clients and the State of Minnesota require some specific insurance products, and we have purchased other insurance products because they make sense for our business and ourselves.

Client required insurance coverage varies from client to client, and most of our clients require the following products and minimum coverages:

- Workers Compensation with limits of $1 million
- Commercial General Liability with limits of $1 million
- Automobile Liability with limits of $1 million
- Errors and Omissions Liability with limits of $1 million

Some clients now require $2 million limits for these products. For the above requirements, except the automobile coverage, we have policies with a single insurance company. This bundling simplifies the process of providing evidence of coverage to clients. We have our insurance company send each of our clients a "certificate of insurance" when we start an engagement and annually thereafter for long-term assignments. For the automobile coverage, since we don't have company owned cars, we make sure our individual personal automobile insurance policies comply with client requirements.

Unemployment Insurance coverage is interesting for a small Minnesota business like ours. Our company is allowed to decline paying Minnesota State Unemployment Insurance (SUI) as long as we pay Federal Unemployment Insurance (FUI). Since FUI is cheaper than SUI we pay FUI, but as owners of a small company who each has more than 25% ownership, we are excluded from collecting Unemployment Insurance benefits. It should be renamed Unemployment "Tax" for the self-employed.

We also elected to obtain life, disability and health insurance coverage, none of which is required by the state or by our clients.

- Life Insurance: We obtained a $50,000 term life policy for each of us naming the company as beneficiary. The purpose was so the company could use the proceeds to pay the heirs of a deceased owner for his financial interests in the company. We rarely have more than $50,000 per owner in cash and receivables in the company. See comments in the Banking Section above about varying the payroll amounts every month to keep cash minimized. We set the term of the life insurance policies to expire at about the same time as our planned retirement dates. An earlier version of our stock restriction agreement, which is described in the Legal Section above, contained a paragraph addressing how this $50,000 death benefit would be used as a payout to heirs, but we eliminated the paragraph when we allowed the life insurance policies to lapse as we got close to our planned retirement ages.
- Disability Insurance: We obtained two different types of disability policies for each of us. One had a flat $50,000 benefit payable to the company for purposes similar to those for the Life Insurance policies described above. The second type of Disability policy named the disabled owner as beneficiary and the amount was for approximately one year's worth of an owner's company revenue.
- Health Insurance: We decided our company would provide health insurance to its employees, all three of us. The premiums were obscenely expensive when we started, and they have only gotten progressively worse over the years. Because the company provided our health insurance, it was paid for with pre-tax dollars which made it somewhat less

expensive, but still quite costly. Frank is single, and Mark and I are both married with kids, so the health insurance costs for Frank were significantly less than for Mark or for me. We compensated for this inequity each year by paying Frank a larger year-end bonus than Mark or I received. Contrary to Frank's claims, he did not receive those larger year-end bonuses because he was smarter and better looking than Mark or me. For more about our objective of equalizing compensation, see the comments above under the Compensation section of this chapter. Now that the Affordable Care Act is operational, there is a possibility that health insurance for the self-employed will become more competitive, but none of us are holding our breath waiting for it.

Office Space

One of our first decisions when we established our business was that we did not need official "offices." During our time at KPMG and at other firms, no client ever asked to meet us at or to visit our offices. The rent and other related costs seemed like a significant and unnecessary drag on profitability, and we chose to eliminate that drag. We each did set up individual home offices, although we did not claim them for tax purposes, as described in the next section of this chapter.

Since we founded our firm, the record remains intact: No client has asked to meet us at our offices. Every client meeting was held in the client's offices.

Tax Filing

We maintain our financial records, do our own billing and perform most other accounting functions ourselves, and these activities are described in Chapter 5. The one accounting function that we outsourced is tax filing. We engaged a CPA, "JL" at the end of our first year in business to file our state and federal tax returns for us. After each calendar year "JL" reviews the financial records we keep, and he then prepares and files our tax returns. We could easily file the returns ourselves and save a few hundred dollars by purchasing a tax preparation software product; however, we want an independent CPA's signature on the returns.

I suffered through a personal IRS audit several years before we established our company, and I swore then that I would do whatever was necessary to never go through another one. My employer at the time, Price Waterhouse transferred me with my family from Minneapolis to New York, and I claimed the allowable moving expenses on my personal tax return. The IRS audited my return for that year, and I spent three days in an IRS office explaining the expenses and showing the receipts I had kept, but most of that time was spent just waiting to see the auditor. After hours of arguing the validity of the various expenses, I finally had to show the auditor, who was a fresh college graduate, the specific IRS regulations that allowed them. I was polite and methodical because I felt that I was dealing with a person who enjoyed his power and who really didn't care about me or about the validity of my claimed deductions. At the conclusion of the process, my moving expense deductions and my entire return remained unchanged, but the time I had spent and lost in the process would never be recovered. It was one of the most frustrating experiences I've endured.

Because of my prior experience with the IRS, when we started our consulting business, I was convinced that we should have a CPA's signature on our tax returns. After hiring "JL" we asked him to advise us on what we should and shouldn't do in order to avoid going through an audit. He provided conservative recommendations to minimize audit risk. For example, "JL" advised us to not claim the home office deduction because it can trigger an IRS audit. By not claiming it, each of us probably pays a few hundred dollars more in taxes each year, but we feel it's worth it to avoid potentially wasting hours with the IRS, hours that we can spend on billable activities with our clients.

Time and Expense Tracking

Tracking T&E (Time and Expense) each month is necessary for client billing purposes. It is also important to keep good records in case the company's tax returns are ever audited. See the description of my irrational paranoia discussed in the Tax Filing Section above.

Prior to starting our consulting business, Frank and I had had experience with the T&E systems and associated tracking sheets/forms at KPMG, Price Waterhouse, Consumer Systems and Cap UK. Each of those systems and forms had strengths and weaknesses. We decided that the systems weren't important to us because we knew we could easily keep acceptable records by using an Excel spreadsheet for our small company. We did want to make use of a T&E form to capture time and expense information each month and for entry into the tracking spreadsheet. None of the forms we had previously used was acceptable to us. They were unnecessarily complicated, consisting of multiple pages; with too much focus on time tracking and not enough focus on expenses.

We decided to create our own T&E form as an Excel spreadsheet using the best of the examples we had, and we focused on what we considered to be most important. The following example is the result. The upper half is devoted to expenses. The lower left quadrant is for time tracking. The lower right quadrant is an automated (using Excel formulas) restatement of expenses organized by the categories that correspond to the IRS tax form we need to complete each year. The form isn't complicated or fancy, but it has worked well for us for over 20 years.

Faulise, Janda & Docherty		**TIME & EXPENSE REPORT**									
Dave Faulise		Employee Number **XXX-XX**						Period Ending **03/31/20xx**			
Date	**Expense Description**	**Eng. #**	**Mileage**	**Auto**	**Airfare**	**Oth Trn**	**Hotel**	**Meals**	**Entert.**	**Other**	**Total**
1-Mar	Auto rental, lease or depreciation			250.00							**250.00**
	Auto license, insurance										**.00**
1-31 Mar	Auto gas, oil, repairs, cleaning - see receipts			164.36							**164.36**
1-31 Mar	Business mileage and parking		320								**.00**
											.00
											.00
16-Mar	Mobile Telephone - business part of invoice									166.44	**166.44**
21-Mar	Internet cable service									48.31	**48.31**
											.00
											.00
											.00
											.00
											.00
											.00
	Total Reimbursable Expenses			414.36	.00	.00	.00	.00	.00	214.75	**629.11**

Week	**Client and Project Description**	**Eng. #**	**Hours**	**Bill Exp**		
1-2 Mar	XYZ Call Center RFP	XYZ-0503	**6**	.00	Automobile Expenses	**414.36**
3-9 Mar	XYZ Call Center RFP	XYZ-0503	**40**	.00	Other Travel Expenses	**.00**
10-16 Mar	XYZ Call Center RFP	XYZ-0503	**38**	.00	Office Equipment	**.00**
17-23 Mar	XYZ Call Center RFP	XYZ-0503	**40**	.00	Office Supplies	**.00**
24-31 Mar	XYZ Call Center RFP	XYZ-0503	**40**	.00	Outside Services	**48.31**
			0	.00	Postage	**.00**
			0	.00	Telephone	**166.44**
			0	.00	Entertainment	**.00**
			0	.00	Non-Client Reimburseable M	**.00**
			0	.00	Health Care Expenses	**.00**
			0	.00	Other Expenses	**.00**
			0	.00	**Total Expenses**	**629.11**
	Total Billable Hours and Expenses		**164**	**.00**	**Signature**	

Work Paper Organization

Being organized during an engagement isn't mandatory, but it is extremely helpful and highly encouraged. We use a standard organization structure to file engagement work papers. The specific work papers for every one of my engagements varies somewhat from our standard structure because I tailor the work papers to fit the unique nature of each engagement. Mark and Frank do the same.

As an engagement is initiated, I create the following file folders on my laptop:

- Administration and Background: This folder contains any client background information I may collect that isn't directly related to the engagement, such as company organization charts, company annual reports, and contact information for the project team and various other people I may need to engage. This folder also contains time entry instructions when the client requires me to enter my hours into their timekeeping system. I also file copies of my invoices to the client in this folder.

- Deliverables: This folder inevitably becomes the largest of all the folders. It is also the one that is most tailored to the unique engagement. Typical sub-folders include
    - A Communications sub-folder containing key presentations, steering committee meeting minutes, timelines, and decision framework/process documents.
    - A Design sub-folder containing analysis, drawings and blueprints.
    - A Financial sub-folder containing the project business case, project budgets and financial performance spreadsheets.
    - A Final Documents sub-folder that may contain the published RFP for an RFP development project, or an Operations Manual for an implementation project, or the Final Contract for a contract negotiations project, etc.
- Issues and Memos: This folder contains an "Issues and Risks" spreadsheet. See more on this in Chapter 14. I also file important memos and emails in this folder that document how issues or critical decisions have been addressed.
- Proposal and Contract: This folder contains the engagement contractual arrangements with the client. It may also contain a Statement of Work and a Scope document. See Chapter 9 for more on this topic.
- Status: This folder contains copies of all project status reports. See more on status reports in Chapter 14.
- Workplans: This folder contains copies of the workplan as it evolves during the engagement. See more on workplans in Chapter 14.

Other folders and sub-folders invariably get added to the structure to accommodate unique engagement requirements.

Summary

Administrative functions are necessary evils, and this chapter describes how my partners and I dealt with the more significant and unavoidable administrivia. We tried our best to minimize and simplify all of them. We engaged other professionals to perform selected functions for us whenever:

- The activity required expertise we didn't have, or
- The activity would consume significant time that was better spent with our clients.

Chapter 5 – Finance

"Facts alone are not sufficient to achieve truth."
-- Aristotle

For the first several months after Frank and I started our consulting business we had no income, and we therefore didn't put much thought into having an accounting system to track and report our non-existent finances. We were spending small amounts of money for office supplies, computer equipment and the gasoline we used when we made sales calls. We simply tracked our expenses using the T&E (time and expense) sheet we had designed, as described in Chapter 4.

Once we started generating revenue however, we found we needed to track our finances, and we created a very simple set of books using Excel spreadsheets. Before you roll your eyes and discount our intelligence for not buying QuickBooks or Peachtree or Sage or some other tool, please understand that there was no low-cost accounting software product available back then. Also, we were confident we could easily assemble a simple accounting system because I had personally programmed a lot of the accounting software that Price Waterhouse sold to their clients, and Frank and I had both implemented accounting systems for dozens of our prior clients. I'll have more to say on this topic later in this chapter.

The following diagram shows the transaction flows within our rudimentary accounting system.

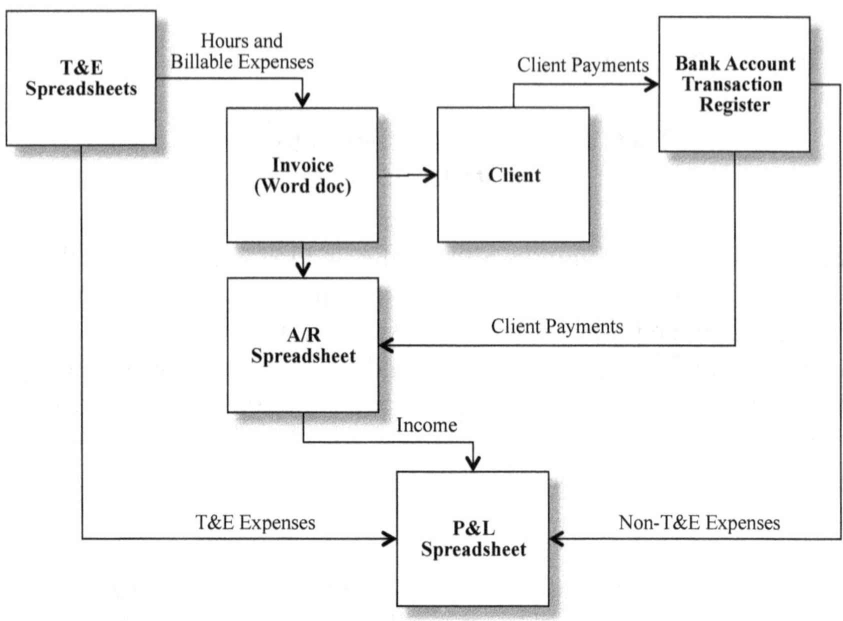

As indicated in the above diagram, our accounting system is driven by transactions initiated primarily from two sources:

- The T&E (time and expense) spreadsheets we each complete monthly. The hours and billable expenses from our T&Es are entered into client invoices that we create with Microsoft Word and send to our clients. Invoice amounts are entered into an A/R (Accounts Receivable) spreadsheet, which in turn automatically feeds into a P&L (Profit and Loss) spreadsheet. T&E expenses (billable and non-billable) automatically feed into the P&L spreadsheet.
- Our Bank checking account transaction register. Our bank provides a web-based transaction register showing all activity on a continuous, up-to-the-minute basis. As client payments show up on the bank transaction register, we enter that information into the A/R spreadsheet. We enter non-T&E expenses, such as payroll transactions, insurance payments, bank fees, etc., into the P&L spreadsheet.

The T&E spreadsheet and surrounding process are described in Chapter 4 and need not be repeated here. Note that the above diagram doesn't show a Balance Sheet because we have no company owned facilities or automobiles or other depreciable assets, and we can literally track our Balance Sheet items on the back of a napkin.

The following sections of this chapter describe the remaining components and processes within the above diagram.

Billing

One of our first clients required us to provide hour and expense details with our invoices, so we copied the information from our T&E spreadsheets onto the invoices we prepared for that client. Eventually we decided that we would provide the same information on all our client invoices because it was easier than trying to remember which clients got details and which got only summary information.

Following is an example invoice. It's simple and concise, but thorough. Note that it includes our contact information, our federal tax identification number, the date, our invoice number and a brief description of the services we provided to the client. Not every client requires all of this information, but we provide it anyway. In over twenty years of sending bills to clients, we haven't had a single question from a client or a request for additional information. We have had a few clients who have been late with a payment, and having the invoice date and invoice number to reference has made it easier for us to track down where the invoice in question is in the client's accounts payable and payment processes.

After we create an invoice as a Word document, we email it to the client. We then enter the amount, date and invoice number into our Accounts Receivable spreadsheet.

The following example invoice is representative of our invoices.

INVOICE

Faulise, Janda & Docherty
P.O. Box xxxx
Bloomington, MN 554xx
(612) 986-xxxx
Federal Tax ID No. xx-xxxxxxx

October 15, 20xx
Invoice Number XYZ-305
Page 1 of 1

Ms. Xxxx Xxxxxx
XYZ Company
1234 Main Street
Minneapolis, Minnesota 554xx

Consulting assistance for the XYZ Big System Implementation Program during the period of October 1, 20xx through October 15, 20xx.

Personnel	Period Ending	Hours	Rate	
D. Faulise	10/04/20xx	23.0		
D. Faulise	10/11/20xx	47.0		
D. Faulise	10/15/20xx	11.0		
Totals		81.0	$125.00	$ 10,125.00

Expenses:

Date	Description	Amount
10/06/20xx	Airfare from Minneapolis to Phoenix	273.00
10/06/20xx	Travel service fee	15.00
10/08/20xx	Two nights at Sheraton Crescent	364.51
10/08/20xx	Avis car rental in Phoenix	129.05

10/08/20xx	Lunch at Tabernina Restaurant	17.50
10/08/20xx	Parking for 2 days at Minneapolis airport	33.00

Total Due $ 10,957.06

Accounts Receivable

We track our Accounts Receivable using a simple Excel spreadsheet. It contains one line for each invoice. The total "Fees," total "Expenses" and total "Paid Amount" for each year are automatically fed into our P&L financial statement.

The following example of our A/R spreadsheet is sufficiently simple so that a narrative discussion of the contents is unnecessary. There is one noteworthy feature: The upper section includes those invoices that we issued in the prior year and were paid by the client in the current year. We keep these separate so we can track invoices and payments by fiscal year. This simplifies year-end reporting and tax filing.

Invoice Number	Invoice Date	Fees	Expenses	Invoice Amount	Paid Amount	Received Date
XYZ-1201	12/10/20xx	2,400.00	0.00	2,400.00	2,400.00	1/26/20xx
XYZ-1202	12/23/20xx	8,200.00	0.00	8,200.00	8,200.00	1/26/20xx
		0.00	0.00	0.00	0.00	
Prior Year		10,600.00	0.00	10,600.00	10,600.00	
XYZ-1301	1/7/20xx	5,700.00	0.00	5,700.00	5,700.00	1/26/20xx
XYZ-1302	1/21/20xx	8,000.00	0.00	8,000.00	8,000.00	2/14/20xx
XYZ-1303	2/1/20xx	7,500.00	0.00	7,500.00	7,500.00	3/1/20xx
XYZ-1304	2/15/20xx	4,000.00	0.00	4,000.00	4,000.00	3/7/20xx
XYZ-1305	3/1/20xx	6,200.00	0.00	6,200.00	6,200.00	3/22/20xx
XYZ-1306	3/15/20xx	7,500.00	0.00	7,500.00		
XYZ-1307	3/29/20xx	8,200.00	0.00	8,200.00		
				0.00		
				0.00		
				0.00		
				0.00		
				0.00		
				0.00		
				0.00		
				0.00		
				0.00		
				0.00		
Current Year		47,100.00	0.00	47,100.00	31,400.00	
Total Open Receivables				**15,700.00**		
Total Payments				**42,000.00**		

Bank Account Transaction Register

Our bank's web-based transaction register contains records of client payments as well as all our non-T&E expenses. We simply copy and paste the bank transaction register contents into a check register Excel spreadsheet we created, and that in turn is linked to our financial statement P&L spreadsheet.

Following is an example of our check register. It looks similar in format to a check register for a personal checking account. The Transaction Description column is noteworthy because it identifies a variety of different transaction types. Similar to QuickBooks, our checking account transaction activity is a primary driver of our accounting system.

****

Check Number	Date	Transaction Description	Deposit Amount	Payment Amount	Balance
	01/01/2013	Beginning Balance			500.00
	01/02/2013	Bank Bill Pay Service Fee		6.00	494.00
	01/03/2013	Insurance Company recurring payment - disability insurance		198.12	295.88
	01/07/2013	Client XYZ Payment	7,650.00		7,945.88
	01/07/2013	Mark expense reimbursement		4,207.48	3,738.40
2554	01/08/2013	Insurance Company - workers comp and liability		1,437.00	2,301.40
	01/09/2013	Bank Bill Direct Pay Service Fee		10.00	2,291.40
	01/18/2013	Bank Year-End and Quarterly Service Fee		92.95	2,198.45
	01/12/2013	Client ABC Payment	19,420.00		21,618.45
	01/22/2013	Client XYZ Payment	6,930.00		28,548.45
	01/26/2013	Client JKL Payment	16,300.00		44,848.45
	01/25/2013	Bank payroll fee		63.79	44,784.66
	01/25/2013	Bank payroll taxes		6,513.15	38,271.51
	01/25/2013	Bank payroll direct deposits		11,550.85	26,720.66
	01/25/2013	FUTA/FUI			26,720.66
2555	01/30/2013	Expense Advance for trip to New York City		1,500.00	25,220.66
2557	01/30/2013	Dave expense reimbursement		926.59	24,294.07
2556	01/31/2013	Frank expense reimbursement		2,468.02	21,826.05
	02/01/2013	Bank Bill Pay Service Fee		6.00	21,820.05
	02/04/2013	Insurance Company recurring payment - disability insurance		198.12	21,621.93
	02/06/2013	Mark expense reimbursement		3,815.39	17,806.54
	02/07/2013	Client XYZ Payment	17,640.00		35,446.54
	02/08/2013	Bank Bill Direct Pay Service Fee		10.00	35,436.54
	02/15/2013	Bank payroll fee		65.59	35,370.95
	02/15/2013	Bank payroll taxes		10,431.73	24,939.22
	02/15/2013	Bank payroll direct deposits		20,130.27	4,808.95
	02/15/2013	FUTA/FUI			4,808.95
	02/14/2013	Client ABC Payment	18,614.83		23,423.78
2558	03/01/2013	Frank expense reimbursement		1,569.16	21,854.62
2559	03/01/2013	Dave expense reimbursement		1,089.75	20,764.87
2560	03/01/2013	USPS P.O. Box fee		60.00	20,704.87
	03/01/2013	Insurance Company - workers comp audit refund	158.00		20,862.87
	02/28/2013	Client XYZ Payment	10,080.00		30,942.87
	03/01/2013	Bank Bill Pay Service Fee		6.00	30,936.87

****

Financial Statement

Our financial statement spreadsheet tells the financial story of our consulting practice. It is a current summary of every financial transaction that has occurred during the fiscal year.

Following is an example of our financial statement spreadsheet. It is generally in the format of a classic Income and Expense statement, and it also includes a summary of Accounts Receivable at the top in order to provide a comprehensive financial picture on a single page.

Expenses are organized in the sequence shown in order to match the sequence of current IRS tax form entries. This makes completing tax forms at the end of the year very simple and straightforward. See the discussion in the Tax Filing section of Chapter 4.

The financial statement example below is a year-to-date summary after about two plus months of activity during one particular year. We are also able to show more comprehensive details in month-by-month financial statements and details by person, as needed.

****

Financial Summary

	TOTAL
Accounts Receivable	
Invoiced Amounts	
Professional Fees	114,900.00
Client Reimbursed Expenses	2,082.88
Total Invoiced Amounts	116,982.88
Cash Received	80,034.83
Net Accounts Receivable	36,948.05
Ordinary Income/Expense	
Income	
Consulting Income	77,951.95
Client Reimbursed Expenses	2,082.88
Total Income	80,034.83
Expense	
Bank Service Charges	38.00
Bank Payroll Fees	222.33
Compensation Of Officers	18,000.00
Insurance	
Disability Insurance	396.24
Liability Insurance	501.00
Unemployment (FUI)	1,260.00
Workers Comp	778.00
Total Insurance	2,935.24
T&E Expenses	
Automobile Expenses	2,689.43
Air and Other Travel Expenses	2,152.88
Office Equipment	507.45
Office Supplies	588.67
Outside Services	653.45
Postage	0.00
Telephone	1,028.85
Entertainment	384.39
Non-Client Reimburseable Meals	671.00
Health Care Expenses	946.46
Other Expenses	6.81
Total T&E Expenses	9,629.39
Reimbursed Expenses	9,629.39
Licenses and Permits	0.00
Misc. Office and Other Expense	1,560.00
Office Supplies	0.00
Taxes	
Payroll Taxes	3,366.00
Total Taxes	3,366.00
Wages	26,000.00
Total Expense	61,750.96
Net Ordinary Income	18,283.87
Net Income	**18,283.87**

****

Summary

Frank, Mark and I have continuously tried to minimize and simplify our company's non-revenue producing activities, and we've therefore purchased most of those services. Financial reporting is the one exception to our "buy rather than build" mantra for administrative and financial services. And we consider it a minor exception because we're using Microsoft Excel and Word to do most of it.

Building a simple accounting system has resulted in the benefit of forcing us to think through how our financial accounting process should work. We clearly understand it. We also have the discipline to keep it current, and our financial records match the bank's records to the penny continuously. Tax filing is easy, quick and accurate.

A few years ago, when Frank and I went into semi-retirement mode, Mark took over the financial record keeping and reporting activities from Frank. Mark was extremely busy with client projects that required well in excess of 40 hours per week from him. We've always put client work at the top of our priorities, and Mark wasn't able to stay current with the financial record keeping and reporting responsibilities. Being semi-retired, I was less busy than Mark was, so I assumed the financial record keeping responsibilities, and we were able to get our financial records cleaned up and brought current fairly quickly. The lesson for us was that our original approach was still the best: Set up the company's financial record keeping with simple tools, and spend the minimum amount of time necessary each month to keep it current.

Chapter 6 – Investments

> "Truth is a demure lady, much too lady-like to knock you on the head and drag you to her cave. She is there, but the people must want her and seek her out."
> -- William F. Buckley, Jr.

When Frank Docherty and I established our business in 1991, we agreed to focus on maximizing contributions to our retirement funds. We only knew the basic fundamentals about investing such as:

- The two broad classes of investments are stocks and bonds.
- Stocks and bonds are classified as either domestic (U.S.) or international.
- Stocks are further classified as growth or value. Growth stocks have high growth prospects, but also high prices and low (or no) dividends. Value stocks have lower prices and higher dividends than growth stocks. A blended stock is classified between growth and value.
- Stocks are also classified by the size of the company. There are large-cap, mid-cap and small-cap stocks.

We had some experience with mutual funds from our KPMG days. KPMG policy did not allow employees to invest in any of its clients, and the Firm required employees to sell shares if the company became a client. This restriction could be avoided by investing in mutual funds where the KPMG employee had no control over the purchase of shares of individual companies.

Neither Frank nor I had the time (because we were too busy doing work for clients), training, experience or knowledge to make competent decisions about how to invest our retirement funds, so we engaged a financial advisor at a large financial services firm based on a referral from a former colleague. As suggested by our advisor, we did not invest in individual stocks, but purchased shares in a variety of mutual funds, each of which was managed by an investment manager who had a solid reputation. Our first advisor retired in 1994, and her firm then transferred our accounts to another advisor who left their firm less than a year later as did the next one, and by 1996 we were on our fourth advisor.

In addition to the qualified retirement funds managed by the large financial services firm we had engaged, we also had non-qualified funds that we invested with other firms such as Janus, Franklin Templeton, Mairs & Power, AIM, Acorn, and Fidelity. These investments also were in mutual funds that were managed by investment managers with solid reputations.

By 1999, we concluded that our investments were consistently not doing as well as they should have. Although some investments like Janus had good years, over the long term the S&P 500 index (the benchmark we used for comparisons) was clearly outperforming all of our investments, regardless of the investment firm. For the prior several years the S&P 500 index was returning approximately 10-11%, but our mutual funds were only returning 7-9%. It appeared to us that the mutual fund managers and our advisors were benefiting more from our investments than we were. They collected their management fees regardless of a fund's performance. We were also paying taxes even when a fund lost money.

Research

In 1999, while having lunch with Paul H., a former KPMG colleague, I mentioned our investment frustrations. Paul recommended a book by Larry E. Swedroe titled "The Only Guide To A Winning Investment Strategy You'll Ever Need." See References at the end of this chapter. The book refers to extensive university graduate school research, especially from the University of Chicago who developed the CRSP (Center for Research in

Security Prices) database, a massive database of market statistics based on over 70 years of daily stock market prices. Some of the results of their research include:

- Stocks (also called "equities") perform better than bonds, although bonds are less risky.
- Small-cap stocks (stocks of small companies) perform better than large-cap stocks, although large-cap stocks are less risky.
- Value stocks (stocks with high dividends and low prices) perform better than growth stocks (stocks with low dividends, high prices and high growth prospects), although growth stocks are less risky.
- The "Efficient Markets" theory which assumes that all relevant information about a stock is known and is reflected in stock prices, making fundamental stock analysis irrelevant. Expensive investment company research departments will increase expense ratios but don't add value.
- "Modern Portfolio Theory" which describes how to optimize an investment portfolio to deliver the highest returns for the amount of risk the investor is willing to accept.
- The average actively managed stock mutual fund replaces its entire portfolio of more than 100 stocks every year. This "churning" incurs trading costs, which are not included or reported in a fund's expense ratio, and these trading costs make it even harder for active managers to beat their benchmark index.
- Asset allocation (constructing an investment model) statistically accounts for nine-tenths of total returns, and selecting specific securities statistically accounts for only one-tenth of total returns. "Asset" is another name for "security" (a stock or bond). Asset allocation is dividing investment money among different markets (groups or classes of investments, like domestic vs. international or

large-cap vs. small-cap or stocks vs. bonds) to achieve diversification.

- In any single year, only 25% of investment fund managers beat their benchmark index (for example, the S&P 500 index), and a manager's success in one year is not a predictor of success in future years. In other words, all fund managers, regardless of recent prior successes, will lose 75% of the time as compared to a benchmark. Exceptions are so rare that it's hard to name more than two: Warren Buffet and Peter Lynch.

The University of Chicago research results certainly were consistent with our experiences using actively managed mutual funds. Larry Swedroe's book contains a lot of useful information, and I highly recommend it.

In addition to Larry Swedroe's book, Frank highly recommends "Common Sense on Mutual Funds" by John "Jack" Bogle, the founder and retired CEO of The Vanguard Group. Bogle's book was first published in 1999, and has had additional updates and releases since then.

Conclusions

There are three basic conclusions we drew from the evidence:

- The higher-risk asset classes (stocks, small-cap, value) provide the best returns. The classes themselves are not risky, only the individual stocks within each class. Therefore investing in a fund that holds all the stocks in a class will significantly reduce the risk so that it is comparable to that of lower-risk asset classes. Classes of investments are groups of similar securities, like domestic vs. international or large-cap vs. small-cap or stocks vs. bonds.
- Stock picking and market timing are a loser's game. Since actively managed portfolios and mutual funds are destined

to miss their benchmarks 75% of the time, passive investing in mutual funds that track the indexes themselves is the only efficient strategy.

- Frequent trading is costly to investors because of the commissions, research expense and tax implications. Passive investing has lower trading activity than actively managed investments.

Index mutual funds provide low risk in all asset classes, hit their benchmarks every year (by definition) and are passive. They have consistently superior returns, and they have the lowest expense ratios.

Applying the Ideas

In 2001, my business partners and I decided to use the University of Chicago's research and conclusions in order to move our retirement investments from actively managed funds to passively managed index funds. First, we each individually set aside enough money to cover our cash needs for at least 6 months plus any large known expenses (looking ahead 5 years) that could not be met by our cash flow income.

Next, we searched for investment companies with a history of good performance in index mutual funds. After investigating several companies, we established our qualified (tax deferred) retirement plans with Vanguard. We also established non-retirement accounts with Vanguard. The following chart depicts the 4 steps in our overall approach. The paragraphs that follow the chart briefly discuss each step.

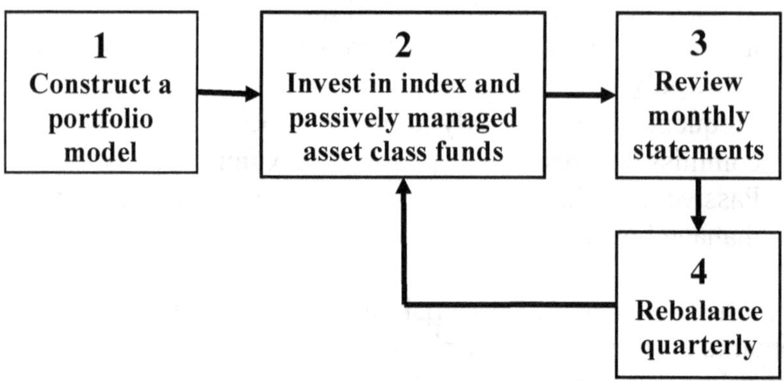

Step 1 of the approach, "Construct a portfolio model" is the most complicated step, but it only needs to be done once. A portfolio model is a list of the mutual funds selected and the percent of money to be invested in each fund. The following table is a basic portfolio model that demonstrates the idea using a total investment of $5,000.

Asset Class	%	Fund Name	Amount
Stocks/Equities	70	Vanguard 500 Index Fund	3,500.00
Bonds	30	Vanguard Short Term Federal Fund	1,500.00
	100		5,000.00

The actual model we constructed has more funds included than the example above. The funds we selected represent the various investment classes we wanted for diversification. We wanted to limit the list to 5-10 funds in order to keep it simple, and we eventually decided on 9 funds. The specific funds we selected worked for us, but they should be viewed only as an example because they won't necessarily be right for anyone else.

The following table (list) is our portfolio model. Items of note in the table are:

- The portfolio is diversified. The first 5 rows (asset classes) are U.S. stock funds, the next 2 are international funds, and the last 2 are bond funds.
- The % column is the most important segment of the model. It indicates what part of the overall portfolio is allocated to each fund.
- The last column shows an example of how an initial investment of $20,000 is to be divided into each fund. The amounts in this column tie to the percents in column 2.

Asset Class	%	Fund Name	Amount
Large-Cap Value	15	Vanguard Value Index Fund	3,000.00
Large-Cap Growth	10	Vanguard 500 Index Fund	2,000.00
Mid-Cap Value	10	Vanguard Mid-Cap Index Fund	2,000.00
Small-Cap Value	15	Vanguard Small-Cap Value Index Fund	3,000.00
Real Estate	5	Vanguard REIT Index Fund	1,000.00
Developed Markets	15	Vanguard Developed Market Index Fund	3,000.00
Emerging Markets	5	Vanguard Emerging Markets Index Fund	1,000.00
1-5 Year Bonds	15	Vanguard Short Term Treasury Fund	3,000.00
1-5 Year Bonds	10	Vanguard Short Term Federal Fund	2,000.00
	100		20,000.00

Step 2 of the approach, "Invest in index and passively managed asset class funds" is fairly straightforward. We wrote a check for

each of us to Vanguard with instructions as to how much to apply the money to each fund. We included a table similar to the one above with our instructions.

Step 3 of the approach, "Review monthly statements" is also easy. This is merely a reminder to stay informed of fund performance. Actually, the whole process is working so well that I stopped my monthly statements after the first few years, and now I merely review results whenever I'm inclined by accessing them at the Vanguard web site.

Step 4 of the approach, "Re-balance quarterly" takes some thought; however, I constructed a spreadsheet that does most of the work. This step is needed because over time, some funds will perform better than others causing the actual percentages to vary from the desired percentages (see column 2 in the above table) in the original model. The purpose of this step is to shift fund amounts to re-attain desired portfolio model percentages. This is done by (1) moving money between funds, or (2) adding more money to selected funds, or (3) withdrawing money from other selected funds, or (4) some combination of the first three methods. The following table is an example of a re-balancing spreadsheet. In this example, the fund values from the current Vanguard statements are entered into column 3 (Old Value); the spreadsheet then calculates in column 6 (Rebalance Amount) how much money should be added to a fund or subtracted from a fund (negative numbers). Instructions can then be sent to Vanguard, or transfers can be executed at the Vanguard web site.

Although periodic rebalancing isn't mandatory, it does slightly improve the return on a portfolio. In general, rebalancing every 2-3 months can be done in about 30 minutes using this simple spreadsheet, and it will add another half a percent or more to the annual gain. The primary reason to rebalance is that it is a foolproof method to "buy low and sell high" consistently and continuously.

Vanguard Fund Name	Old Value	Target %	Actual %	Re-balance Amount	New Value
Cash to be invested or withdrawn		0.00			
Value Index Fund	2,979.26	15.00	14.36	133.56	3,112.82
500 Index Fund	2,298.33	10.00	11.08	-223.12	2,075.21
Mid-Cap Index Fund	2,055.76	10.00	9.91	19.45	2,075.21
Small-Cap Value Index Fund	3,011.74	15.00	14.51	101.08	3,112.82
REIT Index Fund	1,288.28	5.00	6.21	-250.68	1,037.60
Developed Market Index Fund	2,979.65	15.00	14.36	133.17	3,112.82
Emerging Markets Index Fund	1,040.42	5.00	5.01	-2.82	1,037.60
Short Term Treasury Fund	3,009.71	15.00	14.50	103.11	3,112.82
Short Term Federal Fund	2,088.96	10.00	10.07	-13.75	2,075.21
	20,752.11	100.00	100.00	0.00	20,752.11

The calculations in the spreadsheet are fairly simple. Each "Target %" value is a constant. The "Actual %" value equals the "Old Value" in that row divided by the sum of the "Old Value" column. The "Rebalance Amount" is the difference between "Target %" and "Actual %" multiplied by the sum of the "Old Value" column. "New Value" is the sum of "Old Value" and "Rebalance Amount." Experimenting with the spreadsheet is more instructive than reading about it, so I suggest you construct your own version and play with it.

Note that the spreadsheet also allows us to add more money or withdraw funds. We do this by entering the amount to deposit (or use a negative number for a withdrawal) in the Old Value column of the first line, "Cash to be invested/withdrawn," and the spreadsheet will include this amount while rebalancing.

Summary

We have successfully used this approach to investing for more than 15 years, and we are confident that it works. We transferred retirement and other funds to Vanguard before the downturn that started in 2001, and even with the downturn and the "great recession" that started in 2008, we have realized an average annual return across our overall portfolios through 2013 of approximately 9-10%. Our other investments that were not transferred to Vanguard and not applied to this method, have realized approximately 4% (worst performers) to 8% (best performers) during the same time period.

This investment strategy is logical and relatively straightforward. It requires no more knowledge or effort to administer than that needed to work with a financial advisor. Because it can be managed with a relatively simple spreadsheet, it does not require a financial advisor or a portfolio manager.

After our first five years using this method, we began to exit our remaining actively managed investments in favor of index funds. Our experience with Vanguard has been extremely positive; however, we transferred some of those other investments to index funds managed by a firm other than Vanguard in order to not place "all our eggs in one basket."

Making money is important. Keeping it and maximizing its growth are equally important. We reached our retirement goals partially from the revenue we made from our consulting practice and partially from the returns generated from our investment methodology. We could not have achieved our financial goals without a sound approach to investing.

Suggested Reading and Reference

Swedroe, Larry E. *The Only Guide To A Winning Investment Strategy You'll Ever Need.* Truman Talley Books/Dutton, 1998

Bogle, John C. *Common Sense on Mutual Funds.* John Wiley & Sons, Inc., 2010

Part 3 – Sales and Marketing

Chapter 7 – Resume and Interview

Chapter 8 – Client Relations

Chapter 9 – The Contract

Chapter 10 – Exit Strategy

Chapter 7 – Resume and Interview

> "One must not hold one's self so divine as to be unwilling occasionally to make improvements in one's creations."
>
> -- Ludwig van Beethoven

Selling myself as a consultant isn't particularly complicated, but it is hard. And there's never a guarantee of success. The selling process includes use of:

- Existing relationships, which I discuss in the next chapter.
- My resume, which gets me invited to present myself.
- The interview, which is really a specialized sales presentation.

The Resume

I created my first resume long ago, while I was in high school as part of the college application process. As a consultant, I usually update my resume annually because the procurement departments at most companies insist on seeing a current resume regardless how many times or how recently I've done projects for their company. Each company and each hiring manager seems to want a particular resume format with specific content relevant to the project for which I'm being proposed. I sometimes get frustrated when I'm asked to tailor my resume again, but I've learned it's usually easier to comply with mindless bureaucratic policies than to question them. I believe that's an example of "riding the horse in the direction it's headed."

My resume is a required part of my sales process, but by itself, it won't close the deal. In other words, it's necessary, but not sufficient. It only gets me in the door. In spite of requests to the contrary, I don't include all the details of each project I've done because that would make my resume incredibly long and boring, and I would have nothing left to discuss during the subsequent interview.

I try to keep my resume short. Getting it on a single page would be ideal, but I typically use two pages. To make my resume less boring, I turn the projects I'm citing into short stories. Following is an example that is two pages long when on 8½ x 11 inch paper.

****

Dave Faulise

Dave Faulise has worked for more than fifty consulting clients across a broad range of industries and functions. Those clients have engaged Dave as a program manager, as an IT architect, and as an interim director. He manages complex programs, motivates teams, understands organization dynamics, and adheres to proven methods and processes.

Architecture

Dave has led the selection and implementation of two architectural frameworks. For example, at the **ABC Company**, Dave was hired as an enterprise architect. He organized and led the evaluation, selection, implementation and execution of an architectural framework and process to better align IT initiatives with business strategies.

Turnarounds

Dave has helped salvage several troubled client projects. He mitigates problems by examining resources, process discipline, quality of deliverables, and technology usage. He then re-plans and re-organizes the troubled initiative, leading with proven methods and techniques to deliver results, on time and on budget. For example, at **DEF Corporation**, Dave helped salvage a failed initiative by re-planning it, assuming project management responsibilities, hiring new internal and contract team members and setting up continuous communications with business and executive management. The improved processes and organization dynamics helped achieve project goals for all company locations across the U.S. on time and within budget.

Program Management

Dave has assisted several clients by leading large, multi-project initiatives. He has managed the planning, design, development, acquisition and implementation of custom as well as packaged software and hardware solutions for a variety of environments. These programs included offshore and onshore resources representing multiple business and technical disciplines. For example, at **GHI Company**, Dave led a consulting team in the transformation of a software implementation subsidiary with operations on three continents into a more profitable and more professionally managed business unit. The transformation included extensive business process re-engineering, continuous communications throughout the business unit and extensive application of organization change management techniques.

RFPs and Contract Negotiations

Dave has written more than two dozen RFPs for his clients. Using a proven process, Dave assembles business and technical requirements, writes the RFP, facilitates vendor responses, helps evaluate vendor proposals, conducts due diligence and facilitates the client decision. He has also assisted several clients in negotiating contracts with suppliers. Dave works closely with legal counsel, Finance, Human Resources, Technologies and business leaders to execute an effective negotiating strategy. For new or re-negotiated agreements, Dave simplifies and clarifies the terms, conditions, service levels and pricing. Resulting contracts are equitable, enforceable and clear. For example, at **PQR**, Dave led development of a competitive RFP and selection process for technology infrastructure operations. His responsibilities included defining and documenting business and technical requirements, writing the RFP, conducting due diligence, performing supplier evaluations, facilitating the selection decision, and negotiating the final contract.

Outsourcing

Dave has facilitated several outsourcing arrangements for his clients. These engagements have required him to thoroughly understand the business, technical and financial impacts of outsourcing to the organization. For example, at **VWX Corporation**, Dave led virtual teams from multiple disciplines (Legal, Technologies, Human Resources, Procurement, Regulatory Affairs, Business Development, etc.) across multiple time zones while facilitating three different outsourcing initiatives. These engagements included extensive communications and organization change execution. Projects resulted in improved services, risk reduction and significant cost savings.

Faulise, Janda & Docherty **1991 to Present**
Co-founder and co-owner

KPMG Peat Marwick **1980 to 1991**
Partner responsible for the Twin Cities technology consulting practice.

Price Waterhouse **1974 to 1980**
Senior Manager responsible for the Twin Cities management consulting practice. Assistant to the National Partner-in-Charge of U.S. Management Consulting.

Education: University of Minnesota, BA Mathematics

****

Other variations of my resume are similar to the example above. Differences involve which references I include and in what order. Another version of my resume is on LinkedIn. The reason I used LinkedIn is that one of my clients insisted I have my profile on it because her company didn't want to use email to distribute my resume to the other people I would be working with. I have not maintained my profile on LinkedIn, and I am not an active user.

The Interview

The above example resume, imperfect as it is, is usually sufficient to get me invited to an interview. I approach an interview as a sales opportunity, and the interview is where I make or lose the sale.

Interview preparation is as important as the interview itself. I never take for granted that the sale is a sure thing, even when I've done projects previously for the client. Many times there is someone attending the interview that I don't know, and if I'm not prepared, then that "wild card" person is likely to vote "no." Following is how I usually prepare for an interview:

- I review the job specification or position description to make sure I understand the company's areas of emphasis and what's important to the client and his/her organization. Many times job specs are written by HR representatives who are parroting what they've been told and who don't fully understand the work. When I peel away the boilerplate language in the job spec, I can usually discern helpful clues about what's really important to the interviewers. I want to understand the specific needs the organization has that I can satisfy.
- I then prepare a brief two or three slide presentation that answers the question, "Are the project needs a fit with my skills?" I do not use the presentation materials during the interview, but I practice with the materials beforehand and keep them in mind during the interview. Visualizing those materials in my head keeps me on track during the interview so I'm clear, concise and convincing.
- I do bring examples of my prior work products that may be relevant. Showing actual deliverables from prior engagements gives me credibility and makes what the client is buying real. "Show and Tell" is much more memorable than just "Tell". I practice with my examples in advance. Stories about real experiences while showing real examples are highly effective, and that technique is

clearly better than merely talking about theories, concepts or methodologies. Anyone can do the latter.

- I prepare two or three good questions in advance. Near the end of almost every interview, someone inevitably asks me if I have any questions. Examples of questions I've used include: What does success look like? What are the key deliverables signaling that the project is done? How does this project affect your overall business as a whole?
- Finally, I practice closing. As many times as I've done it, I still need to practice because it's hard. In a nutshell, I tell them I believe we have a good fit, and I ask them to hire me. Then I shut up because silence is my strongest ally during the close. It doesn't always work, but occasionally, the client or someone else in the room will agree with me. When I hear words that sound like "yes" I stand up, tell the group I'm pleased we've reached a mutual understanding, and make an exit. When I don't get a "yes" I will inquire about next steps in the process and let the interviewers bring the session to a conclusion.

The interview itself is something I can either enjoy or dread. It's really a matter of attitude and how well prepared I am. I try to arrive a little early so I can spend a few minutes in my car reviewing one last time my preparation materials, my example work products and questions I might ask. Then I tell myself that if the interviewers don't hire me, it's their loss more than mine, and since stupidity isn't a crime, I won't have them arrested. This ritual of a final look at my materials and a quick, humorous pep talk to myself allows me to go into the interview confidently.

Selecting relevant work product examples to bring to an interview isn't difficult for me because I have a large collection of project deliverables. I'm a pack rat, and an organized pack rat. When I create a significant work product during a project, I ask myself if I can possibly re-use it, either as the basis to address another client's needs or to use as an example when talking with prospective clients. Saving prior examples has been highly useful to my consulting practice. I'm careful not to just copy a deliverable from one project for use on another project. Rather, I use deliverables from prior projects as examples to reference when creating similar deliverables for a current project. In other words, even though I could, I don't plagiarize my own work, and yet I don't start from scratch either. And many of my saved examples have been useful during the selling process.

My son Mike, who is also in the consulting profession, has an excellent approach to interviews. When asked to describe a prior relevant experience, he paints a verbal picture using a "fairy tale" like format. There is a beginning that sets the stage, a scary middle that describes the problem, and a heroic ending where his company is the hero. Mike has found this method quite effective, and he clearly wins his fair share (or more) of opportunities.

There's another important point to make about the interview. It should be a two-way street. In other words, in addition to me selling myself to the client, the client needs to sell the opportunity to me. If the engagement really isn't a good fit for me, then I need to have the courage to say so and walk away. In a couple of situations, I've forgotten this basic tenet because I was so anxious to win the opportunity that I wasn't sufficiently critical or skeptical about the assignment. I didn't ask the right questions to determine if the project would have value to me beyond the revenue it would produce. Those engagements turned out not to be good fits for me, and I found myself faced with the unpleasant task of ending my participation. I talk about those situations in Chapter 10.

Also, for many of the opportunities that have not been good fits for us, instead of just walking away during the client's selection process, Frank, Mark and I have said, "We may not be the best consultants for this opportunity, but this would be a great fit for …" and used the situation to refer one of our colleagues in our referral network. See the section on Referrals in Chapter 8.

Lost Opportunities

I know first hand that there are many ways to lose a sale, and I've learned to live with rejection. Not every opportunity is a good fit, and not every hiring company understands the value I can bring to them. After experiencing enough rejections over time, I've grown a thick skin. "Sure" things fall through for lots of reasons.

For example, after I had been in consulting for about four years, I was asked by one of the partners at Price Waterhouse to meet with a client of his. The partner, Mr. Confidence and one of his managers picked me up at the Miami airport at about 9:00 PM the night prior to the client meeting, and rather than briefing me for the meeting, Mr. Confidence wanted to celebrate the new engagement he was sure we'd win. He drove us to a casino where he purchased large quantities of alcohol and expensive cigars, and he didn't drop me off at my hotel until after 3:00 AM. Our 8:30 AM meeting with the client came much too early and was a disaster. Mr. Confidence did most of the talking during the meeting, and his client and his client's managers barely said a word. During the meeting, I never heard anyone describe what the client's specific needs were much less how we were going to satisfy those needs. The client was polite and gracious, but we didn't get the sale, and as I rode home on the airplane that afternoon, I was angry and frustrated because of our lack of preparation, the arrogance of Mr. Confidence and the complete waste of my time and travel expenses.

This next story is about another sales presentation led by a different Price Waterhouse partner for a different client. This partner, Mr. Thorough prepared and delivered a comprehensive presentation. His materials addressed our firm's extensive history in conducting the type of project the client wanted us to do. Midway through his presentation, the client stopped him and said he was convinced we could do the work. Mr. Thorough didn't pick up on the client's clear buy signal, and he doggedly resumed his presentation. After all, he wasn't done. As he finally reached the end of his presentation materials, he asked some questions about the project that the client and the client's staff couldn't answer, nor would it be possible for anyone to answer those questions until after the initial phase of the project was completed. Those questions raised doubt in the minds of the client's managers about their own readiness to proceed with the project. After a few days of re-assessing the project, the client's managers decided to take a completely different approach, and we lost the sale. Because of his inability to accept "yes" from the client, his insistence on completing his presentation and his untimely questions, Mr. Thorough maneuvered the client from "Let's get started" to "Let's re-think this whole idea."

A few years ago, one of my long-time clients called me unexpectedly. He told me about a critical project he needed done and said he wanted to hire me because he knew I could do the work, and he didn't trust anyone else to manage it. He cautioned me that it wasn't 100% sure because he wanted to follow protocol by having his boss OK the arrangement before we started. Neither of us thought much about that because his boss also knew me, and she was as confident in my work as he was. Unfortunately, our timing was exactly wrong. My client's boss had just been confidentially informed that there would be a downsizing in another area of the business, and she agreed to offer any new open positions in her area to the employees about to lose their jobs. There were three project managers who were going to be terminated, and the obvious politically correct action was for my client to engage one of the internal people rather than me. I learned later that the project was successfully completed, but it took longer than my client thought I would take and he had to spend a lot more attention on it than he would have with me. He and his boss did the right thing, and I lost a "sure" sale.

We've encountered a few situations, when we had no chance of winning the project, and we were invited to propose simply to keep another vendor honest or to satisfy a procurement requirement for multiple bidders on a project. These "no win" opportunities usually happened when we received an RFP out of the blue and had no prior connections with the client or their staff. Our proposal and presentation may have been perfect, but we still weren't successful. Over time, we learned to recognize those situations and not waste our time. We tried hard to be selective by investing our time in opportunities that we could win and passing on those we couldn't.

When selling myself, I get hired most of the time. But as the above stories demonstrate, I'm never in control of all the variables, and therefore I don't ever assume I'm getting the contract.

Summary

The selling process includes the resume and the interview, which are addressed in this chapter. The third part of the selling process is the client relationship, which is addressed in Chapter 8. My resume doesn't need to be perfect; it only needs to be good enough to get me invited to an interview.

The interview is where the sale is usually made or lost, and preparation and practice has made my batting average respectable. It's also important to use the interview to find out if the opportunity is a good fit for me as well as for the client. During the interview, I show examples of prior work products to reinforce the fact that I have relevant experience, and I tell stories about prior engagements to make my credentials and me more memorable and real. One of the most important selling techniques is knowing when to shut up. See Rule 5 from the "Ten Pretty Good Rules" listed in Chapter 2.

Selling myself isn't complicated, but it is hard. I have a good success rate, but I certainly don't win them all, and I've learned humility and how to accept rejection.

Chapter 8 – Client Relations

"Life comes in the form of opportunities .....
.... which are easy to recognize ....
.... once they have been wasted."
-- from "Footprints in the Mind" by Javan

This may seem overly simplistic, but I want to define the term "client" before I dive into this topic. On my first day as a new Price Waterhouse consultant, the manager who was assigned to supervise me explained to me that the "client" is the person who hires us. Companies are not clients; they are merely the organizations that employ clients. He went on to explain that before we're hired, we need to focus on achieving a sufficient level of client confidence to allow him/her to engage us. After we're hired, we work for the client and focus on doing what's right for shareholders, not the company.

Client relations is another one of those topics where more has been written than is known. I've never invested time or money in seminars, books or articles on client relations. I didn't need them because I was told by another of my early mentors that the secret to client relations is very, very simple: Deliver good work. Period. That's it. He said that the consultant who does good work and who consistently delivers results that clients expect has laid a reliable foundation of loyal clients who will hire that consultant again and again.

Conversely, the consultant who does not deliver good work won't get re-hired by prior clients, and that consultant therefore needs to continuously find new clients to replace the ones who will no longer hire him/her. While some clients might not bother to check with their colleagues in other companies, most do, and they won't hire a consultant who isn't highly recommended. The consultant with a weak reputation can employ every marketing technique known, have an exhaustive database of contacts and spend numerous hours every day selling, but he/she won't generate much business. Without good work that can be referenced and that creates a positive reputation, the consultant will very quickly run out of clients, regardless of an intensive marketing effort.

How do you know when you've delivered good work? I've yet to meet a consultant who admits to being anything less than brilliant and superior professionally. Mathematically it's obviously impossible for all consultants to be in the top 1% of our profession, but our egos have deluded us collectively. So if I can't trust my own subjective self-evaluation, then how can I objectively know when I've delivered good work? One answer is that I'll know when the client pays the final bill. That answer is attractively simple, but it's wrong. A dissatisfied client will usually still pay the bill, and they may politely thank you during the closing meeting, but that doesn't mean you've delivered good work or that you'll be re-hired. I concluded years ago that the best gauge is when the client tries to convince me to become their employee. The engagement that ends with getting a job offer was probably a good one.

In addition to delivering good work, there is another point to be made here. Don't provide reasons for the client or for the client staff to resent your presence. Pay attention when interviewing and during the first day of an engagement, noting how others are dressed and the cars in the parking lot. Dress consistently with the client environment. Don't wear a coat and tie if no one else does, and don't dress more casually than the managers or directors. Don't drive a car that's nicer than the client's. A flashy Jaguar or Mercedes may possibly result in a request for a reduction in fees. Frank drives a Mazda, Mark drives an Acura, and I drive a Toyota, all very nice cars, but they don't convey that we are over paid. My father-in-law had a similar philosophy; he drove Buicks to the business he owned for 40 years, and it wasn't until after he retired that he drove Cadillacs.

Organization Categories

I evaluate companies based on their abilities (1) to make money and (2) to work as a cohesive team. These two abilities provide a simple two-by-two organization classification scheme:

1. The profitable, highly functional company. Although most organizations would like to classify themselves in this group, I've yet to encounter even a single company in this category, and I suspect that they are as rare as unicorns and flying pigs. If companies in this category do exist, they likely have minimal needs for consulting assistance, which could explain why I haven't run across them, but I prefer to think of them as mythological creatures.
2. The unprofitable, highly dysfunctional company. These organizations do exist, but not for very long, for obvious reasons. On the rare occasion when I find myself consulting for one of these companies, I (a) immediately start looking for another client, and (b) refuse to discount my billing rate because the risk of not getting paid is higher with these companies than with other types of organizations. They will soon be out of business and unable to pay old obligations.
3. The profitable, highly dysfunctional company. I would classify many of the organizations I've worked for in this category. My anecdotal observations indicate that the more profitable a company is, the more dysfunctional it can be. In my view, high profitability is generally not the result of good management, but rather the result of high-demand products/services with limited competition. I've observed very minimal cooperation within some of these organizations and, at times, cutthroat tactics to make colleagues look bad. It seems that the more profitable a company is, the more it can afford the luxury of dysfunctional management. Stated another way, it appears to me that good products create profitability, which in turn allows weak management to survive and thrive.

4. The low profit, highly functional company. I have also worked for several organizations in this category. These organizations are typically in highly competitive industries where price almost always trumps customer loyalty. Well-run companies with thin profitability find themselves constantly in survival mode, and they cannot afford the luxury of stupidity. Employees in these organizations have to work hard and smart every day just to keep the company afloat. They are inclined to help each other, go the extra mile, look for ways to improve, and demonstrate teamwork. As a consultant, helping to solve the difficult challenges these type-four companies face is usually more rewarding than providing assistance to type-three companies. When I feel I am part of a team working hard to solve important problems, I look forward to getting to that client's offices every morning, and I feel a self-imposed pressure to constantly add value to their team.

In summary, although there are theoretically four types of organizations, based on my practical experience, only the type-three and type-four companies provide worthwhile opportunities for consulting work.

A type-three organization engaged me to assess their largest information technology project. I found a classic example of project mismanagement. Many team members, including executive leadership, did not have the education or experience to perform the project-related activities they were assigned. There was no project plan, no status reporting, no schedule, no risk management, nor other generally accepted project management processes. Deliverables did not satisfy company management's expectations, but because there was no formal requirements document to compare against results, the system integrator could not be held accountable. I was hard-pressed to find anything positive to say about this project. After I delivered my findings and conclusions to the president, he asked me to assume overall management to salvage the effort. I agreed and then reorganized the project team and installed new disciplines including a budget and a schedule. What I couldn't do was fire the VP responsible for IT and for the original project because he was the president's brother-in-law. Mr. Ego wanted to succeed, but he wanted to do everything his way, and he wouldn't listen to his IT Director, who I found to be knowledgeable and with good ideas. After I got the project resurrected and moving in a positive direction, my job evolved into blocking Mr. Ego from creating another train wreck. I worked daily with the IT Director to make sure the project was running smoothly and then spent several hours each week getting Mr. Ego to "approve" decisions our team was already implementing. Our new team achieved the project goals on time and within budget. This type-three client was highly profitable, and therefore the multi-million dollar cost of Mr. Ego's prior mismanagement wasn't noticeable to shareholders. However, I knew when I wrapped up my engagement that the dysfunctional situation created by Mr. Ego was unnecessary, was reducing shareholder value and unfortunately would be allowed to continue because the company made enough money to keep on cleaning up his messes. Within a few months after I completed my engagement and I was no longer acting as a buffer to shield the IT organization from Mr. Ego, most of the employees who worked for him had resigned.

One of the type-four organizations I worked for was a small, newly formed business unit within a multi-national company. This unit was tasked with improving shareholder value through technology optimization. I participated as a member of the new unit's leadership team, and my responsibilities included overall program management and communications management. The leader of this unit, Mr. Perspective, selected his team members from a variety of disciplines (technology, legal, human resources, procurement, regulatory affairs, business development, etc.) who he knew were experienced, knowledgeable and proven team players. He gave us a finite timeline and budget to identify and realize significant savings and/or new revenue. He explained early in the effort that "significant" had to equate to several tens of millions of dollars, and that improving efficiency at the margins wouldn't suffice. An evaluation of prior recent budgets indicated that one of the company's largest technology expenditures was telecommunication carrier charges, and we decided to focus our efforts there. We discovered the company was using several dozen different carriers around the globe and paying premium prices to all of them. Our approach included consolidating usage down to a handful of carriers and creating a competitive bidding process between those remaining carriers for each of the company's geographic regions. At the conclusion of the project, this client realized first-year savings in excess of $180 million without reducing employee headcount, and most of those savings were projected to recur annually. Mr. Perspective had a knack for keeping us focused on the big picture while still allowing us to individually pay attention to the details. We knew we had a limited amount of time to produce big results or the unit would be disbanded, so we worked long hours, and we were collectively open to brainstorming ideas offered by any team member. In addition to achieving positive financial results, thanks to Mr. Perspective, we also succeeded in establishing a positive project environment where teamwork and valuing other team members was standard practice. I remember this engagement as exhausting, but also as highly rewarding.

In addition to the four types of companies described in this section, there is another category: companies that we did not want to work for, regardless of their profitability or level of dysfunction. These types of companies included:

- Dysfunctional family businesses which because of excessive nepotism, we knew were train wrecks in the making,
- Companies who made money immorally in our opinion, and
- Companies that we suspected were downright dishonest.

We occasionally received invitations to propose our services to companies in this category, but we always chose to politely decline.

Why Clients Hire

Why do clients bother to use consultants rather than just hiring more employees? My experience indicates that there are two general reasons why my clients hire me:

- Risk Reduction: This generally happens when the client has an uncomfortably visible problem to solve. The client usually wants to engage a prestigious, well-known firm because the client cares not only about results but also about having a defensible position if challenged as to whom they hired to solve the problem. I've heard more than one client say, "No one ever got fired for hiring IBM." A nice by-product of the risk reduction hiring reason is reduced price sensitivity, which is why the big name firms like KPMG, IBM and McKinsey are able to charge billing rates that are double and triple what the rest of us mere mortals can charge. I did a lot of these risk reduction engagements when I was with Price Waterhouse and with KPMG, but since leaving KPMG to start a small firm, I've only done a handful of them. Unless you work for one of the big name firms, save yourself some wasted effort, and don't pursue these risk reduction engagements.
- Staff Augmentation: For this category of engagements, the client may be able to do the work themselves, but they can't free up their internal resources, so they go outside. A variation of this category is "skill" augmentation, when a client may have internal staff with the desired title (such as "project manager"), but they don't have the depth of experience needed to make a difficult project succeed. Because there is typically a lot of competition for this staff augmentation type of work, clients are more price sensitive. If you have a unique skill set, it may help offset some of the

pressure to keep prices low, but that will likely only allow a 20-25% increase, at most, over competing rates. Since my partners and I started our small consulting practice, almost all of our work has been in this staff or skill augmentation category.

Clients rarely hire a consultant for reasons other than risk reduction or staff/skill augmentation. I only have one example from my career when a client engaged me for a different reason, although I wasn't aware of it initially. A privately owned company hired me to conduct an IT strategy study. The owners wanted me to:

- Interview each of their senior executives to ensure I had a broad understanding of the company's technology requirements,
- Review my findings, recommendations and a technology roadmap individually with each member of the executive team to ensure I had their alignment,
- Deliver the final results in a written report to the owners.

The owners gave me only eight weeks to complete the plan, and the project was a logistical nightmare, requiring multiple interviews with each of more than a dozen very busy executives in a tight time frame. The owners announced the project to the organization and asked the executive team to each clear space on their calendars for me. Approximately a week before my deadline, I was called into a private meeting with the owners and was told that I needn't bother delivering the plan. That caught me completely off guard. As it turned out, the owners were in the process of selling the company, and they were using my project first, as a means of collecting information that the prospective buyer wanted and second, as a diversionary tactic to avoid raising suspicions that the company was up for sale. It was a most unsatisfying experience. I felt I had done top-notch work, but I never got to deliver the final results, and I felt used. That engagement taught me to initiate an honest conversation with my client about why he/she wants the project done.

Prospecting

About two months before the end of every engagement, I begin asking myself, "Who is my next client?" In almost all cases, the answer turns out to be the person who (a) has a problem to solve, (b) has the funding and the authority to hire me, and (c) has confidence I can deliver solutions. That last criterion (has confidence in me) is the most critical because it is the most limiting. The person must be sufficiently familiar with my work to believe that hiring me is wise, and there are only a limited number of people with that level of familiarity with my work. My most reliable clients have hired me multiple times, and although I've conducted close to a hundred engagements during my career, I only know a dozen or so people who fit the "who is my next client" profile. For my partners and me, repeat business (doing multiple projects for the same client) represents the vast majority of our engagements.

What all this means is that when I go looking for my next assignment, my list of prospects is quite short. The most obvious person I talk to is the client I'm currently working for. In most cases, my current client is my best source and represents the highest probability for a new engagement. I ask if he/she has another project starting soon where I can add value. If not, then I ask what other executives within the company might need my services. Interestingly, I've found that my current client almost always has mentally pigeon-holed me as a resource who specializes in what I'm currently doing, and I have to remind him/her of the different skills I have and the variety of projects I've done for other clients. When obtaining a referral to another executive within my client's organization, I proceed carefully to ensure I don't cause my current client to regret giving me the internal referral. These internal referrals, which we also call "cross pollination," have been one of our more successful marketing methods.

Although my client list is short, it is constantly changing. People have been added to my list because they are former colleagues or client staff who have progressed in their careers by getting promoted to become decision makers with hiring authority or by moving to new companies. People have been deleted from my list because of retirements and changing professions.

Again, the most critical hiring criterion is sufficient confidence in me, and this variable is the only one over which I have some limited control. My ability to influence this variable comes back to the main point of this chapter: Do good work! Although I'm never in control of all the variables, doing good work provides me with the best opportunity for my clients to have confidence in me.

Referrals

When prospecting with recent clients doesn't lead to a new opportunity, I make use of referrals. Referrals from casual acquaintances are generally worthless. The person providing a referral for me needs to be familiar enough with my work in order to give me a genuinely enthusiastic reference. This is one of many areas where my two business partners and I continuously help each other. When any one of the three of us is getting close to the end of an assignment, the other two start looking for opportunities to provide a referral for the one searching for new work. We've also developed a small network of trusted colleagues who we refer opportunities to when we three are all too busy to take on anything new. We have also referred work that we are unqualified for, such as system development or database management, to other trusted colleagues. And those colleagues regularly reciprocate. We never ask for or pay referral fees, because the referrals are based on mutual respect and trust, knowing that "what goes around comes around." My partners and I and our small network of trusted colleagues have referred dozens of opportunities to each other without a single dollar being exchanged. No one has tracked who owes whom a favor, and we each feel in debt to the others. I do believe that trust and loyalty represent a rare type of currency that is significantly more valuable than money.

One of the benefits of referring work to trusted colleagues is that our clients have learned to rely on our referral recommendations, partly because they know we have no financial incentive and partly because the people we refer are highly competent, like Gary G, Bruce O, Dave J, Diane C, and others. Selective referrals have enhanced our credibility with our clients.

Maintaining Relationships

Another consultant once told me that "the shelf life of client appreciation is only about 24 hours, and after that they don't seem to remember the value we contribute." He was exaggerating for effect, but his message is appropriate. A consultant not only needs to demonstrate value every day for the current client, he/she also should regularly remind former clients that they ought to consider the consultant for future projects.

Clearly it's important to keep significant business relationships fresh, but it's easy to let them get stale, especially when I'm engrossed in a current project that consumes my time day after day. At times, it's difficult for me to keep up with my family and friends, much less business colleagues. My partner Mark is excellent at keeping in contact with former clients, and he sets the standard I try to follow. Mark doesn't just call his clients when he's looking for a new project because that can lead to clients feeling used and eventually not returning his calls. Mark calls to catch up, to find out what's new with the client and to let the client know what he's been doing. His conversations are less consultant-to-client than they are friend-to-friend. It's easier to network when you actually like your clients as real people.

How often I connect with my clients depends on the personality of each particular person. Some people don't mind chatting once a month or so, while others seem to be annoyed if I call more than twice a year. So I let my clients "guide" me regarding frequency. The hard part is remembering to connect regularly like Mark does.

The other important relationships I pay close attention to are those within my current client's organization. If I've not been completely professional with someone, I make amends. I remember a particular meeting at one organization where several project and program managers were in attendance to report their individual statuses (or is the plural of status stati?). When the allotted time was almost up and only a fourth of those attending had reported, I spoke up, stating that I had gotten no value from attending and I felt the entire meeting was a waste of everyone's time. Later, upon reflection, I realized I had likely offended everyone in the room, particularly the overall program coordinator who had organized and run the meeting. The next day, I stopped by the program coordinator's desk with a box of chocolates and an apology. At the next meeting of the same group, I publicly apologized to everyone else. While I was embarrassed to make those apologies, they had a generally positive effect. Most of the attendees were unaccustomed to hearing someone admit an error or make amends, and they indicated my apology was unnecessary. Regardless, most changed from thinking I was a jerk to thinking I was human and perhaps an OK guy after all.

Frank and I decided during the first year we were in business to send Christmas cards to the people on our contact list, and Mark participated in these "festivities" after he joined us. In addition to communicating that we remembered them during the holidays, sending the cards was a strong reminder to ourselves to maintain those relationships. If the card we sent was the only communication we had with a person during the year, then we had to admit we had done a poor job managing that relationship. Our annual ritual of sending Christmas cards became an incentive to connect more frequently.

Client relations are never static. They are like other assets, constantly appreciating or depreciating depending on the quality of attention paid to them. In a small consulting firm like ours, it's easier than in the larger firms to maintain strong relations with our current clients because we're working alongside our clients every day. In a larger firm, the consultants assigned to the client's project are not owners of the firm and are therefore generally more focused on the work than on the relationship. Conversely, with prior clients, the larger firms usually have an advantage because they have dedicated account managers who don't need to neglect a current project to meet with a former client. Regardless of the size of the firm though, as a consultant, I should commit to managing each of my client relationships from the first day of a new project with a new client and never stop until I decide to not do further work for that client.

Contacts

I maintain a contact list. It's not a sophisticated database, but rather a basic Excel spreadsheet that I can sort and search. Naturally, all my clients are on my contact list. The list also includes dozens of other colleagues and acquaintances that I may need to contact occasionally. For example, if my client is looking for expert legal help to draft a technology service contract with a vendor, I can refer my client to one of the attorneys I've worked with previously. Another example is when I have a question about a specific vendor product, I will call a person I trust who works for that vendor so I can be confident I'm getting good information rather than a sales pitch. There are many reasons to add someone to my contact list, but I don't add people just to have a long list. In fact, I throw away 90% of the business cards I receive without adding the person to my contact list. My primary filter is, "Do I trust this person to give me accurate information and to do the right thing when confronted with a moral choice?" If the answer is "no" to either part of the question, then I'm reasonably certain I'm not going to call the person, and I don't put them on my list.

In addition to my Excel contact list, I also have contacts on LinkedIn. I've not found the LinkedIn network particularly useful, and people I barely know ask me regularly to add them to my LinkedIn contacts. As I mentioned in Chapter 7, the only reason I'm using LinkedIn is that one of my clients insisted I have my profile on it because her company didn't want to use email to distribute my resume to the other people with whom I might be working in her company.

There are various popular methods to manage contacts such as with CRM (Customer Relationship Management) databases and with social media sites like Facebook. Call me a Luddite, but my opinion is that these methods, like LinkedIn, involve a lot of effort to set up and maintain with very little, if any, payback. Given the structure of my consulting practice, my small list of true clients and my infrequent use of contact information, a simple Excel spreadsheet works just fine.

Difficult Situations

Occasionally I've found myself involved in difficult client situations that required thoughtful attention to resolve. Those difficult situations weren't caused by technical or process issues which can usually be solved with logic and hard work. The thorniest problems are almost always people related conflicts, and my experience is that doing or saying the wrong thing can easily make a bad situation worse. Following are two examples of how I've addressed difficult client situations.

Without informing the rest of the team, an executive at a company I was working with invited a vendor representative to attend an internal planning meeting. He asked the vendor rep to present the various technical solutions her company could provide that might address a particular need we had. Although her information was educational, it became clear during the meeting that the company executive had led the vendor rep to believe she had a sole source opportunity to make a sure sale. After the meeting, I was asked by my client to inform the executive (my client's peer) of his error and then to contact the vendor rep to correct her thinking without damaging the relationship. My discussion with the executive was relatively easy because he denied leading the vendor astray. Even though we both knew he was weaseling out, I allowed him to "escape" and agreed that the vendor rep must have misled herself. When I called the vendor rep, I initially thanked her for the helpful information she had provided. Then I apologized for the "confusion." I didn't mention the company executive by name but told her "we" should have been clear from the beginning that the company cannot sole source vendor contracts. I then told her that I had been directed to make the bidding competitive and would be inviting another supplier to participate in our purchasing process. She was clearly unhappy, but she graciously accepted my "apology" and admitted she knew about the company's policy regarding competitive bidding. Gratitude and apologies (sincere or otherwise) seem to fix a lot of problems. Also, sticking to the facts seems to reduce negative emotions.

One of my favorite clients, John H. taught me a technique he called the "poop" sandwich. It consists of wrapping good tasting bread on either side of a distasteful message. One occasion that called for this technique involved a colleague, Mr. Teflon who was managing a project that was running in parallel with mine. There were several interdependencies between our two projects, but I couldn't get Mr. Teflon to commit to specific delivery dates for results that my team needed. I invited him to my team's weekly status meetings where we shared our milestone schedule with him, highlighting items where my team needed his team to give us specific deliverables, and he would always indicate he understood, but when the delivery dates came, his team didn't produce what we needed. After the third time this happened, I invited Mr. Teflon to lunch where I told him,

"I appreciate you attending my team's status meetings and the deep technical knowledge you bring to the issues. Thank you. I do need you to stop being polite though and to give us your candid feedback on our milestone schedule. For each deliverable your team is to produce, I need you to:

- Agree the date is realistic and deliver on time, or
- Say the date is unachievable and negotiate a more realistic date with us, or
- I will need to bypass you and go to members of your team directly for information.

We know the long hours you are putting in, and we all appreciate your hard work."

Mr. Teflon left our lunch meeting feeling good about our discussion, and I don't think he understood what kind of sandwich I had served him for lunch. I did start getting more useful feedback from him.

Charitable Contributions

Near the end of our first year in business, Frank and I were grateful for our prosperity, and we decided we would make charitable contributions in December to a few worthy charities. We determined to donate one percent of our top line revenue. We then discussed which charities we should consider, and we discovered that neither of us had particularly strong feelings about any organizations. Then Frank had an epiphany and suggested we stop worrying about it and let our clients decide for us. He said, "It was their money to begin with, so let them tell us what charities they favor." This approach turned into a happy accident for us.

We called each client we had worked for during the year, we told each of them what we planned to do, and we asked them to each identify a favorite charity. All of our clients were pleasantly surprised by our approach to charitable giving, and enthusiastically participated. Our only requirements were that the recipient organizations had to be recognized by the IRS as true charities and they could not have a political agenda. For each client, we calculated one percent of the gross revenue earned from working for that client and rounded the amount up to the next even $100. We then sent a check to the charity with a cover letter acknowledging that our client had named their organization as the recipient, and we sent a copy of our cover letter to the client. Most of the charities sent us gracious letters thanking us. We have continued this practice of asking clients to name charities for us ever since.

Over the past 20 plus years, we've made donations to a variety of worthwhile charities including Ronald McDonald House, St Jude's Children's Hospital, Salvation Army, Red Cross, National Cancer Society, National ALS, Boy Scouts, a college dormitory capital improvement fund, a neighborhood improvement fund and several other world, national and local charitable organizations. One of our favorites was a Special Olympics group in a small Wisconsin community; after our first donation, we received an emotional letter from the director saying our contributions allowed them to purchase new equipment, uniforms and trophies for the participants, and our generosity helped make their event more successful than ever.

We were initially surprised by the reactions and feedback from our clients. Most of them had been contacted by the charities they had named, and our clients in turn called to thank us as well. We consistently heard from our clients that no other supplier or vendor has ever had a similar program, and we would be remembered, not just for our good work, but also for our creative generosity. We started our contributions program solely to give something back to the community. The unintended fallout was to create an enormous amount of client goodwill and to differentiate us from other consultants. The charities benefited not just from the money we donated, but also from the contact information we supplied about the sponsoring client executive.

Letting our clients select the recipients of our charitable contributions had benefits for us that we didn't foresee. First, it forced us to make a purposeful contact with each client that had nothing to do with selling more business. Second, it made us unique from other consulting firms. And third, it gave our clients one more reason to be grateful they hired us. Giving charitable donations is the right thing to do. And as I said earlier, our approach to it turned into a happy accident for us.

Summary

I cannot over emphasize the point I made initially in this chapter. The key to client relations is to deliver good work! Good work is a mandatory prerequisite to securing additional business with a client. It might not be sufficient by itself to getting more work, but without it, repeat business is effectively impossible.

Some of the other lessons Frank, Mark and I have learned regarding client relations include:

- Clearly understand who (which person) your client is.
- Know what category of organization your client works for. I mention four types in this chapter, but you can invent your own classification scheme if those don't feel right.
- Understand why your client hired you.
- Maintain your client relationship by staying in contact.
- Be prepared to handle difficult or uncomfortable situations.
- Do something to differentiate yourself from other consultants, preferably in a positive way.

Suggested Reading and Reference

Levitt, Theodore. *The Marketing Imagination.* The Free Press, 1983

Chapter 9 – The Contract

"Ride the horse in the direction that it's going."
-- Werner Erhard

After a client agrees that I'm the right consultant for their project, I formalize my agreement with the client because I don't start an engagement before getting a written contract. I've used various formats depending on the procurement policies and procedures required by the client's organization and the level of trust my client and I have with each other. The agreements I've used are always one of three types. This chapter describes those three formats, starting with the simplest.

Engagement Letter

An engagement letter, also known as a letter of agreement or a confirmation letter, is an easy way to document and formalize a consulting agreement with a client. While I was with Price Waterhouse and with KPMG, most of our engagements used this format, and I've used it on about half the engagements I've done since starting my own firm. Following is an example.

****

Dear Mr. Client:
Faulise, Janda & Docherty is pleased to confirm our agreement to provide consulting assistance to (client organization). The scope of our assistance includes project management to help develop a new technology architecture for (client organization). Dave Faulise, a consultant in our firm, will conduct this work. He will report to you, and he will be assisted by members of your staff and/or by others you designate. Dave will initiate work the week of December xx, 20xx.

As agreed, professional fees will be based on a $xxx per hour rate through June 30, 20xx. We will submit invoices for time expended at the end of each two-week period. In addition, Faulise, Janda &

Docherty will be reimbursed for travel and other (client organization) approved out-of-pocket expenses incurred on your behalf.

It is the parties' intention that Faulise, Janda & Docherty is an independent contractor. No employee or officer of Faulise, Janda & Docherty is (client organization)'s employee for all purposes including, but not limited to, income tax withholding at the source of income, worker's compensation and unemployment insurance state statute application.

We appreciate this opportunity to assist (client organization) and are looking forward to working with you on this project. Please sign and return the enclosed acceptance copy of this confirmation for our records.

Very truly yours,

David V. Faulise

Accepted by: ______________________________ Date: ____________

Title: ____

****

Although this example engagement letter is brief, it still contains the essential elements of a formal agreement. It specifies:

- What will be done.
- Who will do it.
- When it starts.
- The rate to be charged.
- Expenses are not included in the rate.
- Frequency of billing.

I like the engagement letter format because of its simplicity, its brevity and because it covers all the bases. My clients like it for the same reasons. Attorneys and purchasing departments hate it not because it won't work, but because it does work and because it makes their jobs less necessary.

Statement of Work

I use an SOW (Statement of Work) when I already have a formalized agreement with the client's organization. This happens when the new project is treated as an extension of an existing project or when I've recently done another project for the organization under an existing contract or a master agreement that's still in force. Note that within this chapter, I use the term "SOW" to describe a client contractual arrangement. In Chapter 14, I use the same term to describe a more extensive collection of project management documents used as reference tools throughout the duration of the project.

A contractual SOW is similar to an engagement letter because it's succinct. Although some SOWs might contain all the elements of an engagement letter, many do not because some of the needed elements are already contained in the master agreement or prior engagement letter. The following example is a fairly comprehensive SOW that a client and I agreed to sign a few years ago. This example is silent on some items including expenses and billing terms because those were contained in the master agreement that is referenced in the first paragraph of the SOW.

****

STATEMENT OF WORK

This Statement of Work ("SOW") is governed under the terms and conditions of the Independent Contractor Agreement effective March xx, 20xx between (client organization) and Faulise, Janda & Docherty ("Contractor") and is effective June xx, 20xx ("SOW Effective Date").

1. Services

Contractor is being retained to provide project management expertise for the purpose of assessing and acquiring data center services from external providers.

2. Charges for Services
$xxx per hour

3. Specification of Deliverables
The project manager will coordinate an internal team for the purposes of:

- Reviewing current data center environment (contract, vendor, business needs, etc.)
- Analysis of industry/market trends and vendors
- RFP composition including current, proposed and future needs
- RFP distribution and vendor meetings
- RFP response evaluation and vendor contract negotiations

The project manager will be expected to work full time between now and November 20xx. Total hours will not exceed 600 without prior agreement from both parties.

4. SOW Start Date: June xx, 20xx

SOW End Date: November xx, 20xx

5. The assigned consultant is Dave Faulise. If the consultant assigned does not perform in accordance with (client organization)'s reasonable expectations, (client organization) may accept a replacement consultant from Contractor but (client organization) is not obligated to do so. (Client organization) is only obligated to pay Contractor for hours actually worked by the consultant.

SIGNED:

For and on behalf of: (Client Organization)	For and on behalf of: [Contractor]
By: ________________	By: ______________
Sign: ________________	Sign: ______________
Title: Senior Vice President & CIO	Title: ______________
Date: ________________	Date: ______________

****

Formal Contract

A formal contract is the most complicated and most difficult format to use when documenting the terms of a consulting agreement. It is also the lengthiest, sometimes running to 20 pages or more. I only use a formal contract when required by my client's organization, and I usually use their standard contract as a starting point.

I do not intend this section of the chapter to provide instruction on how to draft or negotiate a formal commercial contract. Rather, this section provides a summary of the general structure and terms contained in most of the contracts I've negotiated. The following table describes in plain language the more significant terms of an actual contract that I negotiated with a client several years ago. I presented this table to the client to communicate my preferred position on these terms. The client found this simple table helpful, and with only minor revisions it became the basis for the eventual contract we signed to formalize our agreement.

Contract Terms & Conditions

Term	Description
Structure	One master agreement with work orders as addendums for each project; a business-to-business arrangement
Parties	(Client Organization) and Faulise, Janda & Docherty, a Minnesota corporation (Contractor)
Term Length	Number of years or months contract is in effect: Prefer One Year, but willing to consider other options
Options	Extension options at the end of the initial term can be added by amendment only
Termination Causes	Contract expiration at end of term, material breach, death by 1000 cuts, or for convenience (with 30 days notice) by either party

Term	Description
Termination Penalty	When termination is for convenience by either party and if less than 30 days notice is given, a penalty of $10,000 is due for each resource released/withdrawn
Reps and Warrants	Both parties provide assurance of non-infringement of 3rd-party intellectual property rights
Indemnification	Both parties hold each other harmless equally
Limits of Liability	Maximum amount either party can recover from the other equals the total fees paid to date at the time of wrongdoing
Confidentiality	Both parties agree to standard confidentiality and non-disclosure terms to keep each other's information confidential
Dispute Resolution	60 days to resolve before litigation can commence; prefer no mandatory arbitration
Services Covered	For each project a detail work order or Statement of Work (SOW) defining project scope, duration, responsibilities and rates
Assignment	Neither party will assign the agreement to a third party without approval by both original parties
Insurance	Contractor shall carry coverage at the limits specified in the Insurance Attachment for Workers Compensation, Employers Liability, Commercial General Liability, Commercial Auto, Commercial Umbrella Liability and Professional Liability
Contractor Rate	For each SOW, determined by agreement with the (Client Company) business unit and pre-approved by the (Client Company) procurement department
Payment Terms	Net 30 Days
Exclusivity	Client limitations to hire other consultants and Consultant limitations to work for other clients: None by either party

Term	Description
Governing Authority	Prefer State of Minnesota, but willing to consider other options
Notices	Address of each party where formal notices are to be sent

Sub-contracts

About half of my engagements over recent years have been sub-contracts, and I've developed relationships with four firms that I use as prime contractors. I've found sub-contracting necessary because many client organizations now have preferred vendor lists and they limit engagements they award to only the large contracting and consulting firms that they have on their lists. Unfortunately my three-person firm is too small to make the lists.

When I find a project through a former client who works for an organization with a preferred vendor list, I invite one of the firms that are on the list to be the prime contractor, and I dictate how much of a cut they get from my billing rate, usually 5 to 10 percent. When a prime contractor finds the opportunity and invites me to participate, they dictate the terms, and their cut of my billing rate will range from 20 to 30 percent.

The contractual arrangement usually involves the prime contractor establishing an SOW with the client organization, and I, as the sub-contractor, establish a formal contract with the prime. The end result is that I do not have a direct arrangement with my client's organization. The section above contains a discussion about formal contracts, and those comments generally apply to sub-contract agreements as well.

Many of the standard contracts I've seen that prime contractors want to use with their sub-contractors are, in my opinion, poorly written and one-sided. One of the prime contractors I had worked with previously came to me with a new opportunity that looked like a good fit. They had re-written their standard sub-contract agreement since I had last worked with them, and they asked me to sign the new version. The non-solicitation clause from their old contract had said that I, as their sub-contractor, would not solicit or engage in business with any client organization to which they had introduced me for one year after my engagement was complete. That old language was acceptable to me. The new clause said, "Sub-contractor promises not to solicit or contract with any existing or prospective client of" the prime contractor. The lack of a time limit was bad enough. The inclusion of "prospective" clients was completely unacceptable. Loosely interpreted, every company on the planet could be considered a "prospective" client. When I discussed my concerns about this clause with the firm's president, he would not adjust the language, and I therefore declined their new opportunity. They've called me a few times since then, and each time they do, I ask about their non-solicitation clause, find out it still includes "prospective" clients, and politely end the conversation.

Rates

My billing rate ranges between $100 and $135 per hour, and it has rarely deviated from this range for the past 20 years. I am usually near the low end of the range when sub-contracting, and near the high end when I have a direct relationship with the client organization. The net result is that the client ends up paying slightly more when I'm sub-contracting because of the uplift by the contracting firm. The economy is another factor that affects rates. When opportunities are scarcer and competition is greater, there is a natural downward pressure on rates.

What are the rates for technology consultants and contractors? It depends on the person's skill set. For example, an experienced web developer who knows Java, C++ and .Net is going to command a rate significantly higher than a developer trainee who took one Visual Basic course while in college. In general, hourly rates are determined by years of experience. In 2013 dollars, the following are reasonable billing rate approximations that clients might expect to pay:

- 1 to 2 years experience $60
- 3 to 5 years experience $80
- 6 to 10 years experience $100
- over 10 years experience $125+

Note that these are rates the client might pay for a consultant from a small firm, and the consultant would collect that amount if he/she were a sole proprietor. The consultant would get less if sub-contracting or if he/she were an employee rather than an owner of the small firm. For consultants from the larger firms with global name recognition, the client should expect to pay double or triple the above estimates, although the consultant won't be paid more.

As a partner at KPMG my billing rate was more than double what it is now. Honestly, I am not less intelligent, less experienced or less competent than I was at KPMG or at Price Waterhouse. The difference is that I no longer have the large, prestigious firm name on my business card. Unfortunately, coming from KPMG distorted our perspectives on billing rates when Frank and I started our own consulting business. We knew our rates should be lower than they had been at KPMG, but we didn't realize how much lower. We thought that $150 per hour was quite reasonable since it was about two-thirds of our KPMG rates. That rate was satisfying to our egos but not to the marketplace. A high rate multiplied by zero hours equals no income. Over the first few months we spoke to several clients and gradually came to realize we needed to push our egos aside and deal with the reality of what the market thought we were worth.

While rates that are too high produce no revenue, rates that are too low reduce credibility. Talking to former clients and other consultants who had started their own businesses brought us eventually to a reasonable balance point somewhere between too high and too low. One nugget of wisdom we mined from our various discussions was that we needed consistency in our billing rates because charging significantly different rates to different clients can create potential problems and conflicts. No matter how confidential a firm tries to make its rates, there are enough clients and others who know what they are, and eventually billing rates are no longer secrets.

Over our years of consulting, Frank, Mark and I have learned to be pragmatic about rates. We are willing to slightly reduce rates (or at least not increase them over time) when the client has re-hired us for additional engagements. This isn't a unique idea. Many other companies in non-consulting industries practice this type of volume discounting for repeat business.

During the last several years, purchasing and procurement departments have become powerful within many organizations, and they have inserted themselves between consulting firms and clients with the result that more formal arrangements are now required in those organizations. Procurement departments justify their heightened activity with claims of reduced rates and lower costs. I will accept a rate lower than my standard rate during a recessionary economy, but that's because there is more competition for fewer projects, not because procurement has created an artificial rate card. The real effect of procurement departments flexing their muscles is that experienced, competent consultants won't pursue projects with sub-standard rates, and the hiring organization ends up compromising on quality by hiring people with less experience. Projects take longer than they should, with the result that, even with lower rates, the longer time frame ends up costing the organization more overall. The math is simple: low rates times more hours equals higher costs. Most of my clients understand this reality, but unfortunately there is no incentive for procurement departments to undermine the power base they've created for themselves. Some procurement people also don't understand or appreciate the services they are buying. They act as if one project manager is the same as every other project manager, a commodity. My clients have numerous horror stories to support an opposite viewpoint. I've worked with some excellent procurement people like Jamie G. and Galit B., but unfortunately, they are exceptions.

Summary

Experience has taught me to be pragmatic and "go with the flow" when it comes to contracts, billing rates and working with procurement departments. Over the years, I've also learned to listen to my clients and to other consultants and to accept the reality of what the marketplace is telling me.

Being pragmatic about rates and contracts has made Frank, Mark and me prosperous for two and a half decades. We're quite proud of the period from 1993 to 2003 when we had no unbilled hours except for vacations and holidays. That remarkable ten-year stretch with no unbilled hours is a testament to the wisdom of "Ride the horse in the direction that it's going."

Chapter 9 – The Contract

Chapter 10 – Exit Strategy

"I don't want everyone to like me; I should think less of myself if some people did."
-- Henry James

As difficult as it is to get entry into a client organization, to secure an engagement and to get paid an acceptable billing rate, there are times when it's equally hard to get out of a client organization. If you do good work, you inevitably will have this enviable problem.

The first time I terminated a client engagement was stressful for me. My client had hired me to plan and execute a technology transformation. I wrote an RFP, acquired equipment, established a communications network, purchased application software, and contracted with custom software developers. After one year, we had replaced all the legacy equipment, applications and databases, and the transformation was well on its way to completion. That was the good news. The bad news was that my client, Mr. Volume who was the CIO, would periodically explode; yelling at the top of his lungs at whomever he felt was responsible to solve whatever problem had set him off. He didn't discriminate, but would vent at all his direct reports, including me, equally. The relative importance of the triggering issue didn't seem to matter, which meant his explosions were unpredictable. After he targeted me for the third time, I decided I had had enough. The next morning I went into Mr. Volume's office, shut the door and explained to him that I was leaving because I would no longer tolerate being treated unprofessionally. He initially pretended to not understand, so I listed the three events when he had screamed at me. I then told him that his staff were afraid of him and were all likely to leave the organization if he didn't change how he treated them. Later that morning, I sent an email to the staff announcing my departure with the explanation that our project was nearing completion and I would be starting soon on another project with a new client organization. Three weeks later I had transitioned my responsibilities and secured another engagement in another company. The day I left, Mr. Volume privately thanked me for my efforts, for the success of our project and for helping him adjust his management style. We've remained friends. Sometimes consulting requires being an amateur therapist.

Most consultants give little thought to the process of leaving a client organization. After all, it's simple because you merely need to finish your project, say your good-byes and walk out the door. Right? Actually, I have the opposite opinion. I believe that leaving a client is one of the most difficult aspects of being a consultant. This is true regardless of how successful the engagement has been and regardless of whether I want to do additional work for this same client. If I want to do further work for the organization and if the termination is handled well, I leave the door open for future engagements. If I handle the termination poorly, I could be slamming the door shut permanently.

Every engagement termination should include a scheduled, formal closing meeting with my client and others as he/she determines appropriate. During the closing meeting I distribute:

- A list of work products (deliverables) with a written summary of each one and where it is stored/located.
- If appropriate, a summary of findings, conclusions and/or recommendations. This may include lessons learned that may be applied to future projects.
- A list of open action items and who is assigned to each.
- Other deliverables, depending on the nature of the engagement.

These documents are obviously important to my client to help him/her tie up loose ends and to bring closure to the effort. They are important to me because they are continuing reminders to my client of my work and they reinforce why hiring me was a good decision. They are much more effective than merely leaving behind a business card.

Even with dysfunctional clients that I have no desire to work with again, I have been careful to make my departure as graceful as possible. I'm convinced that when employees and other consultants from a former client eventually move on to other organizations, they carry long memories with them, and I want them to remember me in a positive light. A good example is a manager who worked in Mr. Volume's organization mentioned above. She joined another company where she became a director and eventually a V.P., and she has hired me several times to help with a variety of her projects.

In general, there are three ways that most engagements are terminated:

- First, the client allows the project to end as planned and as scheduled from the beginning. I don't view this type of ending as positive or negative because the client isn't making an effort to retain me. If he/she feels I have added value, and if I have established a positive relationship, then the client will usually make an effort to offer an extension and/or suggest other projects rather than just let me leave at the natural conclusion of the current project.
- Second, the client initiates an early project termination. This situation is rarely good. Some of the logic from the first type of ending described above applies, but I consider it even more serious because the client is in a hurry to end the project before it comes to a natural conclusion.
- Third, I initiate the termination. This type of ending is the most positive way an engagement can conclude. I am in control. Timing isn't particularly relevant, and I have experience ending projects earlier than the planned end date as well as after an extension or after a follow-on project. Although this third type of ending is positive, I proceed carefully in order to leave behind a happy client.

High School Déjà Vu

If you're skeptical about the above three types of endings, consider the idea that client relationships are like dating relationships in high school. There are many similarities. If I go out for pizza and a movie, and at the end of the evening, my date thanks me but declines when I ask about going out again, then that's similar to ending number one. If my date makes an excuse to end the evening early before we even get to the theater, then that's like ending number two. If the evening goes well and my date wants to see me again, then I have more of an equal say about how long to continue the relationship, and it's similar to ending number three.

For one client, I initiated my termination prior to the end of the engagement in spite of enjoying the people I worked with, my client (our boss) and the work itself. I was leading a business process re-engineering effort for a software implementation company with operations in several countries. We spent the first month identifying various problem areas, and we then divided the corrections we had conceived into two categories: (1) quick fixes that had immediate payback and (2) more extensive programs with longer-term results. We spent the next three months implementing the quick fixes and teeing up the larger programs. By the fifth month, the re-engineering effort was well on its way to transform the company into a more profitable and more professionally managed business. I had a highly competent project manager and two exceptional business analysts working for me who were more than capable of continuing the program without me. While I could have worked on the engagement for several more months for my own financial benefit, I wanted to do the right thing for my client. I spoke with her about my observations, and although she initially asked me to stay, she eventually agreed that the program was running smoothly and that I would transition my responsibilities to the project manager who was working for me. As they say in show business, "Always leave 'em asking for more." I left, and over the next five months the team successfully completed implementing the processes we had re-engineered.

Graceful Departures

I prefer to initiate engagement terminations. This is true whether I want to do additional work for the client or not, and it's especially true when I don't want to work for the client again. Fortunately, most of my engagements have been positive experiences, and I've only had four distasteful engagements working for unprofessional executives. Three of these situations occurred because the person who originally hired me subsequently referred me to do work for another executive in the company who turned out to be a jerk.

One client engaged me to do program management for multiple technology projects to enhance a current suite of systems as well as to completely replace one of them. I managed and coordinated work with several teams including legal, compliance, marketing, product distribution, customer relations, technology operations, technology development and multiple technology vendors. After hiring me, my client had me report to one of his directors who had been with the organization for several years and therefore knew most of the players. They also knew her. Ms. Chaos never wrote anything down. She would hold impromptu meetings with her staff and me to inform us of the latest change in direction based on new information she'd been given that had to remain confidential. She called these urgent, unscheduled meetings multiple times each week, sometimes twice in one day. The scope of my responsibilities expanded, contracted and morphed so frequently that I found myself constantly re-writing the statements of work for the various projects and updating project plans daily. I later found out that two internal program managers had previously been assigned to my position, and they consecutively resigned after each had worked for less than a week for Ms. Chaos. I lasted three months. After making my decision to resign, I waited until my scope contracted again, which it inevitably did. I then wrote the following memo to Ms. Chaos and cc'd my client, our boss:

****

Ms. Chaos:
After reviewing the current state of our program and projects, it is time to end my engagement. Reasons include:

- At your recent staff meeting, we introduced a "divide and conquer" approach with Mr. ABC taking project management responsibility for the XXX project and Ms. DEF taking project management responsibility for the YYY project. This significantly reduced the scope of my work.
- We eliminated the ZZZ project and some components from three other projects, further reducing the scope of my work.
- We now have the XXX project under control, reducing risk and reducing the need for constant attention from me. The XXX project still has issues and will have a few rough spots, but Mr. ABC is fully competent to address those.
- The ZZZ components of the YYY project are now on track and are being well managed by their respective leads.
- Our relationships with sales, marketing and customer relations are significantly improved and currently need only limited attention from me.

The bottom line is there is no longer a need for me to provide program management services, and I am no longer contributing the value we originally anticipated when I was hired. I will spend the next two weeks transitioning my remaining responsibilities to you and your staff.

Thank you, Dave Faulise

CC: Mr. Client

****

Note the generally positive tone of this memo. I was careful to avoid negativity and to not blame Ms. Chaos for my departure. I also did not leave room to negotiate my staying beyond the two weeks notice. Although I had no desire to remain with the organization, I wanted my client and others I had worked with to have a positive last impression of me. I didn't care what Ms. Chaos thought.

Timing

Whether or not I want to continue working for my current client, I start looking for my next assignment two or three months before the current one is scheduled to end. While prospecting and especially while interviewing, it's easier to sound confident and exude credibility when I am currently engaged. I am able to say things like, "I'm sorry I can't meet with you on Thursday next week because of a commitment with my current engagement, but I can free up some time over the lunch hour on Friday if that works for you." That sounds much better than, "I can meet with you whenever you want." The first statement puts me on a more equal footing with a prospective client, while the second statement makes me sound desperate.

Prospective clients want to hire someone they believe is currently busy doing consulting engagements. If other people are hiring me, then that indicates my services are in demand, and you, Mr. Prospect, should be interested in hiring me, too.

Summary

One of the most valuable consulting skills I've learned is how to terminate an engagement. Most engagements are positive, and ending them properly is part of the overall positive experience. Regarding the rare negative situations, my business partner, Mark has said, "Few things in our professional lives are as satisfying as firing a bad client."

With great clients who hire me again and again, the most positive engagement endings are the ones I initiate. Knowing how to properly end an engagement may be one of the reasons my positive client relationships continue to be positive.

Chapter 10 – Exit Strategy

Part 4 – Engagement Execution

Chapter 11 – Assessments

> "There is nothing as easy as denouncing. It don't take much to see that something is wrong, but it takes some eyesight to see what will put it right again."
>
> -- Will Rogers

An assessment is a critical review of a troubled business function or project performed by an experienced consultant. I don't seek out these types of engagements because:

- They typically are completed in a few weeks, and even using a premium-billing rate, they don't generate much revenue.
- As a reviewer, I'm an unpopular person, similar to an IRS auditor, and my opportunities to do other work for the client become limited.

I now refer to assessments as "health checks" because that sounds more positive than an "audit," but I'm likely not fooling anyone, other than myself. When a client organization asks to have an assessment done, usually one of two reasons is behind it:

- A large, high-visibility project or program is considered to be in trouble. The most common symptom indicating a project is failing is multiple delays to the targeted completion date.
- A business unit has developed a reputation for consistently not delivering expected results. The most common symptom that a business area is floundering is an increase in the volume and intensity of sniping from the leaders of other internal departments.

Goals of an Assessment

When I've conducted assessment engagements, I tailor my goals with guidance from and collaboration with the hiring executive. These goals usually include:

- Investigating the problems thoroughly to understand root causes
- Developing practical, targeted recommendations
- Maintaining a fact-based, unbiased and independent perspective
- Completing the work rapidly (in 2-3 weeks)
- Requiring a minimum of time from client personnel

Focus

I organize the work and my thinking for these engagements by focusing on four perspectives as shown in the following diagram:

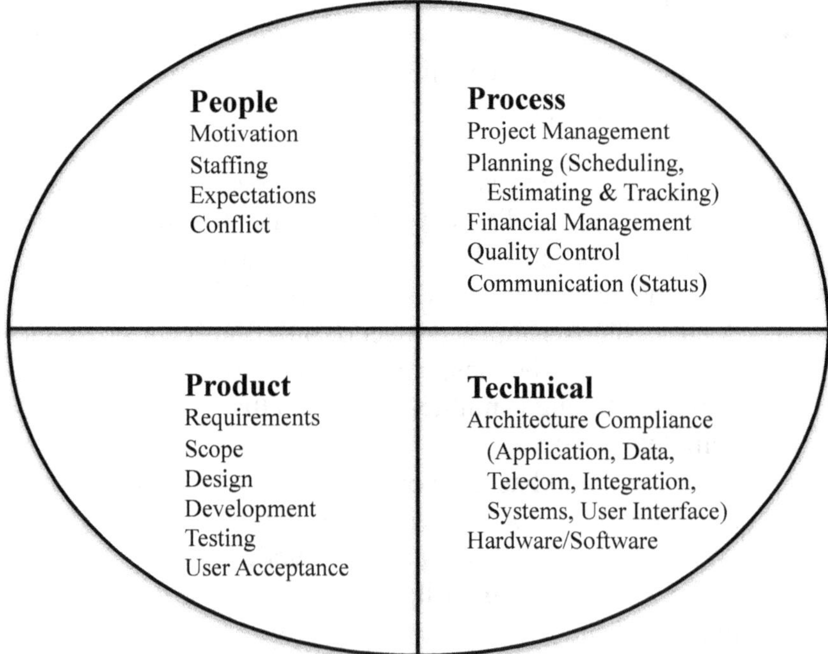

Assumptions

In my experience, no client wants to do an assessment. They want their projects to succeed, and they want their organization units to efficiently deliver valuable results. Clients are forced to have an assessment performed because they know something is wrong that if not addressed may create a career limiting situation for the leader(s) responsible. Also, the manager of the troubled project or business unit invariably assumes that at the conclusion of the assessment, the blame will be laid at his/her feet. As the consultant, I can therefore safely make a few assumptions when starting an assessment:

- The client leader requesting the assessment work is usually doing so out of fear.
- The client has already tried to fix the situation without success.
- Most of those directly involved with the troubled project or business unit are afraid of the assessment.

Let's consider the implications of each of these assumptions individually.

First, the problem situation has the potential to tarnish the reputation of the requesting executive, and he/she ultimately wants to give the appearance of decisively fixing the problem, turning a negative into a positive. Therefore, one of my objectives is to give this executive some highly actionable recommendations at the conclusion of my assignment. While I may or may not recommend long-term and medium-term actions, I must recommend at least some short-term actions that are visible and easily communicated. Also, if the review itself is highly visible, the hiring manager wants to create a safe position by engaging a consultant from an organization with sufficient credibility so as not to be easily challenged. I performed many of these assessments when I was with Price Waterhouse and with KPMG, and I've done far fewer of them since starting my own practice; I'm actually smarter and more experienced now, but obviously the name of my firm doesn't provide the same level of executive air cover. Since leaving the big name firms though, when I have been hired to do an assessment, it's been a result of a trust relationship with the hiring executive and/or I've been hired to perform a larger engagement that requires an assessment to be included as part of it.

Second, I have found that for every assessment engagement I've performed, the client had previously taken actions that did not fix the problem. Typically, the hiring executive had replaced the original manager and was on their second or even third manager of the troubled area. The client also had tried extending the deadline multiple times in the vain hope that more time would solve the problem. Another classic but futile "solution" is throwing money at the problem. I ask about these prior attempts during my initial interview, which I insist is a one-to-one session with the hiring executive. Having this private conversation allows me to reassure the executive that I've previously seen these types of problems many times and that there are always solutions, but those solutions depend entirely on getting candid information, from him/her and from everyone else involved. I state plainly that I need to understand what's been tried already so I can avoid going down blind alleys. I also ask what the executive thinks is the underlying root-cause of the problems. I may or may not get an answer to this last question, and if I do get an answer, it may or may not be accurate. However, more often than not, I'm able to obtain some useful insights that might otherwise take me days to uncover from other company sources.

Third, let's consider those involved with the troubled situation and their fear of my potential findings. They universally do not want me or anyone else to perform the assessment. The success of the assessment depends squarely on the accuracy and completeness of the information I obtain, and therefore I need to extract good intelligence from everyone involved. I typically conduct a dozen to twenty or more interviews over the initial two weeks. I make these one-to-one conversations because I've found that group discussions only provide me with politically correct crap. Having private conversations allows me to assure the interviewees that I will religiously protect their anonymity. Although I've never divulged a source (without their permission), I'm still surprised that most people trust me; I'm not sure I would if the roles were reversed. Fortunately I get some very candid opinions. This is probably because most of the people I interview want their organization to succeed in spite of their fears.

Approach

The assessment process isn't rocket science, and I've found that by using a logical approach and some basic tools, I can gather the information I need to conduct an effective and efficient assessment. The steps are:

- Conduct interviews. I schedule these to be no more than 30 to 45 minutes long. I start with the senior executives responsible and work my way down the food chain. I do as many interviews as possible in a one-to-one setting. I use a checklist of specific questions, but I need to be flexible because not every question is applicable to each person interviewed; in fact, during most interviews I use less than half the questions in my checklist. I don't need to fire every arrow in my quiver to hit the target. I've included an example checklist of questions below. I start the interview with a brief monologue about what I'm doing, why it's important and my guarantee of anonymity. Then I start going through the questions and take copious notes. This next part is key, and it's not on the checklist. During the "Resource" section of the questionnaire, I ask each person, "When you run into a difficult problem that you can't solve, who do you turn to for advice?" I write down the name of the person the interviewee identifies.
- Obtain and review pertinent documentation. I perform this step concurrently with the interviews because I can review documents between interviews and minimize any "dead time."
- Think. This is where experience helps. I use the critical thinking process described in Chapter 1 to mentally move

up and down the levels of details I've accumulated so far. I start jotting down possible conclusions as they occur to me. I resist the temptation to form recommendations at this stage because there's still more information to collect.

- Conduct selected follow-up interviews. I use the names from the "Who do you trust?" game that I played during the interviews to see what patterns emerge. One or two names will be mentioned most frequently, and these are the "trusted experts" with whom I need to do follow-up interviews. Again, I make sure these are one-to-one sessions. Consciously or sub-consciously these trusted experts know what the underlying problems are and what to do to fix them. I ask them directly for their ideas, and I don't let them avoid answering. One question I use a lot is, "If you were king of the world, what three things would you change to fix the problems with this project/organization?" I keep digging by using "Why" questions, such as, "Why would that help?" Again, I take lots of notes.
- Think again. What I learn from the trusted experts is valuable, but it typically isn't politically correct as originally stated to me. Those trusted experts exist in every company, and they lurk in the bowels of the organization rather than rising to positions of leadership because by their nature, they don't particularly care about politics. Note that by definition, leaders are rarely trusted experts because they are too far removed from the nuts and bolts of the company's foundational machinery to understand how things really work. But the trusted experts do know. The raw diamonds you obtain from them will need to be cut and polished in order to be presentable.
- Draft the report findings and conclusions. I write. I think. I edit. I re-write. Writing is hard, and I have to push myself to get my thoughts on paper. I usually don't get near the final version until I'm on about the 6th or 7th draft.

I formerly structured the material in the same sequence I created it:
    - Findings,
    - Conclusions,
    - Recommendations

However, every executive I've known jumps immediately to the recommendations, so now I lead with those. For guidance, I've provided the outline of an actual assessment report at the end of this chapter.

- Have an editor critique the "final" draft. I have one of my trusted colleagues, usually Frank or Mark, do my final editing. Then I use the editor's suggestions to create the final "final" version. The final report will be how the client remembers me after the engagement is completed. The content obviously needs to have value, and the format and readability represent me as a professional.
- Conduct a closing discussion. I send the hiring executive (and only him/her) a copy of the final report in advance. The executive can choose to invite others to the closing meeting and to provide copies of the report to those other attendees at his/her discretion. When the closing meeting starts, I always assume that no one other than me has read the report beyond the first page. I may need to facilitate the discussion for the first few minutes, but generally my role is to respond to questions by clarifying particular points. I answer most questions by referring to a specific page and paragraph in the report. I've had some of these meetings be as brief as 20 minutes and others last for several hours. Because they're unpredictable, I've found it's safest to not schedule any conflicting commitment to start immediately after one of these meetings.

There is typically nothing more to be done after the closing meeting. A few times, I've been asked to follow up on a question or a clarifying point, and twice I was asked by the hiring executive to assume management of the troubled project. But being asked to conduct additional work is rare.

Summary

Conducting an assessment isn't particularly complicated, but it requires being well organized and the use of perceptive interpersonal skills. Interviewing is clearly an art. I don't seek out these engagements, but when they find me, I've enjoyed doing them.

The following pages contain a questionnaire I used and some of the deliverables I produced during a two-week assessment that I conducted a few years ago. Reviewing these materials will likely be more instructive than just reading about assessments.

Example Health Check Questionnaire

Topics	Questions and Documentation Requests
Resources	
Project Organization Structure	• How many people are working on the project and how are they organized into teams? • Are there a sufficient number of resources from ABC and from the Customer? • Are essential project team members assigned full time? • Are all team members identified and committed to the project?
Project Leadership	• Are you, as the PM, assigned full time? • Do you have complete responsibility for managing the project? • How much time do you spend with each team every week?
Team Member's Availability	• Are the ABC and Customer resources able to allocate sufficient time to the project? • How much turnover in team members have you experienced since the project started?
Team Members Experience & Skills	• Do team members have the right skills and experience? • Are experienced and proficient technical resources assigned to this project?
Confidence & Team Energy	• Describe team morale and attitudes.
Geographic Challenges	• Are all or most team members on-site?
Cultural Challenges	• Are some team resources from third-party organizations?
Communi-cations	• Please send me the most recent Customer and/or ABC announcements or presentations about the project.
User Involvement	• Describe the level of cooperation between users and the project teams. • What is the Customer's percent of the total project hours?
Processes	
Phasing	• Is the project organized into phases as prescribed by the

Topics	Questions and Documentation Requests
	XXX methodology? • What phase of the project are you in?
Vision	• Was there any hesitation moving from the Vision to the Strategy Phase?
Strategy	• Was the Strategy phase signed off? • Please send me copies of (or a link to) the final sign-offs for the project Charter, scope, and gate checklist.
Realization	• Was the Execution phase signed off? • Please send me copies of (or a link to) the sign-offs for the User acceptance, and gate checklist.
Deployment & Closure	• How involved was the Customer in the Deployment phase? • Please send me copies of (or a link to) the Training Materials, Procedure Documents, Training Recap.
Scope & Change Management	• Is the project being driven by Schedule, Cost, Scope, or Quality? • Please send me copies of (or a link to) the most recent Change Control Log.
Status Reporting	• Describe the Status Reporting process? Who gets the reports, and who reads them? • Please send me copies of (or a link to) your last two status reports.
Issue Management	• How are problems and issues reported? • What is the process for resolution? • Please send me a copy of (or a link to) your project Issue Log.
Cost/Financial Management	• How many current unbilled hours are there for this project? • Please send me a copy of (or a link to) your most recent project financial report.
Delivery Assurance Compliance	• What checkpoints are in place to ensure quality and to re-assess decision-making?
Linkage & Dependency Management	• Is there a plan for the overall initiative (a master plan) with linkages to detail plans for sub-project components, as well as linkages to other projects? • Are there linkages to other projects, and are the commitments to them on track?

Topics	Questions and Documentation Requests
Schedule Management	• How long will this entire project take? (6 months, 6 – 12, 12+) • What have been the major factors impacting the project schedule, either positively or negatively?
Risk Management	• Please send me a copy of (or a link to) your Risk Management Plan.
Contingency Plans	• Please send me a copy of (or a link to) your Contingency Plan.
Training	• How many Client resources have attended training sessions? • Have there been any training problems or issues?
Results	
Volume of Deliverables	• Have you skipped any XXX methodology deliverables, and if yes, why? • Please send me a copy of (or a link to) the Project Workplan.
Requirements	• What is (or was) the process for gathering the Customer's functional requirements? • Has the Customer signed off on the requirements? • How many changes have been made to the requirements since they were signed off? • Please send me a copy of (or a link to) the Requirements document.
Complexity of Deliverables	• How would you describe the complexity of the deliverables? • Are you using any non- XXX methodology deliverables? • Are non- XXX methodology deliverables replacing existing XXX methodology deliverables, or in addition to? • Please send me a copy of (or a link to) these non-XXX methodology deliverables.
Testing Approach & Quality Management	• Describe the testing approach, plans and who is involved in each of the following? o Unit Testing o Application/Module Testing o System Testing o User Acceptance Testing
Ability to Achieve	• Is the Customer confident in the solution?

Topics	Questions and Documentation Requests
Benefits	
Technology	
Product Compatibility	• Have there been challenges to initial product installation and setup directly related to the ABC application?
Client Installation Environment	• Have there been challenges to product installation and setup unrelated to the ABC application?
Utility and Third-Party Software	• Have there been challenges to implementation related to any Third-Party components?
Conversion	• Describe the data conversion process on this project? • What, if any, were the challenges?
Implementation Tools	• How beneficial are the tools (including conversion tools) your team is using for the implementation? • Are there any tools you feel you are missing?
Support and Service Levels	• Who is responsible (from the client and from ABC) for providing support? • Are there any support issues? • What are the SLAs (Service Level Agreements)? • Send me a copy of (or a link to) your transition plan/checklist to turn over responsibility to ABC Support.
Disaster Recovery	• What is the client's disaster recovery plan, and how does it affect the ABC application and its implementation?
Security	• What are the Customer's security requirements, and how do they affect the ABC application and its implementation?
Summary	
Overall	• If there is one key thought, issue, impression, idea about this project that you would like to express, what would it be?
Other	• Is there anything I didn't ask that I should have?

Example Assessment Report

DATE: January xx, 20xx

TO: Xxxxxx Xxxxxxx

FROM: Dave Faulise

SUBJECT: XYZ Program Health Check

ABC is in the process of implementing (project name). Due to the criticality of these systems to the business, Information Technologies (IT) must ensure that the XYZ program is completed on time and seamlessly with minimal or no service disruptions.

This report is a result of a program "Health Check" conducted from January x through January xx, 20xx. The purpose of the health check was to determine the state of the program and identify any risks that may impact or limit the program from achieving its stated objectives. The health check included 17 initial interviews, documentation reviews, risk evaluation, and follow-up discussions on selected topics. Results were discussed with the Project Manager who is in agreement with the majority of the findings and recommendations. The Project Manager did reserve feedback on the organization restructuring and delivery strategy recommendations pending a more detailed review.

The overall finding of this Health Check is that the XYZ program requires corrective action to succeed. There appears to be sufficient time remaining in the schedule for the recommended corrections, if implemented properly, to preserve the current schedule. Implementation of all of the following four recommendations is necessary for the program to succeed:

- **Resource Adjustments:** To properly manage and lead the program, assign the current Project Manager to perform this role full time, and assign his other role to an individual with xxxxxx experience. Assign a full-time Architect to the XYZ program. See page 4.

- **Linkage and Dependency Management:** To improve resource coordination and synchronization, continue efforts to identify and document linkages and dependencies between each of the XYZ program tracks. See page 6.
- **Architecture and Technical Requirements:** To minimize errors and omissions, create written requirements, including architectural schematics and specifications, in order to clearly communicate what results and deliverables are expected. See pages 6 and 7.
- **Delivery Strategy:** To reduce the risk resulting from the complexity and scale of the XYZ program, change to a phased approach for transitioning to live operations in the new environment. See pages 6 and 7.

ATTACHMENTS:
Attachment A - Summary Profile (snapshot of current status)
Attachment B - Review Findings and Recommendations
Attachment C – Personnel Interviewed and Documentation Reviewed

Example Attachment A – XYZ Summary Profile

Current Status:

Green = progress equal to or better than expected; no significant issues or changes needed

Yellow = Caution; early alert; corrective action is/may be required

Red = Progress less than expected; significant issues or changes needed

Green	Yellow	Red	
			RESOURCES:
	X		Leadership Roles
	X		Organization Structure
	X		Team Members' Availability
	X		Team Experience and Skills
	X		Team Confidence & Energy
X			Geographic Challenges
	X		Cultural Challenges
X			Communications
X			User Involvement
			PROCESSES:
	X		Planning
X			Scope and Change Management
X			Status Reporting
X			Issue Management
	X		Cost Management
	X		Delivery Assurance Compliance
		X	Linkage and Dependency Management
X			Schedule Management
	X		Risk Management
	X		Contingency Plans
			RESULTS:
		X	Requirements
		X	Releases / Phasing Relative to Scope and Scale
X			Complexity of Deliverables
	X		Volume of Deliverables
	X		Testing Approach and Quality Management

X			Ability to Achieve Benefits
			TECHNOLOGY:
		X	Architecture Detail (application, data, network, integration)
	X		Capacity Plan
	X		Performance Requirements
X			Hardware Installation
		X	Utility and 3rd-Party Software
X			Support and Service Levels
X			User Interface Complexity
	X		System Change Synchronization
X			DR
	X		Security
		X	**OVERALL**

Note: Evaluation of the program budget was not included in this health check.

Example Attachment B – Findings and Recommendations

The original version of this attachment is omitted because the content is unique to the client and including it would likely compromise client confidentiality. The material for Attachment B was organized into the following structure:

Resources – 1 page
Findings paragraphs
7 Recommendations

Processes – 1 page
Findings paragraphs
2 Recommendations

Results – 1 page
Findings paragraphs
3 Recommendations

Technology – 2 pages
Findings paragraphs
5 Recommendations

Example Attachment C – Personnel Interviewed and Documentation Reviewed

Resources Interviewed

- List of 17 specific individuals and their titles

Documentation Reviewed

- Project Statement of Work
- Project Approach Description
- Project Plans for individual tracks
- Staffing Plan
- Status Reports (last three)
- Project Financials (most recent summary)
- Issue Log
- Quality Management Plan
- Business Requirements
- Impacted Applications List
- Impacted Databases, Data Sets, Data Structures, GDGs, etc. list
- Batch Job List
- Test Plan
- Test Case List
- Memos and notes documenting changes to scope, schedule and cost
- Project Organization chart
- Communications Plan

Documentation Requested But Not Available

- Overall Program Plan
- Risk Assessment or Risk Management Plan
- External Interface List
- Internal Interface List
- Change Request Log
- Capacity Plan and/or Performance Management Plan

Chapter 12 – Strategy & Planning

> "Vision without action is merely dreaming. Action without vision is just passing time. But, if you can combine the right vision with the right actions, you can change the world."
> -- Joel Barker, "The Power of Vision"

This chapter is organized into two major sections:

- The first section discusses broad-based "Strategic Planning Engagements." I have performed a few of these types of projects, and I have observed a few more that were performed by other consultants. As a result of my experiences and observations, I'm skeptical about the value these engagements provide to clients.
- The second section presents "Planning Tools" and techniques. I include several examples of tools that I have used to address a variety of client needs. The tools and techniques presented in this second section have added considerable value to many of my engagements.

Strategic Planning Engagements

Strategic planning engagements were common during the 1970's and 1980's when every major business magazine had at least one article per issue predicting how technology would revolutionize a particular industry, and most large company executives had no clue how to utilize technology tactically, much less strategically. Those articles sold a lot of magazines, and many of the authors were hired as consultants. Those consultants were mostly MBAs and college professors with commanding vocabularies that included a lot of buzz words, and they had extensive academic training, but little practical experience. Almost none of those consultants were "technologists." A technologist has written program code, or wired a network, or established routing tables, or created a web page, or debugged a core dump (a print out of the

CPU's memory at the time of abnormal termination, usually in hexadecimal format), or gotten his/her hands dirty with ones and zeroes in some other way in the technology trenches.

Clients who hired planning consultants wanted magical answers. They hoped the consultant would predict the future and position their company to take advantage of it. Realistically though, if anyone had a crystal ball and could accurately predict the future, that person would not be a consultant but would be getting rich by either creating a new business of their own or by investing in winning stocks.

As a prelude to digging deeper into this topic, the following technology life cycle chart provides context:

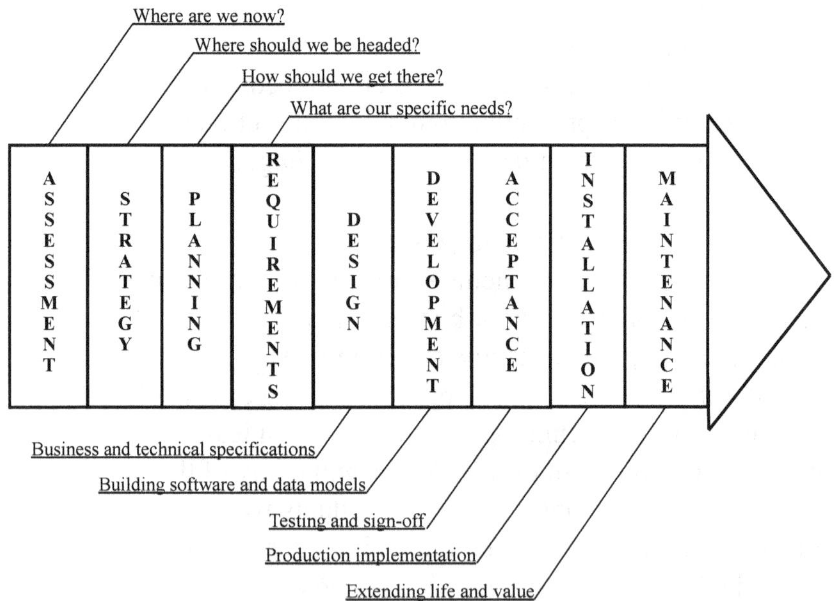

I first created this life cycle chart in the early 1990's as part of a client engagement. It clearly is not a revolutionary inspiration, but it does help in visualizing how different types of technology activities relate to each other over an extended time frame.

Strategic planning engagements typically include the first three phases of the life cycle: assessment, strategy and planning. Most consultants are qualified and competent to perform an assessment. Chapter 11 describes assessment engagements that are focused on a specific client project. The same assessment concepts can be more broadly applied across an entire technology function as part of a strategic planning engagement. If you haven't yet read Chapter 11, you might want to do so now because I won't repeat that material here, and it will be useful to understand assessment engagements before proceeding.

Most strategy engagements I've observed have bogged down in the assessment phase. For some of these engagements, the client eventually halted the work before moving to the strategy phase because there was little measurable progress. The reason those engagements got stuck in the assessment phase might be because the consultants weren't experienced or confident in transitioning into the next phase of work. I've used an 80-20 rule of thumb, such that when the assessment work provides an 80% understanding of the current state, it's time to start phase 2.

The second phase, Strategy is the most difficult of the three phases because it includes articulating a vision of the future. "Vision" work requires many of the skills of an architect. See Chapter 13 for a discussion of architecture engagements. Vision work, within the context of a strategic planning engagement, also implies an ability to predict what emerging technologies are likely to become dominant. While most consultants are competent doing assessments, they aren't very good at doing "vision," and they might subconsciously avoid moving on to that work. It may simply be that technologists are too practical to be visionary, and visionaries don't have enough hands on technical experience to be practical. Teaming a visionary with a technologist might work, but the two generally have such opposite styles and personalities that such a team would likely be dysfunctional.

One of my clients, John R. asked me to do some vision work as part of a market research effort I was doing for him. John painted an analogy comparing his organization to Wayne Gretzky, the hockey great, who had an uncanny ability to skate to where the puck was going to be. John wanted to position his people to "where the puck would be" in the future. I have to admit that the vision part of that engagement was the least successful aspect of the effort, and I clearly would not classify myself as a visionary.

I have met a few visionary people, and I've worked with some of them on shared client assignments. I wouldn't classify any of the visionaries I've met in the same league with Steve Jobs or Bill Gates, but they did each have a reasonable picture in their minds of where the technology world was headed at the time, although they generally lacked the discipline to do assessment projects. Most of them tried to stay abreast of the research efforts being conducted by some of the large technology companies, such as Microsoft, Apple, IBM, Hewlett Packard, Oracle, Cisco and others.

The third phase, Planning is actually fairly straightforward and mundane. After the current state is documented and assuming a future state can be defined, it's merely a matter of connecting the dots to map a logical path from current state to future state. The end result is a roadmap that outlines a series of projects to arrive at the future "point of arrival." The critical and elusive component is knowing that future state. As Rule 8 of the "Ten Pretty Good Rules" states, "If you don't know where you're going, any road will get you there."

Planning Tools

This section of this chapter describes examples of selected planning tools or work products that have proven to add significant client value during several of my client engagements, including many non-planning projects.

Context Diagrams

A context diagram shows at a high level how a system or business function interacts with external entities. The life cycle chart at the beginning of this chapter is one example of a context diagram. Following is another example I created for a hospital client several years ago, prior to the Affordable Care Act, Obamacare.

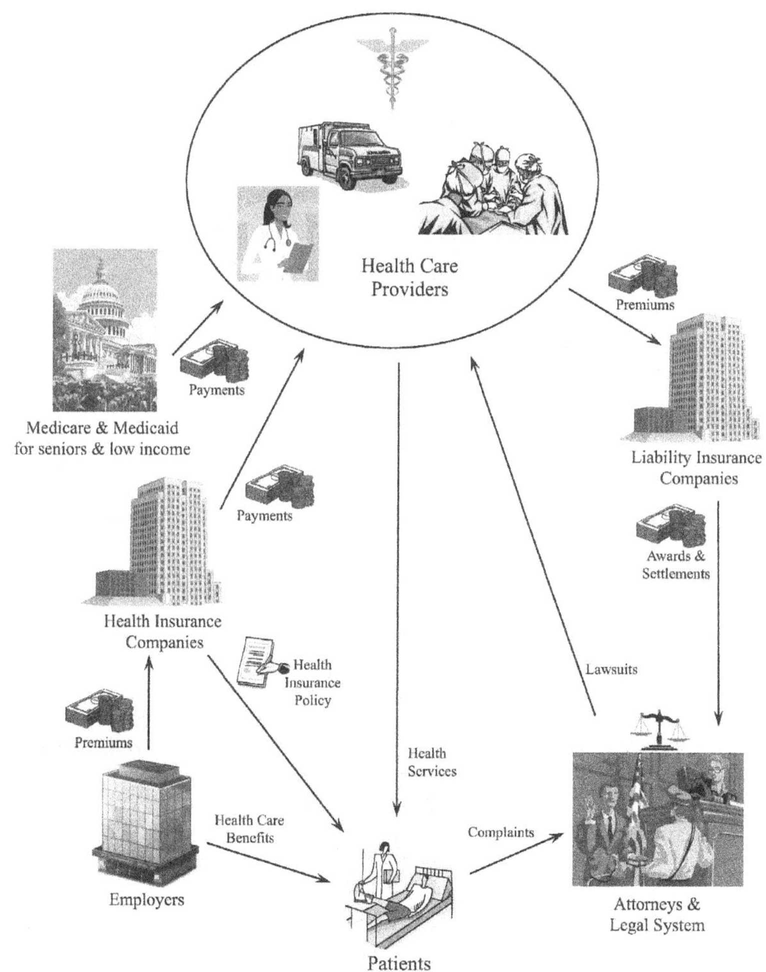

The above example is interesting because it shows that patients are not really customers since they generally do not make payments of relative significance. The definition of a "customer" is one who pays for goods or services. Thus, not being customers, patients have little or no influence over health care providers. Lawmakers might be well advised to construct their own context diagrams when attempting to reform health care, finance or other industries.

The next example shows how a client with a secondary mortgage operation interacts with a variety of external entities such as lenders (banks), investors, etc.

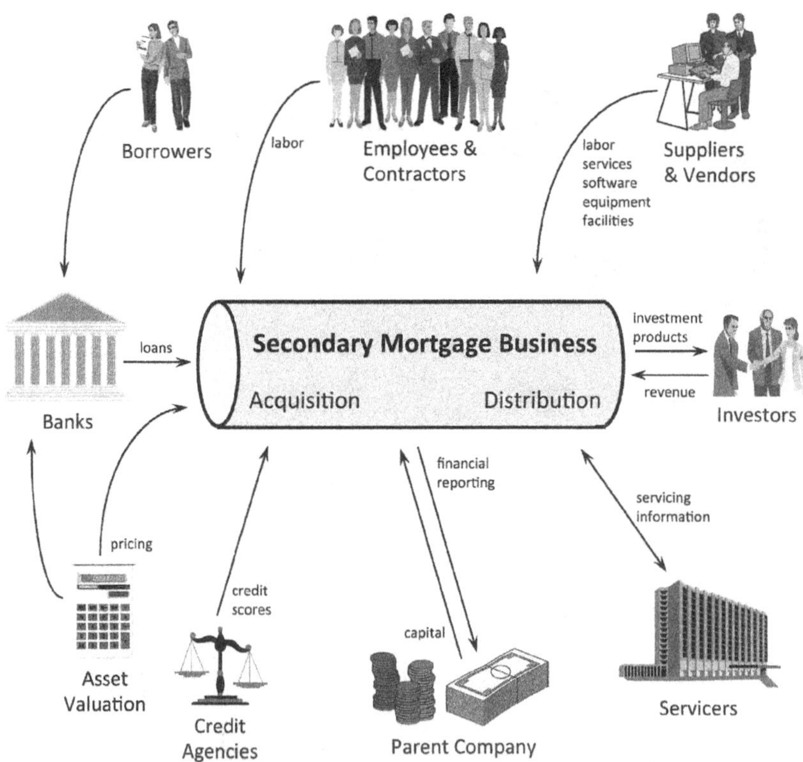

The last example context diagram below shows at a high level how a state transportation department interacts with a variety of external entities.

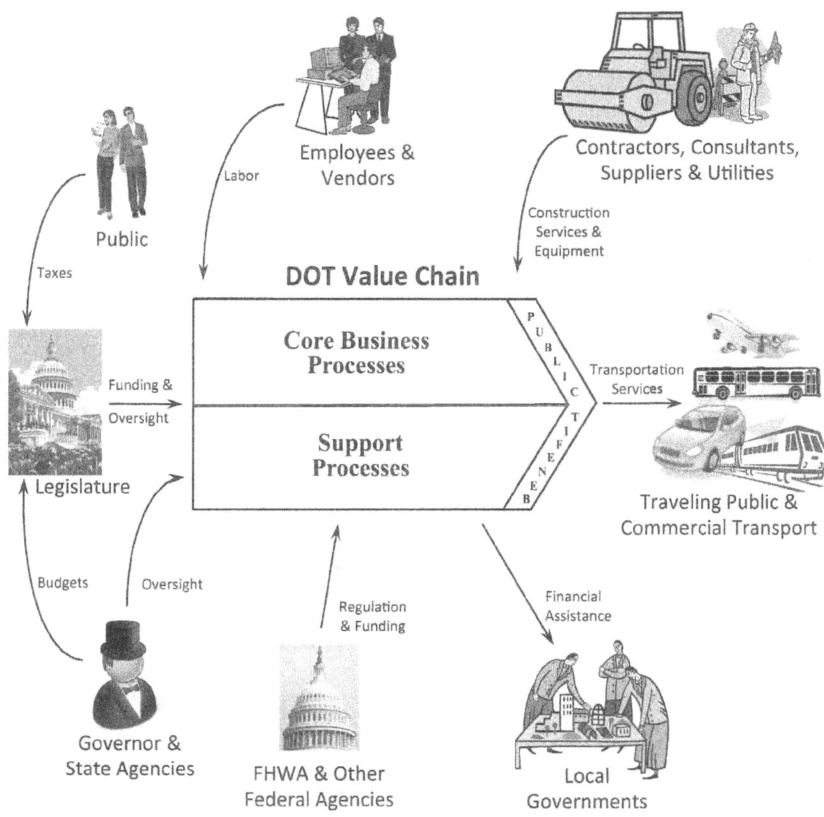

I created each of the above examples to develop a common understanding with members of my then project teams as to how the business function exists and operates within a larger environment. They are not intended to be 100% accurate or to include every possible external entity or transaction, only the most significant ones.

The third example above includes a "Value Chain" to represent the DOT (Department of Transportation) business. Michael Porter conceived value chains in the 1980's, and I've found them to be helpful in presenting how internal business functions relate to each other, as the following tools demonstrate.

Value Chains

This first value chain example was developed for the state DOT client referenced above.

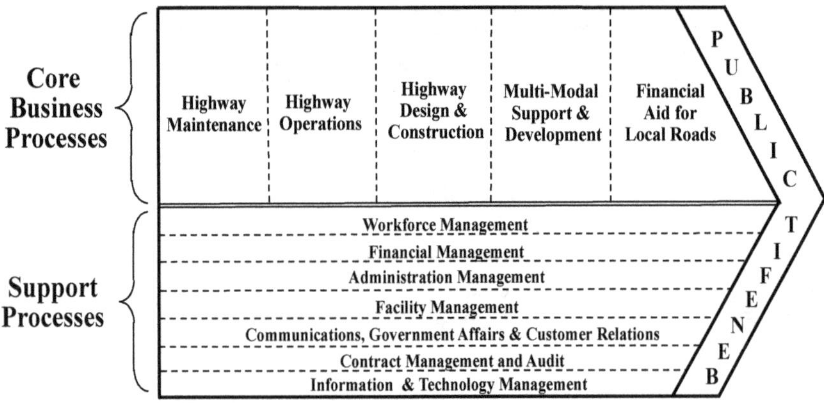

The next example was developed for a banking client.

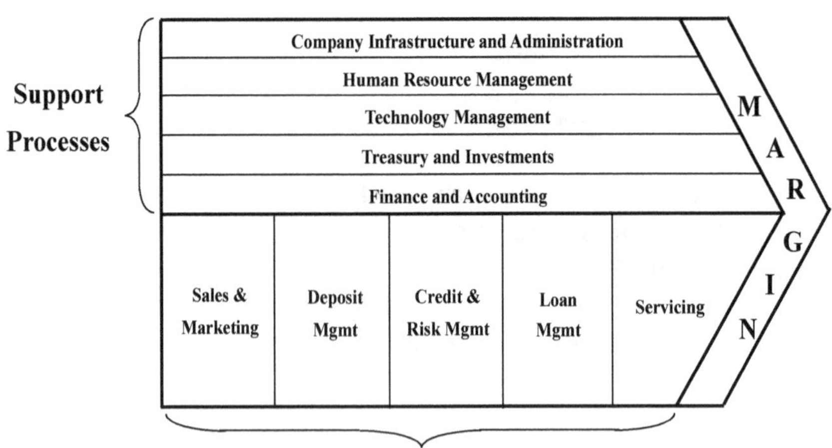

The final value chain example was developed for a health care client.

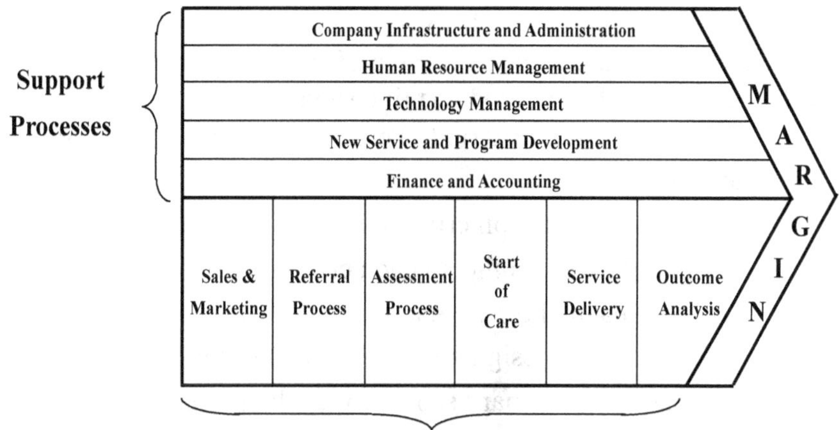

As with context diagrams, value chains are not intended to be 100% accurate or to include every possible process, only the most significant ones. Value chains are helpful in developing a common understanding of the business and its major internal processes. Regardless of the type of project I'm managing or how narrow its purpose, I've found that a project team that understands context is better able to maintain focus on priorities and drive to a successful conclusion.

Decision Charts

Early in my career I mistakenly believed that most executives made their decisions based on well-considered facts and logic. However, my experiences with dozens of client organizations across four decades point to a somewhat different conclusion: Many business decisions are made based on gut feelings, advice from magazine articles, who has the loudest voice in the room or a dysfunctional need of one of the executives to "be right."

About 15 years ago, I worked with another consultant who introduced me to his decision-making process, and I've since simplified and refined the process as I've applied it during my own subsequent client projects. The process is implemented as a group exercise, which needs to include the person ultimately responsible for the decision. This method has five steps:

- Develop a list of criteria to be considered while making the decision.
- Organize the decision criteria into a hierarchy.
- Assign relative weights to each criterion.
- Compare each alternative to the decision criteria (not to each other) and assign a score for each criterion.
- Compare the summary scores for each alternative to identify which has the highest total score.

The mathematics don't dictate the decision. However, using this method helps to quickly eliminate all but the top two or three alternatives, thus simplifying the overall process.

Following are two examples of decision hierarchy charts I've developed for my clients. The first was used to determine which of five vendors would be awarded a multi-million dollar datacenter hosting contract. The maximum possible score as shown in the chart is 1000 points. Vendors received scores ranging from approximately 400 to 600 points, and the scoring results helped our team and our executive sponsor to select the best vendor without emotions getting in the way.

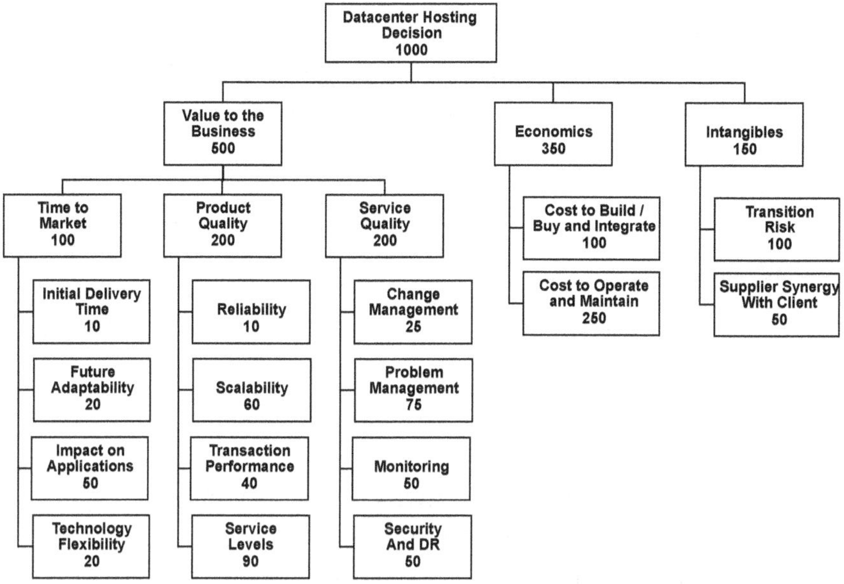

At a more granular level, we defined the above decision criteria as:

- Initial Delivery Time: Includes ability to start the transition immediately, ability to complete the transition within 3 months, and ability to adjust to changing requirements.
- Future Adaptability: Includes ability to add new client locations, ability to close/merge client locations, ability to handle client acquisition of new business units, and ability to add/modify/replace applications.
- Impact On Applications: Includes ability to rapidly deploy new or modified systems, ability to create and remove development and test environments, database support, and technical support.
- Technology Flexibility: Includes ability to readily change topology, ability to increase/decrease bandwidth, and ability to integrate new technologies.

- Reliability: Includes equipment redundancy, failover capabilities, backup and restore capabilities, and technical tools/resources for troubleshooting and problem resolution.
- Scalability: Includes ability to add equipment without downtime, ability to add storage without downtime, and ability to add to the client's footprint without impacting performance.
- Transaction Performance: Includes acceptable latency and physical proximity, ability to monitor performance thresholds, and technical resources to work with client staff to troubleshoot problems.
- Service Levels (SLAs): Includes application performance targets, service fulfillment timeframes, application availability targets, fault and problem resolution times, latency, and release deployment times.
- Change Management: Includes adherence to ITIL and ITSM, compliance with client change windows, ticketing system, ability to rapidly provision added capacity, and load testing capabilities.
- Problem Management: Includes incident identification, severity level classifications, root cause analysis, and escalation procedures.
- Monitoring: Includes real-time view of all enterprise resources, dashboard integration, and predictive analysis.
- Security and Disaster recovery: Includes physical and logical security, identity authorization, intrusion detection, remote access policies, regulatory compliance, and RTOs and RPOs.
- Cost to Build/Buy & Integrate: Includes implementation costs, initial management charges, the client's need to write

off their existing hardware, and the cost to terminate existing circuits.

- Cost to Operate & Maintain: Includes monthly server and storage charges, monthly circuit charges, monthly management charges, and support and maintenance charges.
- Transition Risk: Includes supplier organization stability, process reliability, experience with similar transitions, and mitigation strategies.
- Supplier Synergy: Includes alignment with client standards, compliance with regulatory requirements, supplier's holistic relationship with client, and reputation of doing the right thing every time for their other clients.

To demonstrate, let's look closer at the two Economics criteria, which totaled 350 of the 1000 points. We felt on-going operating costs would be more significant over time than initial start up costs, so we assigned weights of 250 points and 100 points to them respectively. Vendor A, was the incumbent and had no start up costs, so we assigned a maximum value of 100 points for that criterion, but their on-going operating costs were high so we assigned 125 points for that criterion, giving Vendor A a total of 225 points for economics. Vendor B, one of the new contenders had significant start up costs so we assigned only 20 points for that criterion, but their on-going operating costs were relatively low so we assigned 225 points for that criterion, giving Vendor B a total of 245 points for economics. Thus, Vendor B had a slight advantage in the aggregate for Economics despite requiring significant start up costs. Evaluating the economic considerations using this decision methodology allowed us to reach consensus more easily than other methods that could have involved arguments about whether startup dollars are more important or less important than monthly operating costs.

The next example decision hierarchy chart was used to help a client choose a commercial EA (Enterprise Architecture) framework and methodology to implement. This example is similar in structure to the last example and differs primarily in the nature of the decision being made.

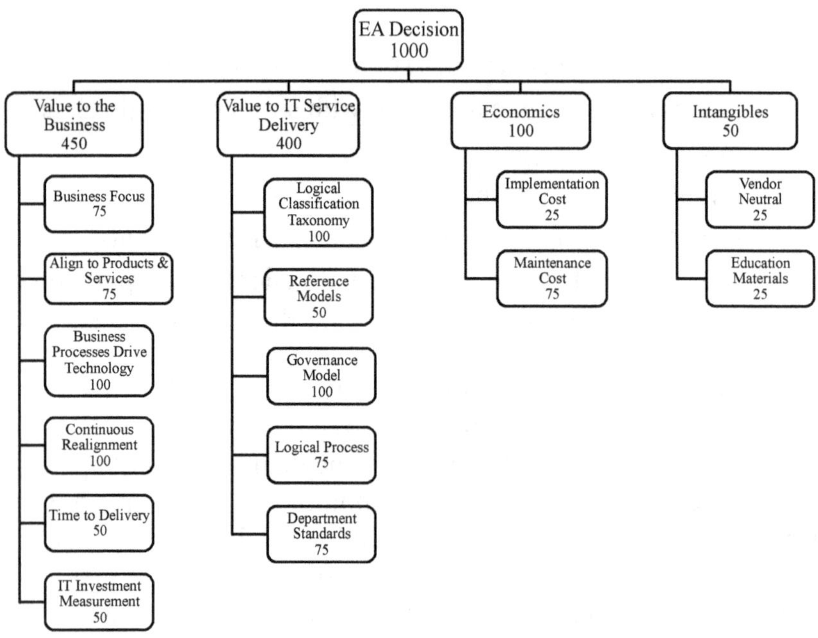

Note that the economics criteria in the two examples have very different relative weights assigned, 350 out of 1000 and 100 out of 1000 respectively. The datacenter hosting client and project team were making a decision to spend several million dollars every year over 7 to 10 years, and we therefore decided economics were highly important. The enterprise architecture client and project team were making a decision to spend less than $250,000 per year for only 3 to 5 years, and we therefore placed greater emphasis on the impact to the business and to IT than on the economics.

Business Case

A business case is a financial analysis of the costs and benefits of a recommended solution. In situations when multiple options are still under consideration, I create a business case analysis for each option.

I have observed a great diversity in the formats and styles that various organizations use to present business cases. My conclusion is there is no single right format or method. When I've introduced a format that the organization hasn't used previously, I usually find myself spending more time "selling" the unfamiliar format than explaining the content. Therefore, I typically ask my client for an example of a previously approved business case from an unrelated project to use as a model or template that I can mimic for the specific business case I'm creating. Although I may not like or agree with the company's format, I would rather fight more worthwhile battles. Only when the client can't produce an example they want me to follow do I present my own business case format.

Because the business case is a future projection, it depends heavily on assumptions, and I document the assumptions as clearly as possible and include them as part of the presentation. I usually divide the numerical analysis into three sections:

- Benefits: These may include the forecasted value of increased revenue, anticipated cost savings, and anticipated cost avoidance, such as avoiding new staff hires or avoiding regulatory fines. Many non-financial benefits can be quantified and included with other benefits based on measurable improvements such as cycle time reduction and percentage of process eliminated. Some benefits are too subjective to be quantified, such as increased customer satisfaction or improved ease of use. I list these separately in a narrative section, and I do not include them in the numerical analysis.

- Costs: These include the project costs, any required capital investments, and any on going costs to operate the project deliverables or new systems.
- Net Gain: This is simply the mathematical difference between the summary benefits and costs. There is generally a negative value during the first year because project costs are highest then and because the resulting value will not begin to accrue until after the project is complete. To demonstrate an overall positive value, I show at least three years in the analysis. I show five years in the following example.

I created the following example business case for a client organization that was in the business of developing and implementing industry specific software for their customers on three continents. I was engaged to lead a transformation of the organization into a more profitable and more professionally managed business through process re-engineering. We planned and executed approximately 20 different projects over a 9-month time frame, and each project was subject to a rigorous cost benefit analysis before it was launched based on its own individual business case. I created the following example for a project to improve how the company performed conversions of customer legacy systems to my client's solutions.

This business case example includes three charts. The first chart shows savings (efficiency) projected for five future years. The base year was the year the improvement effort was implemented. The company employed 107 implementation specialists, and approximately 60 of them were involved with conversion projects. The vice president in charge of the unit believed we could drive utilization (percent of hours worked that were billed to customers) from under 50% to 75%, and the sales backlog indicated the annual number of projects could easily grow from 14 to 45. As per the chart, our calculations showed cumulative 5-year savings of almost $20 million for the overall program. We estimated that the conversion project would be credited with 20% of these savings, and the remaining 80% of value was attributable to other projects within the overall program.

Savings / Value (in millions)

Description	Base Year	Year 1	Year 2	Year 3	Year 4	Year 5	Cum
Implementation Team Utilization Projection	47.6%	55.0%	62.0%	72.0%	75.0%	75.0%	
Anticipated Number of Conversion Projects	14	25	45	45	45	45	
Average Hours Needed to Complete a Project	4,080	3,531	3,132	2,697	2,589	2,589	
Projected Total Hours Needed at Baseline Utilization	57,120	102,000	183,600	183,600	183,600	183,600	**893,520**
Projected Total Hours Needed at Utilization Projection	57,120	88,276	140,957	121,380	116,525	116,525	**640,783**
% of Year's Efficiency to be Realized	0%	25%	80%	100%	100%	100%	
Efficiency in Hours	0	3,431	34,114	62,220	67,075	67,075	**233,915**
Internal Cost Rate per Hour	$82	$82	$82	$82	$82	$82	**$82**
Program Value (Efficiency) in Millions of Dollars	$0.000	$0.281	$2.797	$5.102	$5.500	$5.500	**$19.181**
% of Efficiency Attributable to This Specific Project	20.0%	20.0%	20.0%	20.0%	20.0%	20.0%	
Efficiency Attributable to This Project in millions	$0.000	$0.056	$0.559	$1.020	$1.100	$1.100	**$3.836**

The second chart below includes the consulting and internal costs associated with the conversion improvement project, and we put those in year 1. Because there were no anticipated on-going incremental costs we put zero costs in the future years.

Cost (in millions)

One time / Incremental Costs	Year 1	Year 2	Year 3	Year 4	Year 5	Cum
Consulting Costs	0.108					0.108
Company Internal Costs	0.154					0.154
Travel (10 trips for 2 people at $2,000 per trip)	0.040					0.040
Training						0.000
Facilities						0.000
Capital Investment						0.000
Total	0.302	0.000	0.000	0.000	0.000	0.302

The third and final chart simply combined savings with costs to show net value. We calculated IRR (Internal Rate of Return) and NPV (Net Present Value) using the company-wide standard at that time of 12.0% for the cost of capital.

Business Case (in millions)

	Year 1	Year 2	Year 3	Year 4	Year 5	Cum
Total Efficency	0.056	0.559	1.020	1.100	1.100	3.836
Total Costs	0.302	0.000	0.000	0.000	0.000	0.302
Net Favorable (Unfavorable)	-0.245	0.559	1.020	1.100	1.100	3.535
					IRR	2.78
					NPV	2.28

Based on my suggestion, another of my clients made a decision at the end of our project to re-run their business case analysis one year after the project was completed in order to determine the real value of the project and the accuracy of the original projections. Everyone on the team thought this was an excellent idea, but a year later, it was forgotten and didn't happen. To my knowledge, none of my clients has ever looked back to measure whether or not the anticipated benefits of a project were realized. I bring this up, not to discount the usefulness of performing a business case analysis, but only to observe that I've not had a single one of my analyses proven to be either right or wrong. Interesting. I'm both disappointed and relieved.

Organization Change

Managing organization change ought to be part of most consulting engagements because one of the biggest threats to success is the inevitable resistance to change that naturally accompanies new systems or processes or other project results. That said, my experience is that the most effective method for managing change is simply having solid two-way communications with those most impacted. Those communications typically include:

- Seeking out those impacted by an anticipated change and informing them honestly and as early as possible about the change. Don't sugar coat it.
- Encouraging those impacted to ask questions and giving them honest answers in return.

- Allowing those impacted to voice their opinions and suggestions.
- Listening carefully and incorporating as many suggestions as possible into the implementation process.
- Explaining why some suggestions will not be used.
- Maintaining a continuous feedback loop during and after the change is implemented.

For additional information on communications and communication planning, see the Communication Plan section in Chapter 14.

Many of my colleagues in the Human Resource departments of my client organizations have disagreed with my heavy reliance on two-way communications. They believe that communications are only a part of what should be a much larger and more complex change management program. I agree that communications are clearly part of the change management discipline, and in a perfect world I would also agree that all aspects of change management should be addressed within large projects. However, most of my clients have been unwilling to fund those extensive change management efforts. Pragmatically doing the most I can with limited funding means focusing the change management effort on those tools and methods that provide the most effective results, and for me, that means communications.

The transformation engagement described in the Business Case sub-section above had significant organization change implications, and shortly after I initiated the work, the steering committee assigned Mr. Academia, the change management specialist from the Human Resource department, to work with me. I had not requested the assistance, but I had no graceful way to decline. Mr. Academia had a masters degree in psychology, had attended almost every organization change seminar ever held in the country, and was still taking courses on the subject at night. He quickly demonstrated a complete lack of interest in or understanding of the process changes my teams were implementing, and he wanted the primary focus to be on how to make each person in the company embrace the changes. Mr. Academia was clearly a threat to the success of the program, and I decided to insulate my team members from him. I spent about an hour almost every day working with Mr. Academia creating PowerPoint charts and presentations that he showed to the steering committee but were never used in the project itself. None of my team members spent any time on those activities. Near the end of the initiative, the Human Resource VP invited me to his office for a private chat about Mr. Academia's performance. I stuck to fact-based, non-judgmental comments to avoid the appearance of a personality conflict, but the evidence was clear, and a few weeks later, Mr. Academia's office was vacant. Following is a chart that Mr. Academia and I created that did provide a useful way to think about our overall business process re-engineering program.

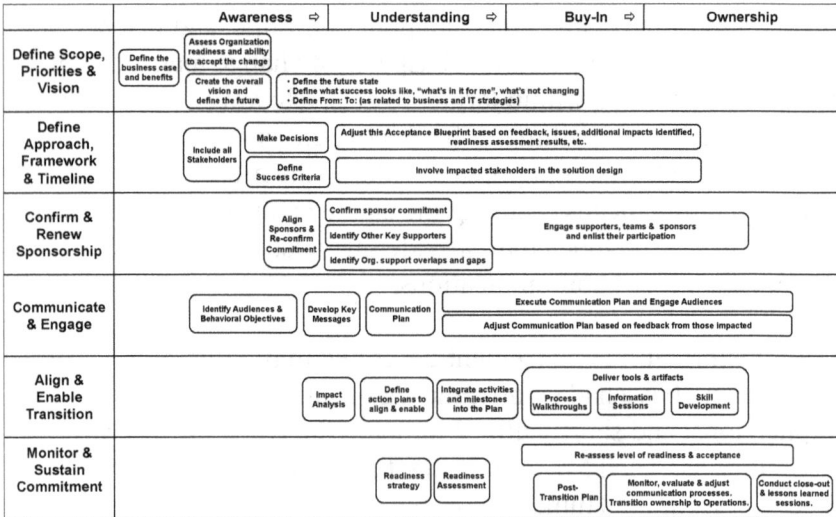

	Awareness ⇨	Understanding ⇨	Buy-In ⇨	Ownership
Define Scope, Priorities & Vision	Define the business case and benefits Assess Organization readiness and ability to accept the change Create the overall vision and define the future • Define the future state • Define what success looks like, "what's in it for me", what's not changing • Define From: To: (as related to business and IT strategies)			
Define Approach, Framework & Timeline	Include all Stakeholders Make Decisions Define Success Criteria	Adjust this Acceptance Blueprint based on feedback, issues, additional impacts identified, readiness assessment results, etc. Involve impacted stakeholders in the solution design		
Confirm & Renew Sponsorship	Align Sponsors & Re-confirm Commitment Confirm sponsor commitment Identify Other Key Supporters Identify Org. support overlaps and gaps	Engage supporters, teams & sponsors and enlist their participation		
Communicate & Engage	Identify Audiences & Behavioral Objectives Develop Key Messages	Communication Plan Execute Communication Plan and Engage Audiences Adjust Communication Plan based on feedback from those impacted		
Align & Enable Transition	Impact Analysis	Define action plans to align & enable Integrate activities and milestones into the Plan	Deliver tools & artifacts: Process Walkthroughs; Information Sessions; Skill Development	
Monitor & Sustain Commitment		Readiness strategy Readiness Assessment	Re-assess level of readiness & acceptance Post-Transition Plan Monitor, evaluate & adjust communication processes. Transition ownership to Operations.	Conduct close-out & lessons learned sessions.

This chart is an organization acceptance blueprint that we adapted from the work of Daryl Conner, an organization change guru. I like the chart because it shows organization change phases on the vertical axis, desired behaviors on the horizontal axis, and individual project activities as boxes in the interior of the chart. The reality is the project teams focused almost exclusively on the "Communicate & Engage" swim lane, and most of the other activities were generally ignored. The overall transformation program was successful, in spite of (or perhaps because of) our selective attention to primarily communication activities.

Summary

Had I known earlier in my consulting career what I know now, I would have informed my clients who asked me to conduct broad strategic planning engagements of the obvious fact that no one can predict the future, and I would have advised them to spend their money on other, more valuable initiatives.

However, there are many useful planning tools and techniques, such as context diagrams, decision hierarchies and others as described in this chapter. These tools can be applied to a variety of situations that I have found add real value to client organizations and to their projects.

Suggested Reading and References

High, Peter A. *World Class IT*. Jossey-Bass, 2009

Porter, Michael E. *Competitive Advantage: Creating and Sustaining Superior Performance*. New York: Free Press, 1985

Conner, Daryl R. *Managing at the Speed of Change*. Random House, 1992

Chapter 12 – Strategy & Planning

Chapter 13 – IT Architecture

> "A rock pile ceases to be a rock pile the moment a single man contemplates it, bearing within him the image of a cathedral."
> -- Antoine de Saint-Exupery

Some of my clients hired me specifically as an IT architect. In addition, I've conducted several engagements that required IT architecture related work as part of the effort, and I've found that an architect's perspective is useful on almost every engagement. One client wanted to establish an IT enterprise architecture function, and that particular effort resulted in an extensive set of deliverables that, for continuity purposes, are collectively the foundation for this chapter.

Background

The client, a department of state government, made a strategic decision to create and execute an IT Enterprise Architecture (EA) program. The work effort required two consultants with IT architecture experience, and the client hired me and another senior architect, Todd T. to deliver:

- A framework for creating, maintaining and communicating IT Enterprise Architecture to the business and technical groups.
- Tactical and operational artifacts (documents and templates) to articulate the framework in each of the four architecture domains: business, data, applications and technology.
- A process to implement and maintain the IT Enterprise Architecture.
- A governance structure to measure and manage the IT Enterprise Architecture and key architectural decisions.

Our approach was to select, tailor and implement one of several commercially available IT architecture frameworks. Todd and I organized the initiative into three phases:

- Phase 1:
    - Identify, clarify and document relevant client requirements.
    - Research EA framework options and narrow those options to a short list.
    - Facilitate an EA framework selection decision.
- Phase 2:
    - Using decisions from Phase 1, roll out initial elements of the EA program.
    - Create, communicate and execute a governance structure.
    - Create, communicate and pilot an EA execution framework.
    - Create and communicate the EA business case and an initial set of EA metrics.
- Phase 3:
    - Transition from definition and pilot mode to an "operational" state.
    - Finalize the initial set of EA domain artifacts.
    - Finish any EA process definitions that were not completed in Phase 2.
    - Establish a continuous improvement process.

IT Architecture Vision

Simply stated, this client's architecture vision was to align IT services with strategic business goals. The following three diagrams represent their vision and that alignment.

We developed a context diagram to identify at the highest level how the organization (represented by the value chain in the center) interoperates with external entities. Note that a context diagram is merely a simple ER (entity-relationship) diagram with pictures.

This particular context diagram and the following value chain diagram were both also used as examples in Chapter 12. If you read Chapter 12 and were not heavily medicated at the time, they may look familiar.

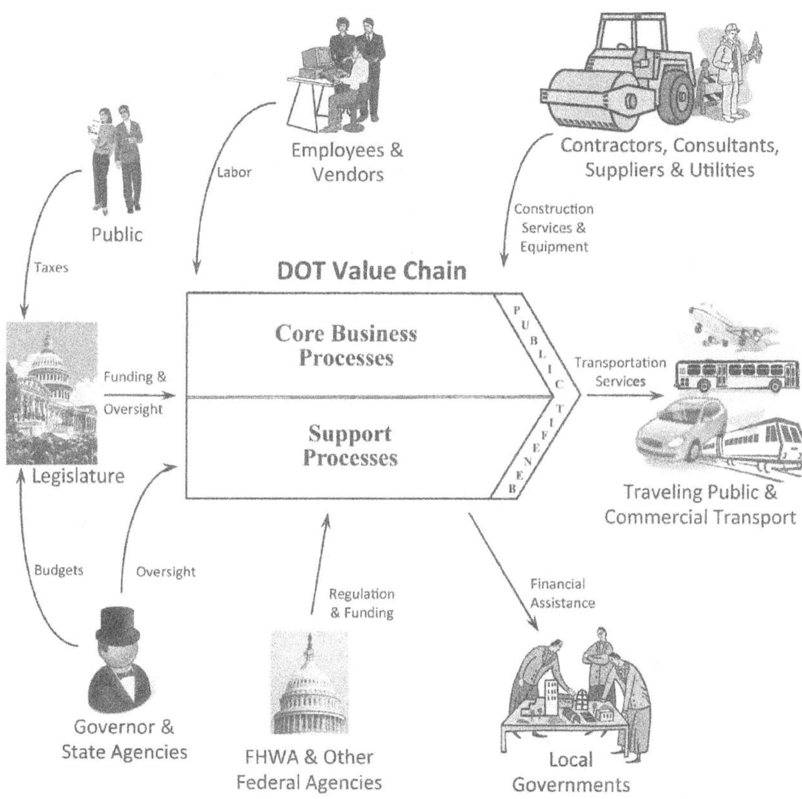

Todd and I then focused on the value chain part of the above diagram. As referenced in Chapter 12, Michael Porter conceived value chains in the 1980's. We expanded the value chain concept to identify and separate core processes from support processes, as the following diagram shows.

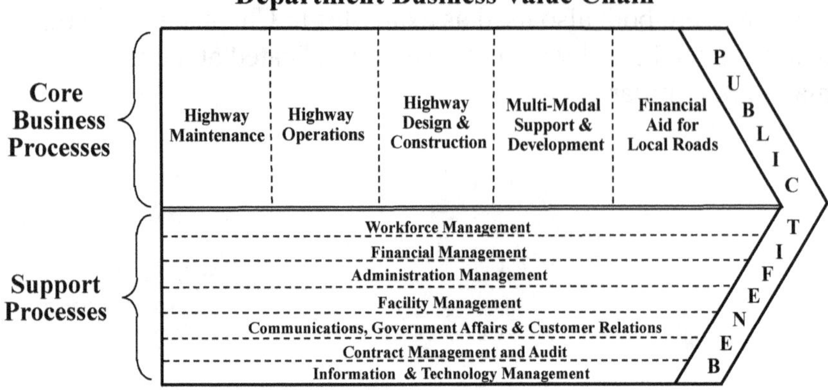

This value chain provided a foundation for us to design a core diagram as follows.

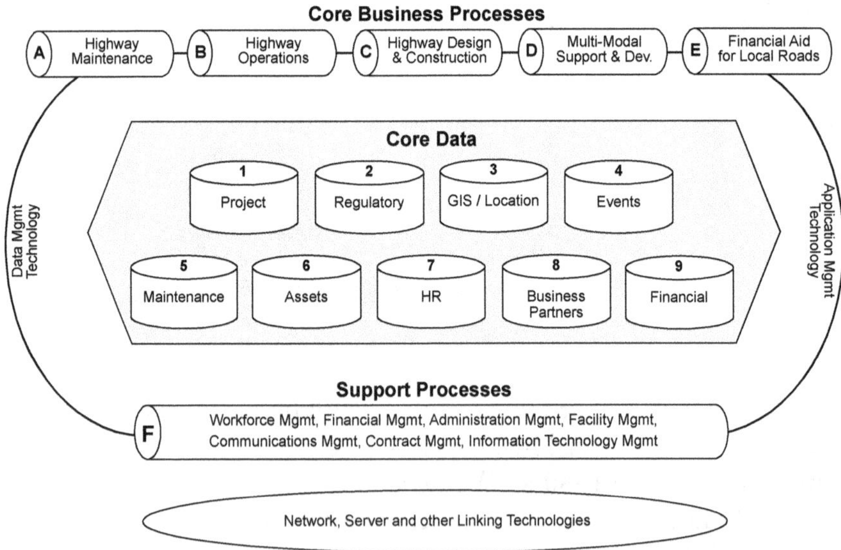

The core diagram begins to introduce high-level technology elements and how those elements support business processes and data. The above diagram shows some of this layered thinking, as we began moving from higher to lower levels and into greater detail.

Achieving the vision requires continuous effort along three parallel tracks representing three EA program components (EA Framework, EA Execution and EA Governance) that I describe in greater detail in the sections that follow.

EA Framework

Enterprise architecture is best represented as cyclical processes of continuous refinement and improvement because architecture must keep pace with evolving business strategies and services. After researching ten commercially available candidate frameworks, Todd and I facilitated a decision to tailor and implement TOGAF (The Open Group Architecture Framework). As implemented by the client, the selected framework taxonomy includes four architecture domains:

- Business
- Data
- Application
- Technology

These domains are useful to organize EA artifacts, rationalize the multiple levels of thought and communicate appropriate messages to target audiences.

A process to develop and maintain architecture artifacts is as important as the EA taxonomy. An EA program must have a process to guide development and should also have a built-in maintenance (continuous improvement) process. The architecture development process we implemented has a simple, iterative approach to defining the enterprise architecture as well as the individual detail domains. Todd and I tailored the methodology for our client, and the following diagram represents the enterprise architecture development process we implemented.

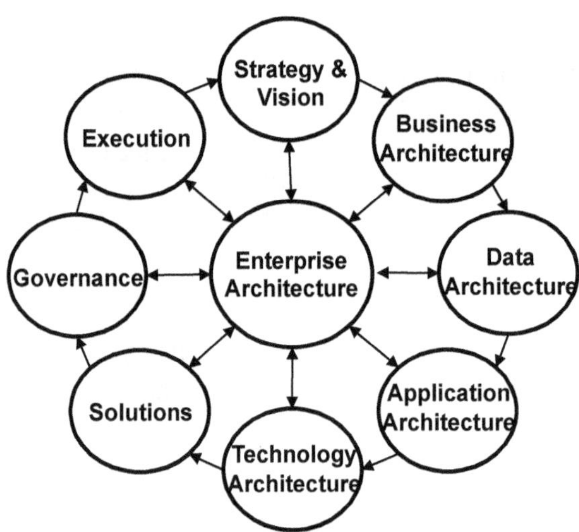

The following sub-sections discuss how we developed the initial versions of the business, data, applications and technology domains.

Business Architecture

Knowledge of the business architecture is a prerequisite for architecture work in any of the other domains (Data, Application, Technology), and in practical terms, it is necessary for demonstrating the business value of subsequent architecture work to key stakeholders.

A target architecture provides a high-level, aspirational view of architecture deliverables. With our client we defined the target business architecture to be comprised of the following artifacts:

- Business and IT Service Catalog
- TCO (Total Cost of Ownership) by Service

- Strategic Planning Documents (business and technology)
- IT Standards
- Organization Charts (business and technology)
- Organizational Support Models
- Location Lists

The first two of these artifacts were classified as mandatory, and the remaining artifacts were classified as useful, but optional.

In addition to the above EA artifacts, we also determined that individual projects would benefit from project-specific artifacts (see the area below and to the right of the heavy black separation line within the gap analysis chart below) including:

- Process Flows
- Entity-Relationship Models
- Functional Decomposition Models
- Use-Case Models

The first of these project-specific artifacts was classified as mandatory for all projects, and the remaining artifacts were classified as useful, but optional.

We identified which of the artifacts existed currently, and that subset became part of the baseline business architecture. Knowing the baseline and the target architectures allowed us to conduct a gap analysis to determine what needed to be done to establish a satisfactory (although not perfect) target business architecture. The results of this exercise are depicted in the following chart. The shading key (for column headings) and the number key below the chart are necessary to decipher it.

Target Architecture

Baseline Architecture

Gaps	Business and IT Service Catalog	TCO by Service	Strategic Planning Documents	IT Standards	Org Charts /w Support Models	Organization Charts	Location Lists	Process Flows	ER Models	Functional Decomp. Models	
Business and IT Service Catalog	2,3										
TCO by Service		6									
Strategic Planning Documents			1								
IT Standards				2,3							
Org Charts /w Support Models					6						
Organization Charts						2,3					
Location Lists							2,3				
Business Principles & Standards											5
Org. Unit by Function Matrix											5
RACI Matrix											5
Asset Lifecycle Program											2,3
Process Flows								2			
Entity-Relationship Models									2		
Functional Decomp. Models										2	
Use-Case Models											2,5

Shading Key	
Shaded	Mandatory
Un-shaded	Optional

Number Key	
1	Include with no changes
2	Include, needs standardization
3	Include, needs to be updated
4	Eliminate
5	Use as an exception as needed
6	To be developed

The gap analysis helped us to identify several business architecture specific projects to develop or refine the underlying artifacts. We followed a similar process for each of the three remaining domains as the following sub-sections describe.

Data Architecture

The data architecture identifies and defines the high-level data domain artifacts that support the client's Business Architecture. During the data architecture effort we were not concerned with database design; the goal was to define the major data entities relevant to the client organization, not to design logical or physical storage systems.

We defined the target data architecture by building on the architecture vision and the business architecture work as described earlier. Through a series of focused workshops and forums, we determined that the target data architecture would be comprised of the following artifacts:

- Business Data Catalog
- Conceptual Data Model
- Business Data Domains Model
- Data Entity by Application Matrix
- IT Data Standards
- Metadata Catalog
- Entity-Relationship Diagrams – Conceptual/Logical

The first six of the above artifacts were classified as mandatory, and the remaining item was classified as useful, but optional. Examples of three of these artifacts are included below.

In addition to the above artifacts, we also determined that individual projects would benefit from project-specific artifacts (see the area below and to the right of the heavy black separation line within the gap analysis chart below) including:

- Entity-Relationship Diagrams – Physical
- Class Diagrams
- Data Dissemination Diagrams

The first of the above artifacts was classified as mandatory for all projects, and the remaining two items were classified as useful, but optional.

Conceptual Data Model

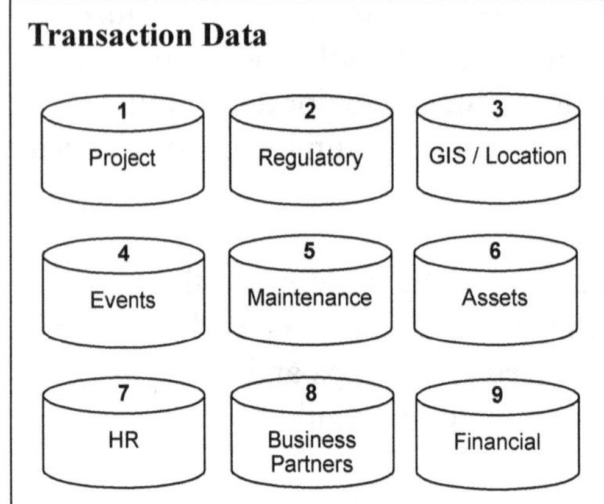

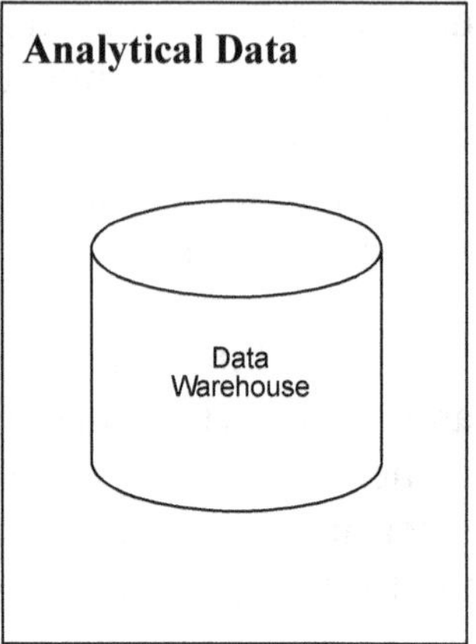

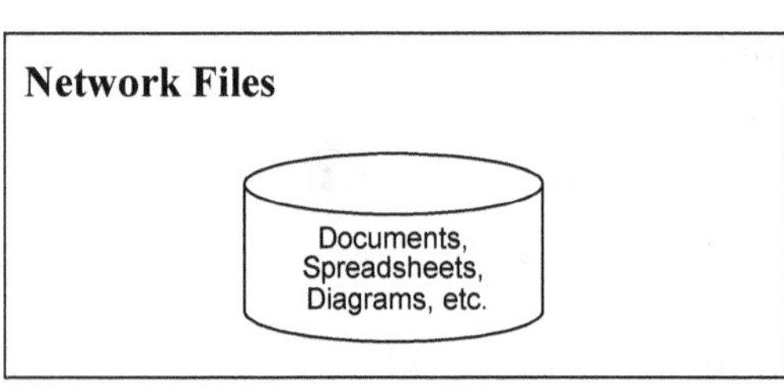

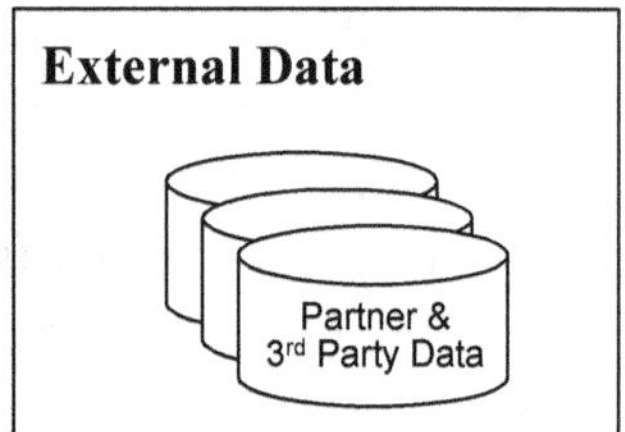

Data Domains Model

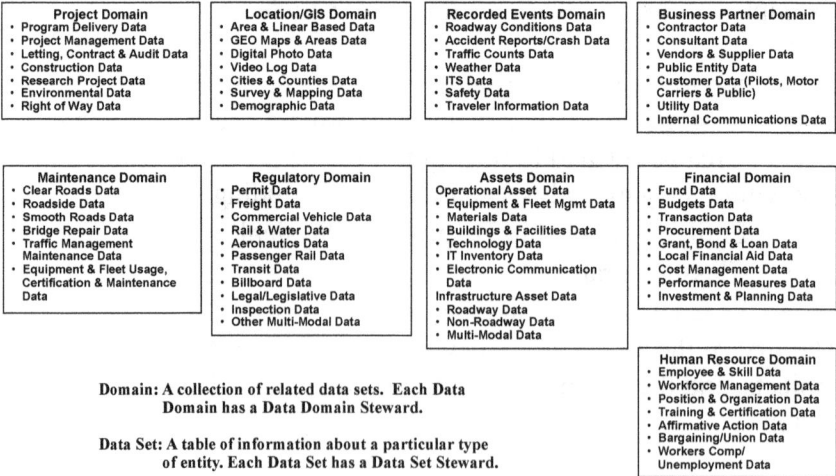

Project Domain
- Program Delivery Data
- Project Management Data
- Letting, Contract & Audit Data
- Construction Data
- Research Project Data
- Environmental Data
- Right of Way Data

Location/GIS Domain
- Area & Linear Based Data
- GEO Maps & Areas Data
- Digital Photo Data
- Video Log Data
- Cities & Counties Data
- Survey & Mapping Data
- Demographic Data

Recorded Events Domain
- Roadway Conditions Data
- Accident Reports/Crash Data
- Traffic Counts Data
- Weather Data
- ITS Data
- Safety Data
- Traveler Information Data

Business Partner Domain
- Contractor Data
- Consultant Data
- Vendors & Supplier Data
- Public Entity Data
- Customer Data (Pilots, Motor Carriers & Public)
- Utility Data
- Internal Communications Data

Maintenance Domain
- Clear Roads Data
- Roadside Data
- Smooth Roads Data
- Bridge Repair Data
- Traffic Management Maintenance Data
- Equipment & Fleet Usage, Certification & Maintenance Data

Regulatory Domain
- Permit Data
- Freight Data
- Commercial Vehicle Data
- Rail & Water Data
- Aeronautics Data
- Passenger Rail Data
- Transit Data
- Billboard Data
- Legal/Legislative Data
- Inspection Data
- Other Multi-Modal Data

Assets Domain

Operational Asset Data
- Equipment & Fleet Mgmt Data
- Materials Data
- Buildings & Facilities Data
- Technology Data
- IT Inventory Data
- Electronic Communication Data

Infrastructure Asset Data
- Roadway Data
- Non-Roadway Data
- Multi-Modal Data

Financial Domain
- Fund Data
- Budgets Data
- Transaction Data
- Procurement Data
- Grant, Bond & Loan Data
- Local Financial Aid Data
- Cost Management Data
- Performance Measures Data
- Investment & Planning Data

Human Resource Domain
- Employee & Skill Data
- Workforce Management Data
- Position & Organization Data
- Training & Certification Data
- Affirmative Action Data
- Bargaining/Union Data
- Workers Comp/ Unemployment Data

Domain: A collection of related data sets. Each Data Domain has a Data Domain Steward.

Data Set: A table of information about a particular type of entity. Each Data Set has a Data Set Steward.

The following diagram is a data entity by application matrix.

High-Level Data Reference Model

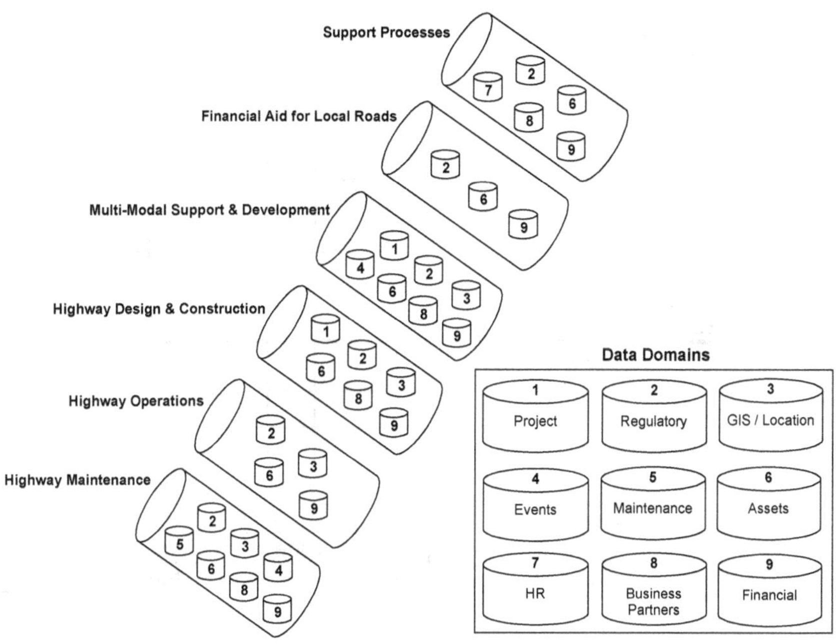

As we did with the business architecture, we identified which of the data artifacts existed currently, and that subset became part of the baseline data architecture. Knowing the baseline and the target architectures allowed us to conduct a gap analysis to determine what needed to be done to establish the target data architecture. The results of this exercise are depicted in the following chart. The shading key and number key below the chart are necessary to decipher it.

Target Architecture

Baseline Architecture

Gaps	Bus. Data Catalog	Conceptual Data Models	Data Domains	Data Entity by Application Matrix	IT Data Standards	Metadata Catalog	ER Diagrams – Conceptual/Logical	ER Diagrams – Physical	Class Diagrams	Data Dissemination Diagrams
Business Data Catalog	6									
Conceptual Data Model		2,3								
Business Data Domains Model			6							
Data Entity by Application Matrix				2,3						
IT Data Standards					1					
Metadata Catalog						2,3				
Entity-Relationship Diagrams – Conceptual/Logical							2,3			
Entity-Relationship Diagrams – Physical										
Class Diagrams										
Data Dissemination Diagrams										

Shading Key	
Shaded	Mandatory
Un-shaded	Optional

Number Key	
1	Include with no changes
2	Include, needs standardization
3	Include, needs to be updated
4	Eliminate
5	Use as an exception as needed
6	To be developed

The gap analysis helped us to identify several data architecture specific projects to develop or refine the underlying artifacts.

Application Architecture

The application architecture identifies and defines the software systems necessary to manage the data objects and support the business functions. The application architecture also supports stakeholder communication by providing conceptual models and application standards. The applications and their capabilities were defined without reference to particular technologies. Thus, we made the process vendor technology agnostic. During the application architecture effort we were not concerned with application systems technical design; our goal was to define what kinds (or generic types) of application systems were relevant to the client, and what those applications need to do in order to manage data and to present information to the client's human and computer actors.

We defined the target application architecture by building on the architecture vision and the business architecture work as described earlier. Through a series of focused workshops and forums, we determined that the target application architecture would be comprised of the following artifacts:

- Application Portfolio Catalog
- Interface Catalog and Application Communication Diagram
- System by Business Function Matrix
- Software Distribution Models
- Application Standards
- Application Communication Standards
- Application Interface Standards
- Technical Requirements for COTS and SaaS
- Value Chain Diagram
- Application and User Location Diagram

The first eight of the above artifacts were classified as mandatory, and the remaining two items were classified as useful, but optional.

In addition to the above EA artifacts, we also determined that individual projects would benefit from project-specific artifacts (see the area below and to the right of the heavy black separation line within the gap analysis chart below) including:

- Software Engineering Models

This artifact is classified as useful, but optional.

As we did with the business and data architectures, we identified which of the application artifacts existed currently, and that subset became part of the baseline application architecture. Knowing the baseline and the target architectures allowed us to conduct a gap analysis to determine what needed to be done to establish the target application architecture. The results of this exercise are depicted in the following chart. The shading key and number key below the chart are necessary to decipher it.

Target Architecture

Baseline Architecture — Gaps	Application Portfolio Catalog	Interface Catalog & Appl Comm Diagram	System by Business Function Matrix	Software Distribution Models	Appl. Standards	Application Comm. Standards	Application Interface Standards	Tech Requirements for COTS and SaaS	Value Chain Diagram	Application and User Location Diagram	Software Engineering Models
Application Portfolio Catalog	3										
Interface Catalog and Appl Comm Diagram		6									
System by Business Function Matrix			2,3								
Software Distribution Models				2,3							
Application Standards					1						
Application Comm. Standards						6					
Applic. Interface Standards							6				
Tech Requirements for COTS and SaaS								1			
Value Chain Diagram									1,5		
Application and User Location Diagram										5,6	
Software Engineering Models											6

Shading Key	
Shaded	Mandatory
Un-shaded	Optional

Number Key	
1	Include with no changes
2	Include, needs standardization
3	Include, needs to be updated
4	Eliminate
5	Use as an exception as needed
6	To be developed

The gap analysis helped us to identify several application architecture specific projects to develop or refine the underlying artifacts.

Technology Architecture

The technology architecture defines the physical realization of an architectural solution, and it represents the technical software and hardware platforms.

We defined the target technology architecture by building on the prior architecture work we had done earlier for the other domains. Through a series of focused workshops and forums, we determined that the target technology architecture would be comprised of the following artifacts:

- IT Technology Standards
- Technology Portfolio Catalog
- Service Hierarchy Reference Model
- System by Technology Matrix
- Network Computing Hardware Diagrams
- Environments and Locations Diagram
- Platform Decomposition Diagram

The first three of the above artifacts were classified as mandatory, and the remaining four items were classified as useful, but optional. This client's technology architecture does not utilize project-related technology artifacts.

As with the other domains, we identified which of the technology artifacts existed currently, and that subset became part of the baseline technology architecture. Knowing the baseline and the target architectures allowed us to conduct a gap analysis to determine what needed to be done to establish the target technology architecture. The results of this exercise are depicted in the following chart. The shading key and number key below the chart are necessary to decipher it.

Target Architecture

Baseline Architecture: Gaps	IT Technology Standards	Technology Portfolio Catalog	Service Hierarchy Reference Model	System by Technology Matrix	Network Computing Hardware Diagrams	Environments and Locations Diagram	Platform Decomp. Diagram
IT Technology Standards	2,3						
Technology Portfolio Catalog		6					
Service Hierarchy Reference Model			3				
System by Technology Matrix				6			
Network Computing Hardware Diagrams					2,3		
Environments and Locations Diagram						3,6	
Platform Decomposition Diagram							4

Shading Key	
Shaded	Mandatory
Un-shaded	Optional

Number Key	
1	Include with no changes
2	Include, needs standardization
3	Include, needs to be updated
4	Eliminate
5	Use as an exception as needed
6	To be developed

The gap analysis helped us to identify several technology architecture specific projects to develop or refine the underlying artifacts. We also crafted approximately 20 recommendations to implement specific technologies such as single sign on, desktop virtualization, blade servers and identity management. In addition, we identified several technologies that we suggested be considered as candidates for retirement such as WAN encryption and unsupported operating system versions.

Enterprise Architecture Execution

The EA Framework described in the above sections provided our client with a rich process to create and maintain architecture artifacts. We were next left with the task of determining how to knit the architecture framework into the implementation engine of the organization. Our approach was to implement "EA Execution" by interjecting architecture participation within the existing Program Management Office (PMO) lean process.

We implemented a process whereby architects would get involved early during projects at the PMO team level to understand and define a conceptual view of the project solution. Based on basic information about a proposed project, EA would create a conceptual model, perform a risk assessment and define how the project fits into the overall architecture framework of the organization. By being involved early with each major project, the Enterprise Architecture team would be able to steadily guide the organization toward the defined target enterprise architecture state.

While closely related to governance, which is addressed in the next section, EA Execution is clearly operational in nature, and it articulates how the EA team interacts with the PMO and with the other IT teams. The following diagram shows how EA Execution "inserts" an element of Enterprise Architecture discovery into the IT project space; whether the project is for Business functionality, IT efficiency improvement or general IT maintenance.

EA Execution Process

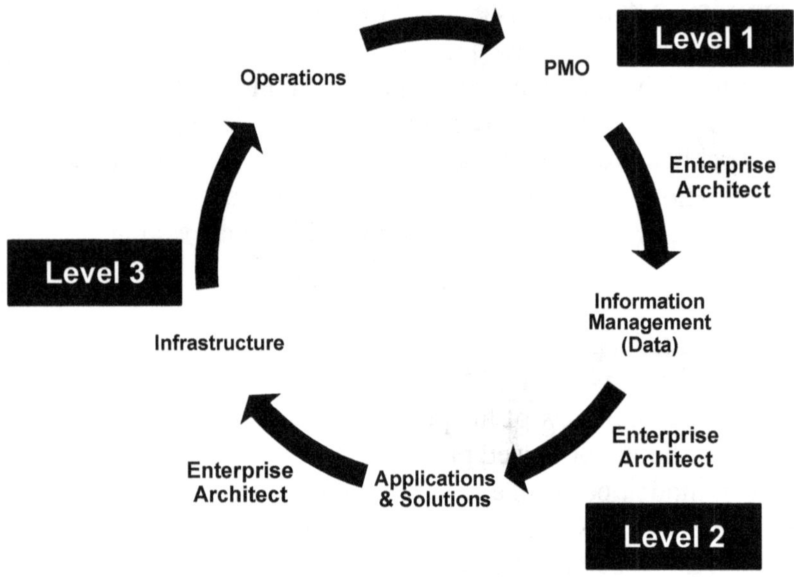

EA Execution is built upon three basic levels.

Level 1: As projects are proposed or considered by the organization, the PMO obtains answers to high-level architecture questions using a structured questionnaire, called an Enterprise Architecture Impact Assessment.

Level 2: The Enterprise Architect uses the information obtained by the PMO during Level 1 activities to:

1. Create a conceptual architectural diagram reflecting the proposed solution.
2. Determine with other architects and/or subject matter experts:
    - What project "type" (i.e. Project pattern) is being proposed.
    - What modifications may be needed to the architecture.

    - What new services or capabilities need to be considered.
3. Create an architecture risk assessment document.

Level 3: The Enterprise Architect meets with the operations support team to review EA component considerations. The Enterprise Architect would use this information to confirm the project can move forward with no alterations or with a list of changes that are required for final signoff.

As the execution process continues over time, the goal is to provide a continuously improving architecture model and a tighter communication process between the EA team, the IT project teams and the Program Management Office. In summary, the client is building the architecture "one project at a time."

EA Governance

Enterprise architecture governance provides guidance and oversight to facilitate successful IT initiatives and to help ensure that the solutions deployed from those IT initiatives conform with standards and to the defined target architecture.

Our recommended approach to EA governance for our client is a blend of processes, organization and performance measures.

- Governance processes are part of the EA execution framework discussed in the section above. Again, EA execution is simply building architecture "one project at a time."
- The governance organization we helped implement includes an Architecture Review Board (ARB) and an Information Standards Group (ISG) as well as the interaction of these two groups with the IT management team.
- Performance measures are embodied in a set of EA metrics

EA Governance Organization

Two groups perform almost all EA governance activities at this client organization:

- The Architecture Review Board (ARB) that we inaugurated during our engagement performs three primary functions. First, it reviews and approves (or disapproves) new projects based on the project's fit with the target architecture. Second, the ARB sponsors and initiates EA design reviews for selected large projects. Third, the ARB initiates revision or replacement work when architecture artifacts or standards need to be updated.
- The Information Standards Group (ISG), which had existed prior to our engagement, establishes and maintains IT standards. The ISG works with the ARB and with IT management to enforce standards, to orchestrate new standards, to change existing standards and to approve exceptions when necessary.

Note that several members of this client's ARB are also members of their ISG, and this overlap of membership facilitates synergy between the two groups.

Metrics

Metrics are necessary to monitor the performance of any business activity including Enterprise Architecture. When instituting metrics, we worked to ensure that each metric be:

- Specific: It must be clearly defined, and it must be clearly owned by an individual.
- Measurable: It must have a baseline starting point, and a desired improvement should be defined.
- Actionable: Information Technology must have control over the metric in order to influence its outcome.
- Relevant: It must be based on value to the business, and it must relate to improved performance of Information Technology.
- Timely: Data for the metric must be readily available.

Following is a list of example enterprise architecture metrics organized by domain. At the conclusion of our engagement, Information Technology leadership was considering which of these potential metrics they would begin tracking.

- Business Architecture Metrics
  Standards Exception Requests and Approvals - These are year-to-date numbers that can be compared to prior years. As new or revised products and services are mapped against standards, they will be classified as in compliance, as an undesirable deviation or as a desirable exception.
  Service Cost Growth – This is the service cost percent increase or decrease from the prior period (year or quarter).
- Data Architecture Metrics
  Database Trusted Source Percent – This is the percent of databases classified as trusted sources of truth.
- Application Architecture Metrics
  Application Re-Use Percent – This is a percentage derived by adding the number of applications (solutions) that are certified for single use plus the number of applications that are shared by more than one business Division or Office and then dividing by the total number of applications.
  Magic Quadrant Ratio – Applications will need to be periodically (annually) classified based on business value and technical quality and mapped to a magic quadrant chart.
  Application Planned Retirements – This is the number of applications planned to be retired in the next 3 years.
- Technology Architecture Metrics
  Hardware Planned Retirements – This is the number of hardware systems (servers, routers, load balancers, etc.) scheduled to be retired in the next 3 years.
- Projects and General Metrics
  EA Project Assessments – This is the number of IT Projects successfully moved through the Enterprise Architecture execution process during the current period.

Summary

For continuity purposes, the methods, tools and artifacts I've included in this chapter are primarily drawn from one engagement. They also are representative of work I've done as part of several other client assignments. I've found that an architect's perspective and the various architecture concepts, as presented in this chapter, are useful to address a variety of client needs.

Suggested Reading and References

Porter, Michael E. *Competitive Advantage: Creating and Sustaining Superior Performance*. New York: Free Press, 1985

Ross, Jeanne W.; Weill, Peter; Robertson, David C. *Enterprise Architecture As Strategy*. Harvard Business Press, 2006

Chapter 14 – Project Management

"Nothing in the world can take the place of persistence.
Talent will not - - nothing is more common than unsuccessful people with talent.
Genius will not - - unrewarded genius is almost a proverb.
Education will not - - the world is full of educated derelicts.
Persistence and determination alone are omnipotent."
-- Calvin Coolidge

A great deal more has been written about Project Management than is known. I'm not going to compound that sin by repeating common knowledge or by stating theories that you can easily find from dozens of authoritative sources. Instead, this chapter includes practical examples of selected tools and techniques that I've used and continuously refined during numerous real projects. These are the project management tools that my clients have found to be most valuable, and I use many of them on almost every engagement.

Project Statement of Work

A good place to start this discussion is with the project SOW (Statement of Work) because it is the initial formal document created to describe the context and framework of a project. There are typically two versions of an SOW, each with its own purpose:

- The first version is the one that is created as part of the client contractual arrangement. I discussed this SOW version earlier in Chapter 9. While it may be identical to the second version, it is typically much more summarized and condensed.
- The second version is intended to be a project reference document with sufficient detail to provide on-going guidance to team members and to other stakeholders. At

minimum it includes the same topics as the first version, and it may also include additional components. The remainder of this chapter addresses this second version.

The project SOW is a non-technical document that answers basic questions about the project, and it is comprised of several components that have continuing value for managing the project throughout its duration. Although many SOWs are Word documents, I prefer using a combination of Word, PowerPoint and Excel because no one tool seems to work well with all the various SOW components. Also, crafting each component individually allows me to construct them such that each will stand on its own, and I can subsequently re-use any one or combination of them for reference and for a variety of other communications.

When properly crafted, each SOW component answers a fundamental question about the project. Some components can be combined, and not all of them always need to be included. There are no rules. Here are the basic components and questions:

- **Objective** – Why are we doing the project? What are the business objectives? This describes the purpose of the project in business terms. I sometimes also include dependencies and assumptions in this section, if appropriate.
- **Priorities** – What is the order of priorities? Relatively speaking, what priority is most important and what priority is least important?
- **Scope** – What activities will we be doing? This identifies the work and deliverables that are included and, equally as important, what is not included. Scope should also specify where the end deliverables will function, especially if more than one location is included.
- **Approach** – How will we proceed? This identifies the overarching methods to be used. For example, if one of the deliverables is functioning software, this section should specify whether a “buy” or “build” approach is to be used,

and if building, whether internal or contract resources or a combination of both will be used.

- **Roles and Responsibilities** – Who are the participants, and where are they located? This identifies project core team members, steering committee members, other project constituents as well as governance considerations. Location information can be important when resources reside in different cities, countries and time zones.
- **Schedule** – When will the project start and end, and what are the major milestones in between? This can be an extensive chart, or it can be a simple timeline.
- **Risks** – What are the threats to success? This is a list of individual risks and mitigation plans for each. This component is typically a separate document, and it is rarely static because new risks seem to be regularly identified throughout most projects.
- **Business Case** – How much will it cost? This identifies benefits, costs and the financial rationale.
- **Communication Plan** – This component is typically a separate document, and it identifies what will be communicated to various stakeholders and how those communications will be delivered.
- **Workplan** – This component is typically a separate document, and it lists what tasks will be done, who will be assigned to each task, and when it will be done.
- **Approval** – This identifies who needs to sign off on the project before proceeding further and how approvals are to be recorded.

The next several sub-sections individually address in more detail the components of the SOW listed above. These sub-sections also contain examples from previously completed engagements.

Objective

One of my clients engaged me to re-organize and re-start a project that had previously stalled. During my first day on that project, I learned that team members had different ideas of why we were doing the project, what was included and what was excluded. During the next two days, I facilitated a working session with the entire team to get all of us on the same page. Many valuable results came out of those two days including the following objective statement.

Objective Statement

> The **objective** of this program is to implement tools and business processes to help protect clients and meet regulatory obligations related to electronic communication capture, archival, supervision and retrieval.

Priorities

At the beginning of most projects, I work with the project Steering Committee to define and agree on relative priorities to help guide team decisions. In this example, taken from the same project as the objective statement above, the relative priorities guided the team to give "scope" the highest importance. Therefore every team member knew we should not reduce scope in order to save money or time.

Priorities Statement

> When project changes need to be made, the project team will make decisions based on the following priority guidelines.

Priority 1	Scope
Priority 2	Schedule
Priority 3	Cost

Scope

Again, continuing with an example from the same project, the following chart defines scope. Note that each of the four boxes has a distinct purpose. Our team members made continuing reference to this chart whenever a stakeholder posed a question. We always had a clear understanding of what our team was working on, what other teams were delivering, what was deferred and what was excluded.

Scope Statement

Our Scope Includes:

- Application integration with vendor tools
- Include email, IM, text
- Unique lexicon lists for each specialty dept.
- Configure and design archiving platform
- Creating and documenting processes
- Vendor supplied standard reports
- Custom reports
- Testing 15 business & system functions
- Training 6 depts. with 150 resources
- Communications

Other Teams Will Deliver:

- Active Directory
- Building the XXX vault
- Environment configuration
- Implementing capture tools
- Deploying data servers
- Linking vendor tools
- Integration with DRP
- Disaster Recovery
- Books & Records

Deferred to a Future Phase:

- SharePoint
- Social Media
- RightNow

Out of Scope:

- End User archiving (personal vault access)
- Enterprise vault consolidation
- Non-Corp. access to vault

Approach

The project team needs to be flexible in how they achieve objectives, and while the approach might change during the course of the project, it is valuable to start with a common understanding of how the team intends to proceed.

Project Approach

Our approach is to build on the work done to date by the Architecture group and the software tools selection project team. More specifically, we will use the requirements from the selection project body of work to construct test cases.

We will enlist resources from the following teams:

- ABC Program Team
- Business teams from 6 locations, including India, for UAT testing
- Infrastructure teams to validate that hardware and telecommunications components are working properly in both remote data centers
- External Contractor for development of interfaces and custom reports

Program code development will be minimized whenever possible:

- Requirements will be satisfied by using parameter settings and "levers" that are available within the vendor supplied software tools.
- Functions that absolutely require programming will be designed with the assistance of a senior architect, and the code will be created in the PowerShell scripting language.

The project team will need to address known difficulties in the current interfaces:

- Instant messaging formats are incompatible with email formats.
- Text messaging formats are incompatible with email formats.
- Different sets of 'baseline' code are being used at the two data centers.

Roles and Responsibilities

Publishing a project organization chart, like the one below, is useful for everyone involved. This part of the SOW might also include a discussion of governance; however, I've found that governance is not a subject where creativity is welcome by most clients, and when governance verbiage is required, it's been easiest to merely cut and paste a governance paragraph from another of the client's existing or previous SOWs.

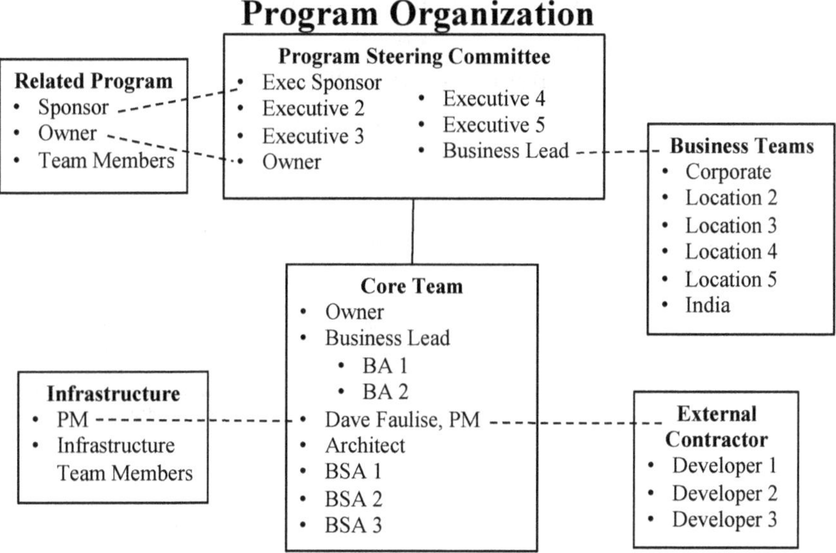

Schedule

A timeline is a useful visual tool that helps manage a project. It is also a wonderful communication device when developed properly and tailored to the audience. Unfortunately, most timelines are overly complex and nearly impossible to decipher because the author feels compelled to include far more detail than any audience is willing to digest. Once again, brevity and simplicity are my strong preferences. I provide two examples, one for a single project and another for a complex program consisting of 19 projects.

The first example is taken from the salvaged project that I mentioned previously in this chapter. The workplan included dozens of deliverables, but I constructed this timeline to show only the significant milestones, which allowed company executives to maintain their focus on priorities rather than getting caught up in minutia. It also was a continuing reminder to the project team that while we would likely be forgiven if we slipped a few days on one or two of the deliverable target dates, the milestones on this chart were sacred and would not be compromised.

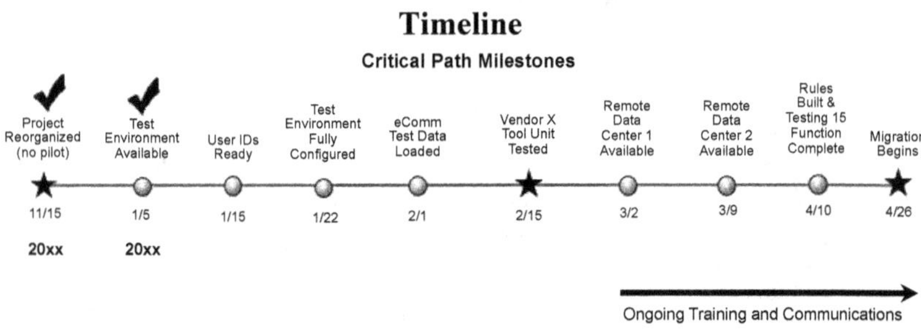

The second timeline example below is taken from a service company with major operations in Asia, Europe and the Americas. They were replacing obsolete software to support their core service offering at hundreds of customer locations, but the replacement effort had gone poorly, and I was asked to lead a team in turning the initiative around. The timeline shows multiple projects within two major phases. Phase I included nine projects that collectively were intended to correct deficiencies within the product. Phase II included ten projects that each focused on making the software implementation process more scalable so we could execute more customer implementations at the same time. This second timeline chart simply shows a single line for each of the 19 projects. Linkages and dependencies between projects were detailed in a separate document and were intentionally omitted from this chart in order to keep it simple and focus the Steering Committee and each team on when each project was scheduled to happen.

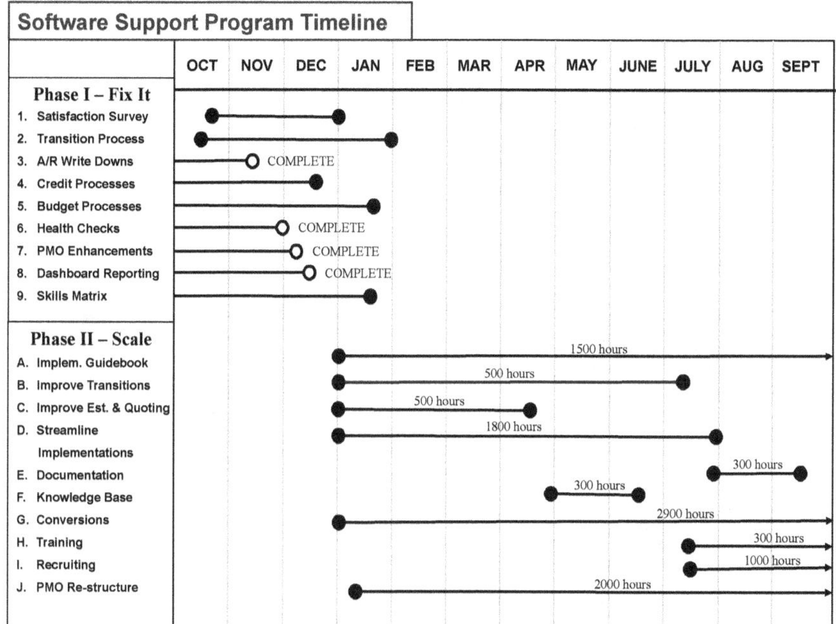

Risks

From the first day of a project, I start documenting risks in a "risk log." The log is easy to start because there are always risks, such as contention for resources. Risks can also surface from seemingly benign sources. For example, team members located in different cities may present language, geographic and/or time zone challenges that create risks to the project.

Terminology varies from client to client. Some organizations want to maintain a "risk log" while others prefer an "issues" log. An "issue" seems to me to be a "risk" that has materialized into a problem; however, some organizations want to reverse the importance by making "risks" more urgent than "issues." I've found it's easiest to go along with whatever terminology the client is using as long as I understand their use because it doesn't matter as long as we're addressing the most important problems and tracking threats that could become problems.

Following is an abbreviated risk log example. Note in particular the last three columns. I assigned a priority for each risk based on the odds that the risk would become a problem (probability) and how badly that problem was likely to harm the project (impact).

Risk Log

Risk	Description and Impact	Mitigation Plan	Owner	Probability	Impact	Priority
XYZ Project Success	We are dependent on the XYZ project to stand up their new release.	Make this dependency highly visible.	DF	Med	High	1
SEC and State Approvals	SEC and State approvals are not assured, and we may have a low number of states at launch.	Use the prior release for unapproved states.	DF	Med	Med	2
Resource Constraints	Multiple concurrent projects may require the same resources.	Re-confirm all resource commitments and priorities. Consolidate scheduling to identify potential problems. Escalate any conflicts.	DF	Med	Low	3
Outsourced Develop-ment	Development of the ABC module will be outsourced.	Include SLAs and penalties in the contract.	DF	Med	Low	3

Business Case

The business case is a financial analysis of the costs and benefits of the recommended solution. Many of my clients have required me to provide a business case for the project or program I'm managing.

See the Business Case section in Chapter 12 for a discussion of business cases and an example from one of my projects.

Communication Plan

The purpose of a project communication plan is simply to document the approach and actions for communicating with those impacted by the project. Ironically, the plans created by many project managers are poor communication tools themselves because, in spite of good content, each one is so lengthy that only the author has bothered to read it. I've found that creating a good communication plan requires brevity and structure as well as good content.

My communication mentor was Kathie W. She was brilliant at boiling a complex topic down into a simple message. She also taught me the value of structure. Instead of immediately focusing on the message content, Kathie always started by identifying and understanding the various audiences and what behaviors we wanted from each audience. She introduced me to the ABCDE communication approach:

- Audiences: With whom are we communicating, sorted into logical groups.
- Behavior: What we want each audience to do after receiving the information.
- Content: The messages we are communicating.
- Design: The delivery medium for each message and the frequency and/or timeline.
- Evaluation: The feedback mechanism to determine if the communication is effective.

I've used the ABCDE method of critical thinking to structure numerous communication plans. Kathie was not initially in agreement with the short plans I drafted because she felt that I was sacrificing clarity, especially in the Content section, for the sake of brevity. We eventually agreed to supplement my single page plans with additional verbiage that expanded the detail content of individual messages. I've continued to prefer and refine the one-page approach. Similar to Kathie, some team members are initially unsure about my proposed communication plan because it is so brief; however, after studying the plan more thoroughly they usually agree that the plan is in fact comprehensive and a highly useful tool for managing project messages.

Following is a communications plan example. I've not included the supplemental expanded content messages. This example is from a planning and architecture project that had broad impact across every IT group and most business units in the organization. Note that column headings represent the ABCDE method and that the Evaluation mechanisms in the last column intentionally tie directly back to the Behavioral Objectives for the individual Audiences. As you review each row in the following example, think about the content of each cell for that row, and then consider them holistically. I think you'll agree this tool has value.

Communication Plan Example

Audience	Behavioral Objectives	Content (key messages)	Design	Evaluation
Business Stake-holders	• Understand business rationale of the project • Align with and support framework models and processes	• Project results align with business strategies and priorities • Risks are known, managed and mitigated • Summary models, concepts and plans	• One to one discussions between business and IT leaders	• Direct feedback from business leaders indicating under-standing and alignment

Audience	Behavioral Objectives	Content (key messages)	Design	Evaluation
IT Steering Commit-tee	• Understand and accept recommendations • Assist in managing business stakeholder expectations • Approve plans and deliverables	• Project results align with business strategies and priorities • Risks are known, managed and mitigated • Summary models, concepts and plans	• Workshops and forums • Recommen-dation presen-tations • Status updates	• Direct feedback from IT leaders indicating under-standing and approval
Project Core Team	• Define project require-ments and plans • Understand and apply the principles and priorities • Understand and apply the framework models and processes • Provide information rapidly • Deliver results	• What information is needed by whom and when • On-going status and plans • Risks and mitigation options • Pros and Cons of alternatives • Recommen-dations • Scope and scope changes	• Weekly Core Team meetings • Written directives • Weekly status reports focusing on issues and decisions needed • Shared directories and folders	• Open questions are answered • Assump-tions become decisions • Project results are delivered on schedule

Audience	Behavioral Objectives	Content (key messages)	Design	Evaluation
Subject Matter Experts (SMEs)	• Understand business and IT leaders' purpose for the project • Provide feedback and requested information rapidly	• Guidance detailing what and when feedback and other information is needed	• E-mail requests, instructions and reminders	• Timeliness and quality of feedback and requested informa-tion
Other IT Teams	• Align with the project vision & framework and ask, "What does it mean to me?" • Accept temporary ambiguity • Use project models for their own planning	• Project goals • Project models and processes	• Written guidance • Presenta-tions • Open meetings • Shared directories and folders	• Other projects incorporate the principles and tools from this project
Parent Company IT Group	• Be aware of this IT project initiative • Understand roles • Provide support and information	• Project initiative objectives, approach, timeline and status	• Access to the shared directories and folders	• Direct feedback from Parent IT Leaders and SMEs indicating alignment and support

Audience	Behavioral Objectives	Content (key messages)	Design	Evaluation
Vendors and 3rd-Party Suppliers, as necessary	• Align with the project vision and framework	• Summary models and concepts	• One to one discussions between suppliers and IT leaders	• Direct feedback from supplier representa-tives indicating alignment

Workplan

The initial workplan construction process forces me to think in detail about what tasks we're doing, how we'll do them, who will do them, and when we'll do each one. My experience is that the value of a workplan follows an 80-20 rule during its life. 20% of the overall effort goes into the initial creation, which provides 80% of the value. 80% of the effort is spent maintaining the workplan throughout the remainder of the project, and that provides only 20% of the value. The workplan clearly needs to be kept current, but I try to minimize the time I spend maintaining it after it's built.

Over the years I've worked with several different project-planning tools, and I'm agnostic about all of them. I will use whatever tools my client is using. My concern with any project planning software is that it can easily become an end unto itself. In other words, the project manager can get so involved with making the tool work and so invested in the elegant charts and graphs the tool can create that he/she spends an inordinate amount of time maintaining the tool. I have observed some project managers spending as many as 20 hours each week maintaining their MS Project workplan. In my opinion, this is crazy. These project managers are terrific administrators with great paper trails, but they are terrible at adjusting to changes and heading off threats before they become major problems.

I've created several example project workplan templates that I maintain in my personal library. For example, I have templates for waterfall development, agile/rapid development, software selection, architecture, planning, database design, etc. I maintain these as Excel files because Excel files are easier than other formats for porting into various client environments. I will select one of these templates as a starting point for a new project because I find it simpler to tailor from a template than to start with a blank page. Also, after I complete a project, if it was sufficiently unique, I may make a generic version of that project's workplan and save it in my template library.

Following is one of my example templates that I've used for software and infrastructure acquisition projects. I've omitted four of the spreadsheet columns from this example because the cells of those columns are generally blank in the template. The four missing columns are Method/Tool, Responsibility, Due Date, and Deliverable Work Product.

Evaluation and Selection Workplan Template

I.D.	Phase/Task	Description
1.0	**Planning & Initiation**	
1.1	Review Project Request	Conduct initial fact-finding with project sponsor/initiator and business user. Define objectives, scope, assumptions, constraints, priority, success factors, timetable and deliverables. Create summary context diagram.
1.2	Tailor Approach	Confirm suitability for software package evaluation and selection. Review and adapt standard workplan phases and tasks.
1.3	Estimate Cost	Develop high-level cost estimate.
1.4	Obtain Approval	Submit project charter, proposal and preliminary workplan to Sponsor/Steering Committee for approval. Assign Project Manager.

1.5	Recruit Team	Select team members. Identify and confirm Steering Committee members. Hire contractors and consultants.
1.6	Arrange Facilities	Obtain team workspace & meeting room. Set up team Novell directories. Set up login I.D.'s as needed. Obtain security cards for contractors.
1.7	Develop Detail Workplan	Define deadlines, responsibilities, dependencies and deliverables for each task.
1.8	Conduct Kick-Off Meeting	Conduct formal kick-off session with Steering Committee. Review charter and workplan.
1.9	Conduct Team Training	Schedule and conduct initial team education and team building exercises.
2.0	**Requirements Definition**	
2.1	Model Current Process	Obtain or develop models of current processes.
2.2	Assemble Background Docs	Obtain copies of all pertinent background documents needed to define related enterprise goals, functions and information areas. Identify current process performance and capacity metrics.
2.3	Draft Table of Contents	Draft a table of contents for final requirements document. Draft preliminary Executive Summary section.
2.4	Identify Data Requirements	Confirm business data rules and relationships. Identify input and output file requirements. Identify volumes and frequencies. Define a high-level data conversion strategy.
2.5	Identify Process Requirements	Define external interfaces. Define process threads. Define reports and screens. Define transaction processing. Develop use case diagrams.
2.6	Define Acceptance Criteria	Identify test cases and scenarios. Identify performance and capacity requirements. Define security and control requirements. Review and confirm with user sponsors.
2.7	Define Technical Infrastructure Requirements	Determine where processing and data will be distributed. Determine technical requirements for each node (Location). Determine telecom requirements between nodes. Define facility requirements.
2.8	Define User Impact	Understand how the users will interact with and use the system. Develop business workflow model. Determine organization impact.
2.9	Identify Project Issues & Risks	Document issues and risks identified during requirements gathering.
2.10	Create Deployment Strategy	Identify transition issues, business constraints and release dependencies.

2.11	Prepare Evaluation & Test Environment	Divide evaluation, test and selection work into time boxes. Establish dependencies. Initiate technology acquisitions necessary for testing.
2.12	Assemble Requirements Definition Document	Edit and finalize all document sections. Proof, assemble and print document.
2.13	Review with Steering Committee	Review application requirements and final document with the Steering Committee.
3.0	**RFP**	
3.1	Identify Alternatives	Identify vendor population. Select participating vendor candidates based on user requirements and priorities.
3.2	Develop draft RFP	Include company background, project background, processing requirements, technical requirements, instructions and conditions, proposal format, proposal content requirements, schedule.
3.3	Develop Evaluation Criteria	Identify evaluation areas such as proposal responsiveness, requirements fit, vendor stability, cost, and other considerations. Identify weighting and scoring scheme.
3.4	Review with Steering Committee	Review draft RFP and evaluation criteria with Steering Committee. Identify enhancements and revisions.
3.5	Finalize RFP	Incorporate enhancements and revisions as appropriate.
3.6	Distribute RFP	Eliminate any non-qualified vendors from original list. Send RFP to qualified vendors. Confirm receipt with each vendor.
3.7	Develop Contact Instructions	Document anticipated vendor tactics, and develop a response script for anyone inappropriately contacted by a vendor.
3.8	Review with Steering Committee	Review final RFP, contact instructions and other general recommendations with Steering Committee.
4.0	**Acquisition**	
4.1	Evaluate Proposals	Read and score proposals individually. Develop composite team scores for each vendor.
4.2	Contact References	Conduct telephone reference checks. Conduct on-site visits as appropriate.
4.3	Recommend Finalists	Identify top 2-3 finalists.
4.4	Negotiate Deal	Conduct face-to-face negotiations with finalists. Identify recommended winner.
4.5	Conduct Legal Review	Have legal counsel review contract terms.

4.6	Review with Steering Committee	Document recommendation. Review results with the Steering Committee.
4.7	Obtain Software	Order and obtain package software and documentation.
4.8	Order Infrastructure Components	Order required new equipment and utility software.
5.0	**Installation**	
5.1	Refine Design	Review interface and conversion designs and revise for development. Design test criteria.
5.2	Construct Objects	Create and/or update interface objects, support objects and components.
5.3	Complete Programming	Finalize interface programs. Finalize conversion programs.
5.4	Create Test Data	Create, update and load all test data sets.
5.5	Conduct Time Box Tests	Integrate components. Execute integration testing. Execute volume and stress testing. Test security and control features.
5.6	Conduct Acceptance Tests	Guide user execution of acceptance testing in the Model Office. Obtain user sign-off.
5.7	Finalize Documentation	Taylor and publish technical and user documentation. Update all affected models.
5.8	Review with Steering Committee	Review results with the Steering Committee.
6.0	**Deployment**	
6.1	Schedule Deployment	Finalize and publish deployment schedule.
6.2	Mitigate Risk	Develop a detail back out plan to de-install new release and re-install prior release. Include all data and software.
6.3	Conduct Training	Train users and operations personnel as appropriate.
6.4	Install Infrastructure Components	Accept, test and install equipment, utility/operating system software and other infrastructure components.
6.5	Convert Data	Initialize production database(s) and files. Load converted data.
6.6	Stage Release	Load all software and data into a "new release" directory set.
6.7	Deploy Release to Production	Initiate production operations. Execute parallel operations, if appropriate.

6.8	Monitor Transition	Monitor and support production operations. Manage and correct bugs. Document needed changes and enhancements for next release.
6.9	Review with Steering Committee	Review results with the Steering Committee.
7.0	**Post-Project Activities**	
7.1	Document Lessons Learned	Circulate team survey to collect knowledge gained from the project. Improvement areas include standards, staffing, processes, tools, and approach.
7.2	Assemble Global Recommendations	Assemble issues and ideas for possible inclusion in a global recommendation set to be created at conclusion of the project.
7.3	Summarize Suggestions for Future Projects and Releases	
7.4	Publish Final Report	

Approval

I have not included a discussion of or an example for the Approval component of an SOW because that is typically a single signature page for the sponsor and key stakeholders to sign. Also, with the advent of document management systems such as SharePoint, many approvals are now handled electronically.

The remaining sections of this chapter address additional project management activities that are typically not part of a SOW.

Status Report

Project status reports are a pain, but they are necessary to maintain continuous communication with project constituents, and I force myself to religiously publish weekly status reports during my projects. Unless the client organization has a mandatory status report format, I keep the report format as simple as possible. I try to keep them to a single page and use repetitive sections in order to minimize the effort needed to produce the report each week. The examples below demonstrate two simple, but effective status report formats. What's important to note here is the formats, not the contents of the reports. The first example uses four quadrants:

- Upper Left contains high-level purpose and results.
- Upper Right is for recent and near-term activities.
- Lower Left shows schedule and milestones.
- Lower Right identifies risks and financial status.

Project Status Report

Program Number: XXXXX
Sponsor: XXXXXXXXX
Leads: XXXXXXX, XXXXXX
IT Project Manager: Dave Faulise
Update Date: 08 May 20XX

Project Objective

Consolidate and replace outdated technology within the XXXXX and XXXXXX datacenters and move to a scalable Infrastructure environment that enables high availability, redundancy, 24/7 response, and security.

Project Deliverables

1. RFP released to the market before January 31, 20XX
2. Contract negotiations completed before April 30, 20XX
3. Services in the new location initiated before June 30, 20XX

Project Benefits

- Consolidated services in a centralized location.
- Upgraded Systems and OS to a contemporary architecture.
- Improved availability, resiliency and redundancy for all applications.
- Reduced infrastructure maintenance overhead.
- Improved Security & Compliance controls.
- Real-time Scalability to support growth of our business.

Current Update:

- Conducted the design session and transition planning with Vendor A.
- Scheduled twice-weekly status meetings with Vendor B.
- Finalized transition detail workplan.

Upcoming Key Activities

- Define transition "waves" and phases.
- Document additional required server details.
- Initiate acceptance test planning.
- Continue executing communications plan.

Y	Project Schedule				
Start	RFP	Vendor Selection	Contract	New Services	Go Live
	✓	✓	✓	○	△
Dec	Jan	Feb-Mar	Apr	May	Jun

	Key Milestones/Deliverables	Due Dates Original	Due Dates Act./Forecast	# Re-plan
G	Architecture framework	Dec 31	Jan 8	1
G	Requirements complete	Jan 15	Jan 14	2
G	RFP distributed	Jan 21	Jan 21	2
G	Vendor selected	Mar 16	Mar 18	3
G	Contracts signed	Apr 30	Apr 30	1
Y	New services provisioned in new location	May 29	May 29	1
Y	Existing system transition begins	Jun 1	Jun 1	1

Likely/ Severity (H/M/L)	Project Key Risks / Issues/Dependencies	Mitigation/Resolution	Owner
H / M	Time for carriers to provision circuits into the new datacenter	Place orders immediately after contract is signed	XX
H / M	Time and availability of internal resources	Communication and advance scheduling	DF
M / M	Unforeseen issues within our environment	Adhere to change management procedures	XX
M / M	Dependencies on other projects	Collaboration with and between IT leaders	DF
L / M	Network bandwidth constraints external to Datacenter	Carrier capacity monitoring and updates from them	XX

G	Project Budget	Planned	Actual To Date	Variance
	1,000,000	1,000,000	575,000	425,000

The next example is similarly simple. Note that the timeline part of this example is one of the timelines I provided earlier in this chapter. Re-use is a good thing. I repeated this same timeline on each status report during this project; and as the project progressed, I merely added more checkmarks to indicate completed milestones. This only took a few seconds each week and allowed me to focus on important items like the risk section. Even the risk section didn't require a lot of time because many of the bullet items were retained from week to week.

Project Status Report

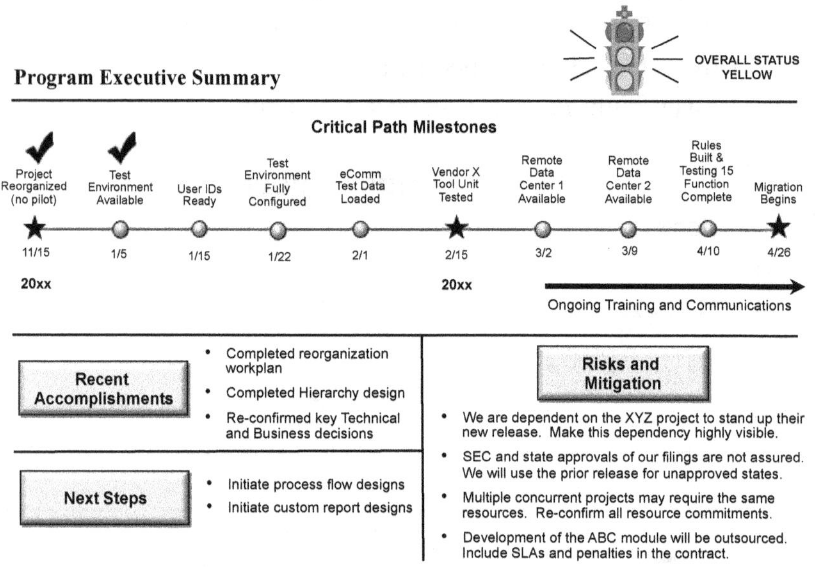

Program Executive Summary
OVERALL STATUS
YELLOW
Critical Path Milestones
Project Reorganized (no pilot)
Test Environment Available
User IDs Ready
Test Environment Fully Configured
eComm Test Data Loaded
Vendor X Tool Unit Tested
Remote Data Center 1 Available
Remote Data Center 2 Available
Rules Built & Testing 15 Function Complete
Migration Begins
11/15
1/5
1/15
1/22
2/1
2/15
3/2
3/9
4/10
4/26
20xx
20xx
Ongoing Training and Communications
Recent Accomplishments
Completed reorganization workplan
Completed Hierarchy design
Re-confirmed key Technical and Business decisions
Next Steps
Initiate process flow designs
Initiate custom report designs
Risks and Mitigation
We are dependent on the XYZ project to stand up their new release. Make this dependency highly visible.
SEC and state approvals of our filings are not assured. We will use the prior release for unapproved states.
Multiple concurrent projects may require the same resources. Re-confirm all resource commitments.
Development of the ABC module will be outsourced. Include SLAs and penalties in the contract.

The above examples both show an overall status of "yellow." One of my favorite clients, John H. believes that it is important to report project status as yellow as soon as there is evidence that something is not going smoothly. John's counsel was to always resist reporting green, and I agree with him. Regardless of a client's unique organizational dynamics, there are useful psychological principles for managing executive expectations. Some project managers always report status as green, but I believe this creates a "no win" position. Executive sponsors and steering committees want to contribute, and they will, one way or another:

- If the status is reported to be green, they will pick at issues and eventually find something to "fix" while making the project manager look silly for not bringing it up first.

- If the status is reported to be yellow, and the project manager asks for their guidance about the concerning issues, the sponsors feel useful and are less likely to get in the way.
- If the status jumps from green to red, the project manager risks being criticized for springing a surprise on the sponsors and for not managing the project properly. This can cause executives to lose confidence in the project manager.

I'm going to deviate briefly here to comment on managing expectations. Following is a simple but powerful chart that another client, Paul S. shared with me early in my consulting career. The underlying message is that when my project is perceived as easy, then I'm in a no-win situation, and when the project is perceived as hard, then I'm in a no-lose situation. As Paul admonished me before showing me this chart, "Don't ever tell my boss again that what we're trying to do is 'a piece of cake.'" As in diving and gymnastics, while successful execution is clearly important, the degree of difficulty should not be ignored.

Expectation Management

Difficulty Scale	Failure	Success
Hard	"Good try, and we forgive you."	"You're a Hero!"
Easy	"You Fool!"	"We're not impressed."

Achievement Scale

Team Building

There is no rule that says you can't have fun during a project. Humor and having some occasional fun builds allegiance and loyalty among team members. When I've assembled a project team that hasn't worked together previously, I employ "ice breaker" games early in the project to get the team to know each other and to determine who might take some initiative when necessary.

Following are descriptions for two of the several games I've used for these purposes.

****

"4-3-2-1" Team Building Exercise

Purpose: Have team members get to know each other better on a personal level.

Divide group into 4-person teams. Some teams may have more than 4 people.

Each team has 10 minutes to identify 4 different events:

- Something exactly 4 people have done.
- Something exactly 3 people have done.
- Something exactly 2 people have done.
- Something only 1 person has done.

Example Events: Scuba diving, being arrested, playing the banjo.

After 10 minutes, each team presents their 4 events to the full group, keeping the team members who did them anonymous.

The objective is to identify the team with the most unique or unusual or humorous 4 events.

****

"Birthday Lineup" Team Building Exercise

Purposes: Develop cooperation. Identify who takes initiative to lead the group to a solution.

Instruct the group that no one is allowed to talk during this activity.

Explain to them that you want them to line up in chronological order, according to the month and day of their birthdays. Year of birth is not relevant.

After they have lined up, have them discuss how they arrived at their formation. Note if there are any errors in the formation. Note if there are any shared birthdays. Identify who assumed a leadership role and how others reacted to that person's direction.

****

As the above examples demonstrate, I like to use simple, easy to execute games that don't require elaborate supplies. I found these and others on the Internet using a simple search of "team building games." The Girl Scout and the Boy Scout web sites are also good sources.

PMO Experiences

I have been hired by two different clients to be an interim PMO (Project Management Office) director. The first of these engagements occurred in the late 1990's when PMOs were first being established within the technology divisions of many companies. My client asked me to plan, create, organize and manage their PMO. More specifically, I:

- Recruited several project managers,

- Helped launch an improved project management methodology,
- Designed prioritization, funding and approval processes,
- Established tools and techniques to conduct project audits and risk assessments,
- Helped initiate monitoring mechanisms including a master schedule,
- Provided day-to-day Project Office management, and
- Recruited my permanent replacement.

Several of the tools described in this chapter were used during that engagement.

During my second experience as a PMO director, my client's organization used the PMO for business as well as technology related projects so the scope of my work was quite broad. I was engaged as the interim Enterprise and Business PMO Director, and I focused primarily on implementing PMO process improvements. The workplan templates, the scheduling tools and the communications planning techniques described in this chapter were used extensively during that engagement. I also employed some of the planning and organization change tools described in Chapters 12 and 18.

Summary

This chapter intentionally contains very limited discussion about project management theory. Instead it includes several practical examples of tools and methods that I've used during numerous real projects. This chapter also contains client stories that describe how I created and how I used some of those tools and methods.

Chapter 15 – Requirements

> "We do not need, and indeed never will have, all the answers before we act.
> It is often only through taking action that we can discover some of them."
> -- Charlotte Bunch

Experience shows that successful projects almost universally have clearly defined business and technical requirements. While good requirements do not guarantee success, it's almost impossible to succeed without them. In mathematical terms, they are necessary, but not sufficient. Well-defined requirements are essential to do proper development, and they are also necessary to define appropriate test cases. If you are an Agile proponent, please don't discount this chapter. Agile is a software development approach based on rapid, iterative development cycles that might include only partially complete requirements. I too believe in Agile, and I've been using Agile techniques since before they were labeled "Agile." Those who participated in IT projects in the 1990's should be familiar with the "Rapid Development" movement that included many of today's Agile concepts. Agile clearly does work, but it can also fail, and the failures I've observed were caused in part by poorly defined requirements.

In contrast to projects with poorly defined requirements, I have observed a few projects that were at the other end of the spectrum and were intently focused on creating perfect requirements. Most of those projects got incredibly bogged down because, as the project team spent weeks and months nailing down details, the business changed as a result of new as well as obsoleted products and services, changing customer demographics, regulatory changes, etc. Those business changes caused the requirements to change, which caused the project team to back up and revise their work products. The only way out of this cycle of frustration is to compromise perfection in favor of speed. That's not to say it's OK to do a sloppy job, but getting requirements 95% right at the beginning is usually good enough because the remaining 5% can be nailed down during design and development. See the Charlotte Bunch quote above. Enough platitudes. Let's get practical.

How long should it take to get requirements defined? Even for the most complex projects, requirements should be 95% complete in four to six weeks. It can be done even faster. How does a team rapidly nail down requirements?

- First, an experienced BA (Business Analyst) is worth his/her weight in gold. I tell my clients that the BA position is not one where they should try to save costs. In fact, if the BA on my project doesn't have a billing rate higher than mine, then I get concerned.
- Second, process is important. Most BAs will employ a variety of techniques, such as ER (Entity-Relationship) diagrams, Venn diagrams, process flows with swim lanes, etc. Examples of ER diagrams (I also refer to them as context diagrams) are included in Chapters 12 and 13, which discuss Strategy and Architecture. A fairly sophisticated process flow diagram is included as an example below. Many times, part of the overall requirements process is to work towards a proof-of-concept phase. In other words, classify those critical requirements that will later be used to prove (or disprove) the validity of an eventual solution.
- Third, business participation is necessary. Even if the BA knows the business cold, participating business users can speed the process by challenging results, and they approve deliverables more easily when their fingerprints are on them. Finally, users who are intimately familiar with requirements make excellent testers later in the project and can help keep the QA and acceptance testing processes properly focused.

- Fourth, use checklists. This may sound simplistic, but checklists can eliminate weeks of work, and they increase confidence that the team hasn't overlooked an important feature. I maintain a library of requirements documents that I've developed over the years, and I use generic versions of them as checklists to jump start the requirements definition phase of my projects. I include an example below.
- Fifth, borrow ideas from commercially available solutions. When the project approach is to buy rather than build a solution, the BA should research features and functions available from multiple competing commercial products. Even when building a solution, the BA might find similar products to research. Many requirements can be identified while reviewing product features and functions; although the team needs to be cautious because there can be a tendency to include "really cool" features as "requirements" when they aren't needed. This hard-to-resist tendency, called "gold plating" should be avoided.

Process Flow Examples

I am including two examples of process flow diagrams. The first is a typical or traditional process flow that might be included in a requirements definition effort. The second example is somewhat unusual because it includes features not usually found in most other process flows.

I created the following traditional problem work flow diagram as part of a process re-engineering effort for an internal help desk that was servicing several hundred stores of a retail operation. The chart contains horizontal "swim lanes" for the five business functions involved in the process. The numbered boxes represent individual activities, and the arrows show various paths through the process that are possible, depending on the nature of the particular problem being addressed.

Help Desk Problem Management Work Flow

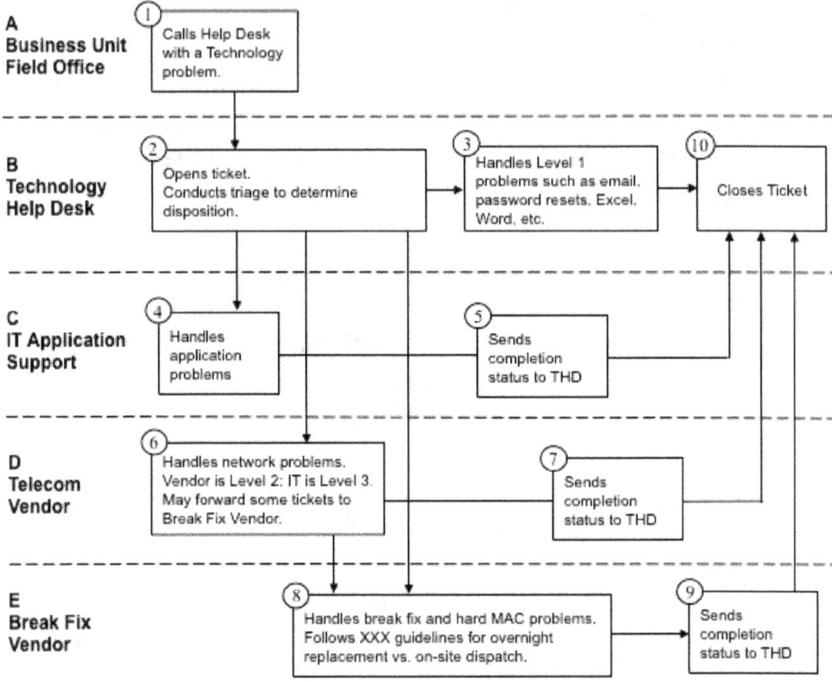
A
Business Unit
Field Office
1
Calls Help Desk with a Technology problem.
B
Technology
Help Desk
2
Opens ticket.
Conducts triage to determine disposition.
3
Handles Level 1 problems such as email, password resets, Excel, Word, etc.
10
Closes Ticket
C
IT Application
Support
4
Handles application problems
5
Sends completion status to THD
D
Telecom
Vendor
6
Handles network problems.
Vendor is Level 2: IT is Level 3.
May forward some tickets to Break Fix Vendor.
7
Sends completion status to THD
E
Break Fix
Vendor
8
Handles break fix and hard MAC problems.
Follows XXX guidelines for overnight replacement vs. on-site dispatch.
9
Sends completion status to THD

The next process flow diagram, showing a project governance process, contains several non-typical features. My apologies, but I had to turn this diagram 90 degrees to fit on the page. Specifically the diagram shows:

- Project (or product) life cycle phases as column headings.
- Deliverables (in lighter text) and specific responsibilities (in black text) identified in the appended bottom row, which is not one of the swim lanes.
- Gating inserted as the heavier vertical line labeled "Division Directors Commissioning Gate." This gate separates Request processes from Execution processes. I have created similar charts for other organizations that employ multiple approval gates.

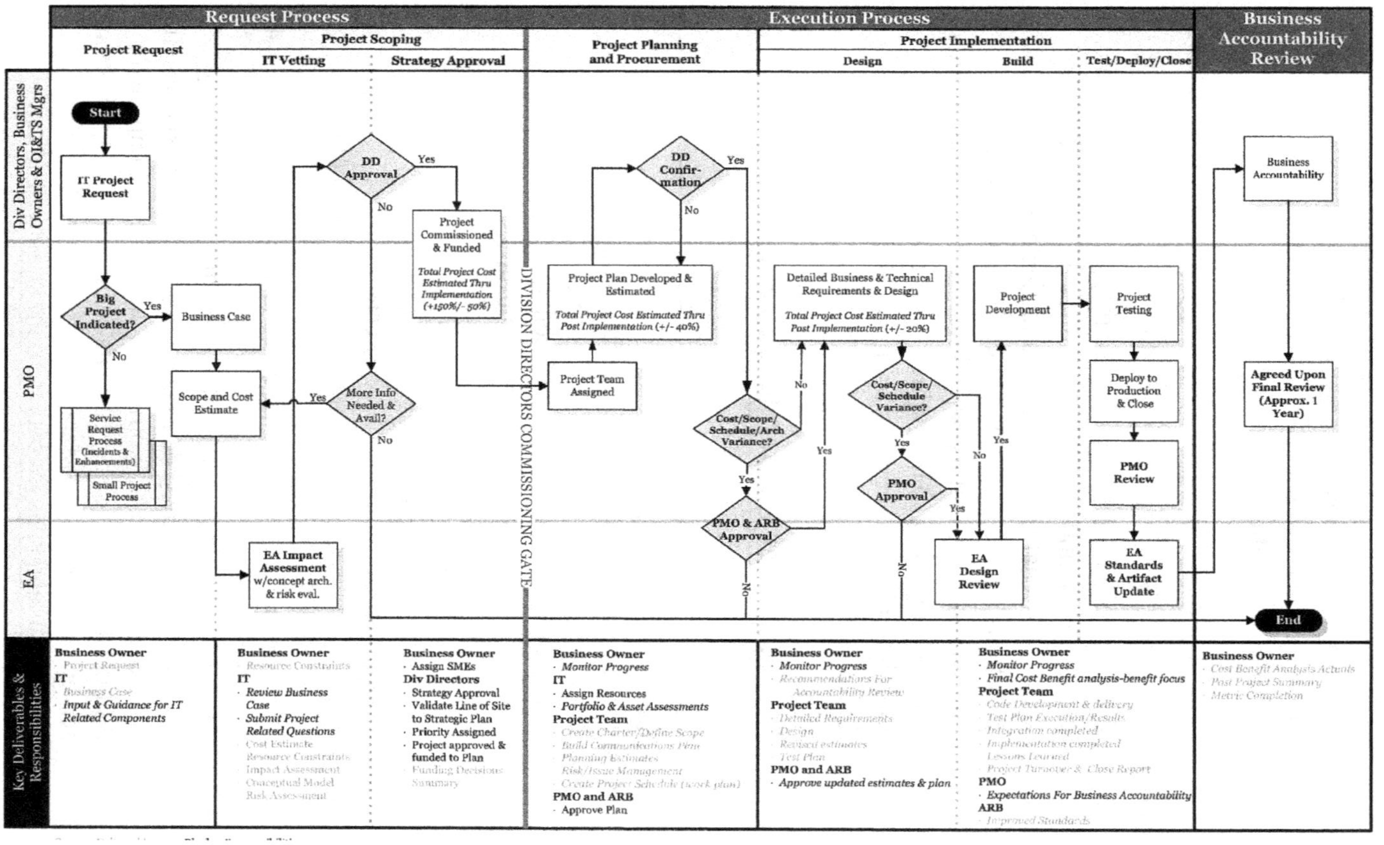
Request Process
Execution Process
Business Accountability Review
Project Request
Project Scoping
IT Vetting
Strategy Approval
Project Planning and Procurement
Project Implementation
Design
Build
Test/Deploy/Close
Div Directors, Business Owners & OI&TS Mgrs
PMO
EA
Key Deliverables & Responsibilities
Start
IT Project Request
Big Project Indicated?
Yes
No
Business Case
Scope and Cost Estimate
Service Request Process (Incidents & Enhancements)
Small Project Process
EA Impact Assessment w/concept arch. & risk eval.
DD Approval
More Info Needed & Avail?
Project Commissioned & Funded
Total Project Cost Estimated Thru Implementation (+150%/- 50%)
DIVISION DIRECTORS COMMISSIONING GATE
DD Confir-mation
Project Plan Developed & Estimated
Total Project Cost Estimated Thru Post Implementation (+/- 40%)
Project Team Assigned
Cost/Scope/ Schedule/Arch Variance?
PMO & ARB Approval
Detailed Business & Technical Requirements & Design
Total Project Cost Estimated Thru Post Implementation (+/- 20%)
Cost/Scope/ Schedule Variance?
PMO Approval
EA Design Review
Project Development
Project Testing
Deploy to Production & Close
PMO Review
EA Standards & Artifact Update
Business Accountability
Agreed Upon Final Review (Approx. 1 Year)
End
Business Owner
· Project Request
IT
· Business Case
· Input & Guidance for IT Related Components
Business Owner
· Resource Constraints
IT
· Review Business Case
· Submit Project Related Questions
· Cost Estimate
· Resource Constraints
· Impact Assessment
· Conceptual Model
· Risk Assessment
Business Owner
· Assign SMEs
Div Directors
· Strategy Approval
· Validate Line of Site to Strategic Plan
· Priority Assigned
· Project approved & funded to Plan
· Funding Decisions
· Summary
Business Owner
· Monitor Progress
IT
· Assign Resources
· Portfolio & Asset Assessments
Project Team
· Create Charter/Define Scope
· Build Communications Plan
· Planning Estimates
· Risk/Issue Management
· Create Project Schedule (work plan)
PMO and ARB
· Approve Plan
Business Owner
· Monitor Progress
· Recommendations For Accountability Review
Project Team
· Detailed Requirements
· Design
· Revised estimates
· Test Plan
PMO and ARB
· Approve updated estimates & plan
Business Owner
· Monitor Progress
· Final Cost Benefit analysis-benefit focus
Project Team
· Code Development & delivery
· Test Plan Execution/Results
· Integration completed
· Implementation completed
· Lessons Learned
· Project Turnover & Close Report
PMO
· Expectations For Business Accountability
ARB
· Improved Standards
Business Owner
· Cost Benefit Analysis Actuals
· Post Project Summary
· Metric Completion

The shaded diamonds represent decision points within the flow that determine how a request becomes a project and how it then flows through the execution process.

Requirements Checklist Example

Following is a set of tables that comprise many of the requirements that my partner Frank and I helped define for a Contact Center (Call Center). Note that the last table identifies out-of-scope features, functions and capabilities. Note also, that after the requirements tables, we included an exhibit listing acronyms used by this client organization. The requirements refer to other exhibits containing schematics and technical specifications, but I have not included those exhibits for confidentiality reasons.

Contact Center Requirements

Section 1 - Architecture
1. **Volumes and Statistics:** The current environment includes the following volumes and statistics: • Our Contact Center in Location 1 contains: – The 400 Contact Center employees – The PBX systems – The Avaya ACD system – The Intervoice systems – Obtains data from the data center – Connects with the strategic partner with both voice and data • We have satellite offices in Location 2, Location 3, Location 4 and Location 5. • We have 70% of voice traffic local and 30% long-distance. • We have an outsourced data center in a Twin Cities suburb. It is far enough from Location 1 to be unlikely to be impacted by a single disaster incident. The data center contains application servers and applications data, provides applications to Location 1, and receives data from the strategic partner.

Section 1 - Architecture

- We have a strategic business partner in Minnesota that is far enough from Location 1 to be unlikely to be impacted by a single disaster incident. The strategic partner location contains the voice portal, contains self-service applications, contains our data, connects to the Location 1 office by both voice and data, and connects to the data center.
- We currently process 2.2 million inbound calls per year, and this volume is projected to increase in the next three years to 2.6 million calls per year. We want to retain all calls for 60 days and then retain a reduced number of calls for a longer period of time. Assuming an average call time of 5 minutes, this would result in a need for approximately 2,600,000 (messages) / 6 * 5 minutes to be saved for 60 days. This is 36,000+ hours. Allowing an additional 25% for longer-term storage would suggest a need for approximately 45,000+ hours of available storage.

We require the architecture to be cost effective, perhaps matching incremental expenditures with incremental growth. We are not in a position to consider dramatic changes in architecture due to:

- Financial considerations because of investment in current locations, equipment, etc.
- Existing business dependencies and agreements, in particular our outsourced data center and a strategic business partner who is hosting certain applications and data

2. **Infrastructure:**

We require an architecture that:

- Has minimal single points of failure
- Has high availability equipment
- Uses primary and redundant features to provide near-instantaneous recovery, possibly through mirroring and fail over processes
- Has flexible process routing, possibly by using load balancing capabilities
- Uses open standards rather than proprietary technology

We require the network architecture to include data switches and

Section 1 - Architecture
routers to operate a fully converged voice and data network for the contact center. We require the network to support a distributed voice architecture. We require the network to be VoIP (Voice over IP) ready. We require the network to support multiple locations (home or office) for agent positions. We require the network to be sized to handle growth projections of a 50% increase in call volumes over the next 5 years. Schematics of network connections and hardware are attached in Exhibit C.
3. **Disaster Recovery:** We require the network to be optimized for disaster recovery/business continuity. We require a distributed architecture that: • Supports business continuity in the case of hardware or software failure • Supports survivability in the case of a serious disaster We require a working environment within 48 hours of a major disaster. We consider a "survivable" working environment after a major disaster to be one where: • Employees can perform their business functions. Flexibility may be required, and working from home or from another location is acceptable. • Members can reach our employees with minimum disruption to normal procedures. • Providers can reach our employees with minimum disruption to normal procedures. We consider "business continuity" to include almost immediate

Section 1 - Architecture

recovery from a less catastrophic failure, with no noticeable impact on operational performance. As examples, failures may result from:

- A specific communications piece of equipment
- A specific piece of hardware
- An external influence, such as a building contractor cutting an underground cable with a backhoe

Section 2 - Core Applications

1. **Call Routing:**

We require an intelligent call routing application with universal queues to support phone, email, Chat, and FAX transactions.

We consider the Contact Center to be the means of providing a value added service through agents who are knowledgeable and skilled in a variety of areas. The needed skills vary widely so a key requirement is to route the call to the correct "skills", represented by an agent or group of agents. These "skills" may include for example:

- Knowledge of a particular process such as "Eligibility" or "Claims"
- Knowledge of a particular customer company's plan
- Ability to speak a particular language

Currently, most of the voice routing is successful due to interaction with the IVR systems that helps identify variables that allow routing to a skill. However, alternative contact entry points are growing or have the potential to grow, and these do not yet have the same level of routing capability.

For example, email is a growing alternative method of contact and is staffed by a separate dedicated team of agents. We do not see a separate email team as an appropriate approach to achieve intelligent call routing objectives as it grows in the future. The

Section 2 - Core Applications
preferred method will be to: • Support email as a contact method • Collect data that can allow emails to be routed successfully to the same skilled agents who support voice calls • Provide the skilled agents with the tools to respond via email efficiently Another alternative contact method is Chat. Currently, we have no Chat applications, but we are considering the potential. There are similar considerations for Chat as for the email scenario: • Support Chat as a contact method • Collect data that will allow Chat conversations to be routed to the correct skilled agent • Provide the skilled agent with the ability to respond efficiently In summary, we require the call routing application to: • Route contacts, regardless of source (voice, email, Chat, etc.), to the correct skill for resolution. • Manage the different sources so that customer response is acceptable and fair, regardless of source (the universal queue concept).
2. **Campaign Management:** We require outbound dialing/campaign management including preview and predictive dialing. Campaign management consists of contacting large numbers of members by phone and providing a generic information message. This is an outbound capability that is partly outsourced currently but will be brought in-house. See volumes and statistics in Section 1 above.
3. **Disease Management:** Disease Management is an outbound process similar to other campaign management processes, but we are listing it separately because of its unique requirements. Disease Management consists of contacting individual members on a regular basis to manage an on-going condition. It is currently outsourced but will be brought

Section 2 - Core Applications
in-house and expanded. The major unique requirements of this application are: • The ability to get to the member who is enrolled in the disease management program (not just the correct household telephone number) • The use of personalized disease management programs • The use of live agents • The ability to maintain the schedule dictated by the Disease Management program See volumes and statistics in Section 1 above. We expect to invest in this opportunity and double the number of calls in five years.
4. **Reporting and Analytics:** We require enhanced reporting, cradle to grave. This includes the integrated reporting of data collected between: • The time the call is answered by the ACD and • The time the call is completed or sent to a live agent or alternative destination such as voice mail or external 800 # Currently data is collected independently during each of the steps by each of the systems: • ACD data • IVR data • ICM data The data is merged for reporting using a variety of third party tools such as SMSI and Crystal reports. Standard reports and ad hoc reporting is performed for: • Business use • IT use A desktop ticker application is used by agents and provides real-time data to the agent desktop. Excel spreadsheets are also created for subsequent end user ad hoc use. Data is collected over extended time periods to produce:

Section 2 - Core Applications

- Monthly reporting
- Trend reporting

In the future, we intend to continue to support key existing reporting features, for example:

- The ROC real time reporting
- Desktop ticker
- Reports from existing systems such as IVR
  - Customer Survey Report
  - Coordination of benefits report

In the future, we intend to improve other current reporting capabilities by use of the following approaches:

- Using more real time data to produce information for non-ROC users, for example
  - Contact Center Managers
  - Agents
  - IT
- Combining data from multiple sources into one data warehouse for reporting
  - Removing our "data silos" that exist today due to different pieces of hardware and vendors
  - Incorporating data from the Strategic Partner
- Considering that not all Contacts occur through voice, and planning for
  - Email contact reporting
  - Chat contact reporting
- Providing reporting tools to end users to build ad hoc and custom reporting capabilities

We require an analytics solution that integrates data and reporting from:

- Core call center applications
- Workforce Management application
- Quality Monitoring application
- IVR, bundled or not
- CTI, bundled or not

Section 2 - Core Applications

We require the ability to eliminate manual analysis by deploying an analytics tool for:

- Corporate visibility, monitoring progress of strategic initiatives
- Scenario planning
- Trends in agent performance
- Trends in call types and volumes

We require an end-to-end view that consolidates data sources for reporting and presenting information to all levels of the organization.

We require the ability to automatically deliver scorecards/dashboards.

We require the ability to evolve manual databases (On-Target, Escalated Call, and Quality Databases) to a data warehouse.

We require the ability to report on system outage impact and availability.

5. **Email management:**

We require email management.

The use of email as an alternative method of contact has grown quickly over the last few years but is expected to stabilize in two years. See volumes and statistics in Section 1 above. The methods and capabilities to manage the receipt and processing of email requests have not matured at the same rate.

The Call Routing requirements above discussed the integration of email into the overall routing process.

6. **Fax:**

Currently the Contact center does not use desktop faxing capabilities.

Section 2 - Core Applications

Some inbound and outbound contact is performed by fax to support the "lowest common denominator" of technology. We would like to:

- Centralize, file, and possibly route incoming faxes
- Offer outbound faxing from the desktop

See Section 1 above for volumes.

Section 3 - Interactive Voice Response

1. **Current Application Support:**

We require the ability to support applications across the existing IVR platforms. This includes using:

- The Avaya PBX menu
- The Avaya and Intervoice IVR
- The strategic partner voice portal
- AT&T network prompts to front-end Passport 2/4 calls

We require the ability to rationalize the use of the current Avaya and Intervoice IVR and a strategic business partner's IVR platforms and evaluate future options.

Currently, voice calls may be received and routed for initial processing in two different locations:

- Our Location 1 by the Avaya and Intervoice systems
- Strategic Partner location by the voice portal

In either case, the end user has the ability to provide data that results in subsequent call routing to a self-service application or a live agent, which may actually be a re-route to the other location. See volumes and statistics in Section 1 above.

There is sufficient difference between the "sound and feel" of the two entry points to affect the end-user experience. For example:

- Voices are different – different tones, different styles
- Prompts are different

Section 3 - Interactive Voice Response
• The Avaya system requires entry of digits only from a touch tone phone • The Strategic Partner Voice Portal accepts touch tone entry and limited voice recognition prompts The anecdotal evidence (no hard statistics) indicates that a certain volume of live agent requests is caused by: • End user not being comfortable with the user experience and requesting live assistance for items that could have been satisfied through a self-service application • End user not wishing to use a key pad to enter data, particularly those with small cell phone key pads We have an opportunity to improve the initial end user experience and also reduce the number of calls being unnecessarily sent to live agents. We want to do this in a cost effective manner, considering that the Strategic Partner and we both have an investment in the current equipment and applications and that the same business functionality will be required in the future. We intend to replace proprietary technologies with those that satisfy industry standards (non-proprietary) in an Open Architecture environment, such as Voice XML and text to speech.
2. **Self Service:** We require the ability to expand self-service features and improve self-service menus. As our business changes, so do the self-service applications. These applications require development, maintenance, testing and re-installation to production, just like any other application. We want to improve the development and maintenance processes for self-service features.
3. **Data Directed Routing:** We require the ability to gather additional information for data directed routing.

Section 3 - Interactive Voice Response

As described in the Call Routing requirements of the Core Applications table above, calls are routed to "skills". Two sets of information are required to make this routing connection successful:

- Sufficient information to identify the required "skill"
- Where that "skill" is currently located

Data collection is performed in a variety of ways:

- From the incoming called number
- From data entered via touchtone as requested by prompts
- From data entered verbally as requested by prompts
- By an automated application looking up data in the Operational Data Store

We require the ability to gather information using each of the above methods.

Section 4 - Computer Telephony Integration

1. **Data Integration with Agent Desktop:**
   We require improvement in the delivery of data to the agent desktop.

   Currently, we have CTI (Computer Telephony Integration) capabilities but have not implemented them due to technology conflicts with the strategic partner. A high priority project is currently under way to resolve those conflicts.

   Currently, very limited "CTI" type data can be passed to the agent when it is available via the telephone 32-digit display. This is limited to numeric data; typical fields are group and member numbers, both of which are likely required by the agent.

   There are two related areas of opportunity:

   - Routing to the "skills" agent using Intelligent Call Routing

Section 4 - Computer Telephony Integration

  - Derive data from other data by using additional data look up. For example, derive company from member number.
  - Determine which agent dealt with this user the last time, for follow up situations where "same agent" is the best routing.
- Providing data to the agent via "screen pops" as the voice call is received using CTI
  - Knowing where the user was before requesting an agent and provide that data.
  - Knowing previous interactions with this same user, retrieving relevant data, and supporting the "same agent" scenarios.

A future goal is to merge some of these opportunities with Customer Relationship Management applications.

Sources of data to support routing and screen pops are:

- ODS – the Operational Data Store Oracle database maintained at the outsourced data center
- QSTAR and IDT – operational application systems containing claims and some customer information
- IVR data – as collected by user entry
  - Available from our Avaya and Intervoice system
  - Transferred from the Strategic Partner Portal through the Cisco ICM (Intelligent Contact Management) connection

2. **Cisco ICM Integration:**
We require the ability to leverage the Cisco ICM infrastructure to support as many of the new requirements as possible, for example, Outbound calling, email, and Web Chat functionality.

Section 5 - Quality Optimization Tools

1. **Call Recording and Retrieval:**
Currently we only record a sample of calls. Outbound calls are not recorded. Recording includes voice and screen capture of data. In the near future, we will require the infrastructure components to

Section 5 - Quality Optimization Tools
record all calls for compliance and liability. The same recordings may also be used for Quality Assurance and Training. Quality monitoring and other optimization tools are not in scope. In the future all contact center inbound and outbound calls will be recorded. In the future email and chat will have the same retention and retrieval business requirements. We currently process 2.2 million inbound calls per year, and this volume is projected to increase in the next three years to 2.6 million calls per year. We want to retain all calls for 60 days and then retain a reduced number of calls for a longer period of time. Assuming an average call time of 5 minutes, this would result in a need for approximately 2,600,000 (messages) / 6 * 5 minutes to be saved for 60 days. This is 36,000+ hours. Allowing an additional 25% for longer-term storage would suggest a need for approximately 45,000+ hours of available storage. Retrieval of messages will be required by: • Agent • Date • Dialed number • VDN, DNIS or ANI • Audio key words

Section 6 – Maintenance, Support and Training
1. **Maintenance capabilities:** We require 7x24 maintenance capabilities and support that includes coverage for hardware, software, and upgrades.
2. **Technical training:** We require training for 10 technical staff on new functionality.

3. **End User training:**
   We require end user training for 400 contact center staff.

Section 7 - Security

1. **System Access Controls:**
   We require all telecommunications lines to be secured in a manor that will ensure availability while preventing tampering.

   We require the ability to have restrictions either built-in or customizable for toll-calling capabilities.

   We require authentication mechanisms that are available for systems connected via analog telephony lines to protect the analog circuits from attack.

   We require the ability to secure backdoor communications (IE: "out of band modems") from dial-back functions, etc.

   We require controls to support secure communications for transmission of User-IDs and passwords (IE: SSH).

   We require the system preserve the confidentiality of the authentication information that is stored within the system (IE: passwords, pins, etc.).

   We require the ability to automatically disable or remove User-IDs that have been inactive for a period of time.

   We require the ability to expire standard user and administrative users' passwords after a specified period of time or inactivity.

   We require user-selected passwords to have a minimum password length of 8 characters, use both alpha and numeric characters, and use both upper and lowercase characters.

2. **System Auditing and Monitoring:**
   We require the ability to continuously monitor and track system activity.

Section 7 - Security
We require a means to view all user access to the administrative console. We require an audit log containing at a minimum: • Types of events. • Dates and times of events. • User identification including associated terminal, port, network address, or communication device. • Name of the resource accessed. • Success or failure of the event. We require that all administrative actions within the system be logged and that administrators are unable to disable or modify those logs. We require security notifications. Audit logs must have the ability to log: • Changes to the system security configuration. • Modifications to the software. • Invalid user authentication attempts. • Unauthorized attempts to access resources such as data, the password file, and transactions. • Changes to a user's security profile and/or attributes.
3. **System Architecture Security** We require the ability for administrative access to the system on dedicated communication ports to be separated from normal voice and data traffic. We require the ability to disable the communications port after unsuccessful login attempts to access the system in a set period of time. We require security controls to protect emailing and faxing capabilities to minimize information leakage.

Section 8 – Out of Scope
1. **Out of Scope:** The intent of the following list is to identify the non-contact center related IT products and services that are out of scope: • Internal company Help Desk • End User Computing • Data Center Management • File and Print management at our facilities • Voice Telecommunications Management • Data Telecommunications Management • Architecture and Design • Strategy • Standards • Applications software development and data management • Applications maintenance and support • Business relationship management • Charges from IT to the company business segments • Supplier contracts and governance

Exhibit A – Contact Center Requirements Acronyms

The following list of acronyms was included with and made part of the requirements for the client's contact center because the project team felt it was necessary to foster clarity of communications with the supplier community. Some acronyms are unique to an organization, and others may not be universally understood. Regardless, I prefer to err on the side of "clarifying the obvious" rather than risk a vendor misunderstanding a requirement. I have been thanked by suppliers, attorneys and business representatives for including these lists.

ACD - Automated Call Distribution.	**LAN** - Local Area Network
ANI - Automatic Number	**LMS** - Learning Management

Identification	System
APO - Aspect Performance Optimization	**LOE** - Level Of Effort
ASR - Automatic Speech Recognition	**MPLS** - MultiProtocol Label Switching
BI - Business Intelligence	**NCC** - National Call Center
BU - Business Unit	**ODS** - Operational Data Store
CC - Contact Center	**OEM** - Original Equipment Manufacturer
CDHP - Consumer Directed Health Plans	**PBX** - Private Branch eXchange
CHA - Center for Healthy Aging	**PMPM** - Per Member per Month
CRM - Customer Relationship Management	**QM** - Quality Monitoring
CSF - Critical Success Factor	**RFP** - Request for Proposal
CVP - Customer Voice Portal	**RFQ** - Request for Quote
CTI - Computer Telephony Integration	**ROI** - Return on Investment
DB - Database	**SIP** - Session Initiation Protocol
DNIS - Dialed Number Identification Service	**SLA** - Service Level Agreement
DRP - Disaster Recovery Plan	**SMSI** - Systems Management Software Inc.
FCRR - First Call Resolution Rate	**SOA** - Service Oriented Architecture
HP - Hewlett Packard	**SPP** - State Public Programs
HW - Hardware	**SW** - Software
ICM - Intelligent Contact Management	**TBD** - To Be Determined
IDT - Intelligent Desk Top	**TCO** - Total Cost of Ownership
IP - Internet Protocol	**VDN** - Vector Directory Number

IT - Information Technology	**VoIP** - Voice over IP
IVR - Interactive Voice Response	**VXML** - Voice eXtensible Markup Language
KM - Knowledge Management	**WAN** - Wide Area Network
KPI - Key Performance Indicator	**WFM** - Workforce Management

Summary

Regardless of the project methodology used, getting business and technical requirements clearly defined is necessary for almost any project to succeed. Requirements can and should be defined quickly by using:

- A smart and experienced BA (Business Analyst)
- Proven processes
- Participating business users
- Checklists and examples
- Ideas obtained by reviewing features and functions of working products

The examples I've included in this chapter are representative of a variety of the engagements I've conducted. The primary purpose of including these examples is to demonstrate format and structure; the content of the examples is merely interesting.

Suggested Reading and Reference

Orr, Ken, *Structured Requirements Definition*. Ken Orr & Associates, Inc., 1981

Chapter 15 – Requirements

Chapter 16 – RFPs

"It is not because things are difficult that we do not dare.
It is because we do not dare that they are difficult."
-- Seneca

During the first six years of my consulting career, I gained a lot of experience as a project manager, implementing software solutions and writing requirements. During my seventh year, I was engaged to help a mining company that was headquartered in Denver to document the organization's financial applications requirements as a first step to replacing all of them. I used checklists I had previously developed for accounts payable, billing, accounts receivable, fixed assets, payroll and general ledger. See Chapter 15 for a discussion of Requirements engagements. The checklists allowed me to complete the initial assignment much faster than my client expected. He was pleased, and he then asked me to use the resulting requirements documents as a foundation to create an RFP (Request For Proposal) and to solicit bids from competing software vendors. I was delighted. I had a highly satisfied client; I was given a significant follow-on engagement; and I would be paid to learn a new skill.

In addition to the opportunity to learn how to construct an RFP, I also got an education about mining operations during this project, and I'm taking you on a short side trip here to share some of what I learned. The company owned coal and copper mines in Pennsylvania and Minnesota, but their most interesting operation was a gold mine in Nevada. One of the applications we were replacing was cost accounting, and because of the gold mine's unique processes, their senior cost accountant and I decided to visit it.

The gold mine was an open-pit operation in the middle of the desert, and we had to fly there from Las Vegas in a four seat, single prop charter plane. It was hot and desolate. The only buildings for 75 miles in any direction were the mine processing building, a store and a restaurant owned by the company and a few trailer homes also owned by the company and rented to their employees. I was instructed to leave the suit and ties at home, so I brought jeans and short sleeve shirts that had been laundered recently. I was still incredibly over dressed.

The mine was extracting roughly one ounce of gold from each ton of raw ore they processed. Their approach included brute force followed by sophisticated chemical engineering. The mine pit was circular, and the walls consisted of about a dozen layers or "benches" that were each about ten feet high. It looked like a football stadium for giants with enormous steps going up the sides. One end of the pit had a long sloped rock road built up to provide access for dump trucks and front-end loaders. When I first saw the pit, all the vehicles were coming out because they were getting ready to "blow down a bench." The dump trucks all parked side by side, very close to each other facing the buildings and raised their dumping beds towards the pit. The front-end loaders also parked close to each other and raised their buckets towards the pit. It looked like a military formation of vehicles "saluting" the pit. I was instructed to get in front of a dump truck. Then I heard a series of explosions, and it started raining rocks. I was most happy to be protected by that dump truck because several of the rocks that landed near me were the size of baseballs, and I saw a few that looked like cantaloupes. After the dust settled, I saw that about 100 yards of one of the benches was now about ten feet lower than it had been. The explosives team had cored out ten-foot vertical holes every few feet along the back of the bench and stuffed the holes with dynamite. Using synchronized fuses they blew down the bench. After the blow down, the vehicles returned to the pit, and front-end loaders filled dump trucks with the resulting boulders and gravel, which was driven out of the pit and unloaded onto a conveyer belt that led to the primary crusher.

The primary crusher was a large conical-shaped container whose interior was lined with steel plates. The narrow end was at the bottom where there was a two-foot wide hole. Hanging inside the crusher was a large conical shaped solid piece of cement covered with steel plates. The whole contraption looked like a pestle and mortar that a giant might use. As the boulders and gravel, fed by the conveyer belt, dropped in through the top, the interior cement and steel cone was swung around by a crane breaking up the larger boulders into basketball size rocks, and eventually everything dropped through the hole at the bottom to another conveyer belt that led to the secondary crusher, which was similar in design but smaller. The secondary crusher broke the rocks into baseball-sized chunks and, via another conveyer belt, led to the tertiary crusher that reduced the rocks down to pebbles.

A conveyer belt from the tertiary crusher loaded the crushed ore into dump trucks that drove to the leach pad where they were unloaded. The leach pad was about ten feet wide and 100 yards long and was surrounded by a shallow pool. After the crushed ore from the prior batch was removed, the dump trucks deposited the newly crushed ore onto the empty leach pad. This was the end of the brute force process and the beginning of the chemical engineering magic. The leach pad had a sprinkler system with heads every few feet along its length, and the sprinklers began spraying the crushed ore with a solution of sulfuric acid and water. The diluted sulfuric acid was strong enough to melt the soft gold but too weak to liquefy other minerals. The liquid gold drained off the leach pad with the sulfuric acid and water into the surrounding toxic pool, and the mixture was pumped into the electrowinning building.

Inside the electrowinning building, the mixture was channeled through a series of filter plates that looked like furnace filters, except these were covered with steel wool. As electricity passed through the filter plates, gold molecules adhered to the steel wool. After plates became saturated, they were removed, and the steel wool was placed in a cupola, a conical shaped ceramic cup about 12 inches tall and 6 inches wide at the mouth. Using tongs, the cupola was placed into a blast furnace until the contents became liquid. After cooling, the cupola was broken away and the resulting solid item was gold on the bottom (it's heavier) and steel on the top. The steel part was broken off and discarded, leaving a 9-10 pound "button" of almost pure gold. Ta da! Each button was worth about $45,000 to $50,000 then, and at 2014 prices, they would be worth close to $200,000 each. Once or twice each week, an airplane would ferry three to five buttons to the Federal Reserve.

Although the extraction processes were quite interesting, from a cost accounting perspective, the unique aspect of this mine was that more than half of the staff were security personnel who carried rifles and wore side arms. Security was a constant concern, and the biggest risks were from employees. The week prior to our arrival, a disgruntled former employee had been throwing lighted sticks of dynamite over the fence at the buildings and equipment, and the mine had to shut down for a few days until the culprit was captured. Full body metal detection scanners were used for anyone entering or exiting the electrowinning building. They didn't want guns brought in or gold smuggled out. In addition to the body scanners, we had to have our hands scanned by another more sensitive device because a few years earlier an employee had scratched the gold buttons and smuggled small amounts of gold out under his fingernails. People can be creative.

One reason I included the above story is to demonstrate some of the added benefits of being a consultant: I get to learn about how a lot of businesses work, and I find myself in unexpected places learning interesting things.

Let's get back to the main discussion of this chapter. That mining company engagement to develop and issue an RFP happened in the early 1980's, before laptops, before the Internet and before search engines. Therefore I looked in my own firm's physical library and found a couple of state and county government RFPs to which my firm had recently responded, and I used them as templates for the format of the RFP I was building. Since then, I've developed dozens of RFPs for a variety of clients, and I've continually refined the format during each RFP engagement I perform so that it has become increasingly useful over time. Before looking at the format of an RFP, let's first consider context. What should the client's process be when considering the acquisition of an external service? As one possible answer, I created the following model for one of my clients.

The process starts in the lower left box with a requirements definition effort and proceeds through the model, eventually reaching the lower right delivery box. Note particularly the RFP and contract negotiation activities, which are discussed in this chapter and in Chapter 17.

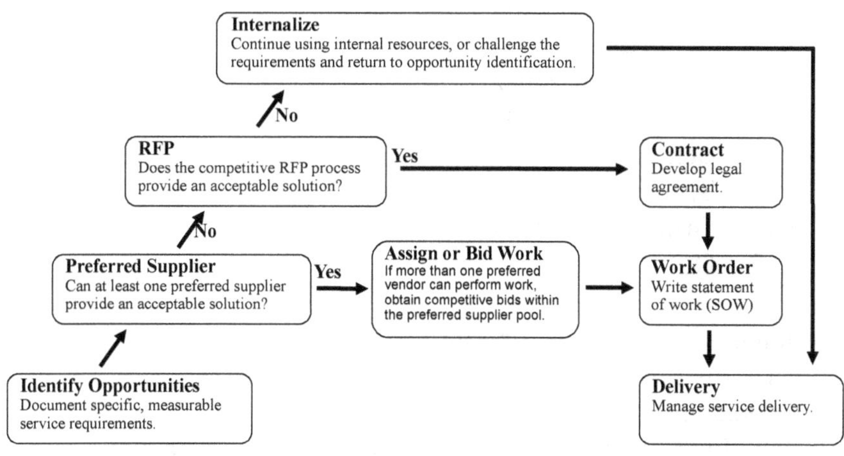

Chapter 16 – RFPs

Following is the Table of Contents from an RFP I developed for a Health Insurance client. The purpose was to solicit bids for managing the client organization's data center.

The above example table of contents is representative of the format I've used for many of the RFPs I've developed for my clients. The following paragraphs discuss the individual sections and describe some of the variations in format I've employed.

Section 1

Section 1 is a summary of the entire document. I typically include two or three paragraphs that briefly describe the client company's business and IT (Information Technology) environment in the Introduction. I will also include a statement informing the respondents that they should not interpret the requirements or any part of the RFP as eliminating possible solution options because I don't want to restrict their ability to create the best value proposition for my client. Background information includes a summary of the circumstances within the client organization that have prompted issuance of the RFP. Within the Value Proposition, I describe the dimensions of the desired supplier relationship, typically including:

- Speed to solution
- High adaptation and flexibility to technology changes
- Scalability
- Clear service components and easily understood billing
- Competitive unit cost economics

The Purpose describes the expected end result of the RFP process. The RFP Structure discussion includes one or two sentences about each of the RFP sections and exhibits, and it identifies the client contact person who can answer questions during the process, who is usually, but not always, me. Finally, the Submission Format and Deadline identifies how electronic and/or paper copies of proposals should be submitted and a date and time by which they must be received.

Section 2

Section 2 includes several paragraphs that provide a more thorough discussion of the business environment than is included in Section 1. I usually include a context diagram to assist suppliers in understanding the business. See Chapter 12 for examples of context diagrams. I also include lists of primary operating and support functions, and I may supplement those lists by including a Value Chain diagram. See Chapter 12 for examples of Value Chain diagrams. This section also describes the IT environment, including a list of the IT departments and primary work units. The IT description identifies any currently outsourced functions, and it usually refers to technical diagrams that would be included as exhibits at the end of the RFP. Interestingly, half or more of the RFPs I've written have been for outsourcing initiatives, and almost all of the awards for those outsourcing efforts have gone to domestic suppliers.

Over the years, a few suppliers have commented that the charts and lists I include in the company environment section have helped them understand the organization structure better than the organization charts they've seen. My experience supports those anecdotal observations. While organization charts may detail who reports to whom, they usually don't accurately indicate what the primary business functions are or how those functions relate to each other.

Section 3

Section 3 is the "heart and soul" of the RFP. It contains the detail requirements that should have been documented during a requirements definition effort prior to assembling the RFP. See Chapter 15 for a discussion of Requirements projects.

When I begin working on this section of an RFP, unless I conducted the prior requirements definition effort myself, I invariably need to supplement the existing requirements document. This is always a bit tricky, because I don't want to offend the business analysts and others responsible for the original requirements document by implying their work is insufficient. I need to work with those same people to complete the RFP, and it's easier to get them to contribute when they are enthusiastic rather than resentful. I solve this dilemma by saying that the format and structure of the RFP require us to revisit how some of the requirements are worded. This usually works.

When the requirements are sufficiently detailed and complete, I format them into tables to be inserted into this section of the RFP. Each table has two columns. Column 1 contains the requirements organized into major categories and numbered. See the above Table of Contents for Section 3 for an example of the numbering scheme. I leave Column 2 blank because it's intended to be filled in by the supplier later with their responses to the requirements. The instructions for suppliers indicate that their proposals should follow the same format, sequencing and numbering as this section of the RFP, and I suggest that the suppliers simply copy this section in its entirety, insert their responses into the tables and include the resulting document with their proposal. The primary reason for this approach is to allow the evaluation team to proceed in a systematic and organized fashion after receiving proposals. If each vendor were allowed to present its own format, sequencing and organization, then the resulting evaluation process would be chaotic. Following is a partial network management example of a requirements table taken from an RFP I wrote.

Network Management	Supplier Response
1. **Software and Hardware:** We require the supplier to support and proactively manage Cisco network equipment and operating systems. Versions no longer supported by the manufacturer are not included. Customer will provide all LAN and WAN hardware, software and licensing. We require the supplier to provide all hardware, tools, software and licensing for network monitoring. If we purchase spare equipment, please describe your policies and pricing to store cold spares.	
2. **LAN:** We require redundant 100 Mb or 1000 Mb fiber or copper Ethernet connections between the Customer Client System and the supplier data center core-switching infrastructure. The Customer Client Systems will be placed on a private sub-network behind a Customer-owned firewall.	
3. **WAN:** Customer may order telecommunications services from a remote Customer location to the Customer Client Systems hosted in the supplier data center. We require the supplier to allow Customer to provision WAN circuits with no restriction to the carrier or to the technology approach offered by all major carriers. Please describe any carrier restrictions that you may have for private connectivity to Customer back-end resources. Please describe any limits on the type or number of circuits that Customer can route to or through your data center. We require WAN capacity to be monitored	

Network Management	Supplier Response
and appropriate capacity anticipated and maintained. We require a minimum of 10Mb guaranteed Internet bandwidth (Committed Information Rate or CIR) with a minimum burstable port speed of 100Mb. We require the supplier to support direct network connectivity between Customer and the supplier location. In addition, we require the supplier to support direct network connectivity between the supplier location and 8-10 Customer partners. It is possible this number may grow. Please describe your traffic distribution and traffic shaping techniques and your use of hardware and software load balancers.	
4. **VPN and Remote Access:** We require the supplier to manage VPN remote user and system access for our strategic business partners, customers and employees to our servers in the supplier data centers using secure multi-protocol access over the public Internet.	
5. **Communication System:** We require the supplier to manage and monitor, on Customer's behalf, the delivery of network services by the telecommunications providers. These network services include, but may not be limited to, leased lines and switched telecommunications services linking the supplier data center with: • Customer's Minnesota location • Other Customer-owned remote sites • Customer employees working remotely • Customer business partners	

The scope of an RFP is usually easy to identify. It is limited to the requirements contained in this Section 3. To provide additional clarity, I include a final list in the requirements section titled "Out of Scope." The intent of the Out of Scope list is to identify non-RFP related IT products and services. For example, the Out of Scope list for the data center management RFP (see the table of contents at the beginning of this chapter) included items such as:

- Help Desk
- Voice Telecommunications Management
- Architecture and Design
- Strategy and Standards
- Applications software development, maintenance and support
- Data management
- Business relationship management
- IT accounting and charges to business segments
- Supplier procurement contracts and governance

When scope is unusually complex, I have created a separate Scope section within the RFP document. For example, one of my clients needed to contract with a third-party data center to process selected customer transactions independently of the client company's internal transactions. Some of my client's customers considered one of the client company's internal business units to be a competitor, and those customers wanted to guarantee that the business unit in question would not have access to customer transaction data. Therefore, while assembling the RFP to solicit managed hosting services from independent suppliers, I needed to write a separate scope section in order to clarify that certain requested products and services were in scope for some business units but out of scope for other business units.

Other variations in the requirements section may involve adding columns to some of the requirements tables. For example, for an

RFP soliciting data center management services where the client was supplying all the equipment and the supplier was only providing the facility, I created a requirements table that identified all the infrastructure hardware components the client used, and I added columns to specify specific manufacturer model numbers and quantities. The blank Supplier Response column allowed suppliers to indicate whether or not they would support the specific devices in the quantities specified.

A final variation I want to mention for the requirements section is the use of Case Studies. I've included a separate Case Studies sub-section in two different RFPs. The purpose of the case studies is for my client to gain a thorough understanding of the supplier's processes and costs associated with potential unusual events. I ask suppliers to include their assumptions as well as costs in their responses. For a data center hosting RFP, some of the Case Studies included:

- A new release of client owned software. The supplier was asked to describe how they would manage the new release into their environment, including testing, training of help desk personnel, documentation updates, etc.
- A capacity upgrade. This case study assumed the client has acquired a major competitor, doubling their transaction volumes. The supplier was asked to describe impacts to their capacity monitoring and projection processes, provisioning additional equipment, change control processes, SLA (Service Level Agreement) processes, etc.
- Disaster Recovery. This case study described a hypothetical broken water pipe that flooded part of the supplier's telecommunications infrastructure including connectivity to the Internet. The supplier was asked to describe immediate actions, provision of temporary relief to comply with SLAs, and longer-term actions to recover and restore operations at the supplier's main data center.

Section 4

Section 4 provides specific instructions to suppliers about the format and content of their responses to the RFP. There are three specific items this section requests from suppliers:

- A formal commitment letter, signed by an executive authorized to bind the supplier organization to their proposal.
- Requirements satisfaction details. This item should be a copy of the client's RFP requirements tables, with blank columns filled in with supplier responses to each particular item or question.
- Pricing details. I ask that the supplier identify all pricing assumptions, and I state that all costs, expenses, fees, taxes, duties, and any other charges to my client associated with provisioning services must be specified in the pricing section of their proposal. Failure to include a cost in the pricing section will be interpreted as a no cost item to my client. Pricing must be stated in U.S. dollars. I also specify that the supplier's pricing must clearly show what my client will pay if the client's transaction volumes increase. Experience has taught me that if I provide an Excel spreadsheet for the supplier to fill in with their pricing information, there is less confusion and less of a need to go back and forth to finalize pricing information.

If the requirements are detailed and logically structured in Section 3, then this Section 4 usually falls into place nicely, and I can focus primarily on the pricing part of this section.

Section 5

Section 5 provides most of the legal language needed, and it helps tee up the eventual contract negotiations. The major provisions within this section address:

- Confidentiality. This provision refers to a Confidentiality and Non-Disclosure Agreement that I require each RFP recipient to sign prior to giving them the RFP. The language states that an authorized representative of the supplier company has previously signed the Confidentiality and Non-Disclosure Agreement, which requires the supplier to regard and preserve as confidential the existence of the RFP, the fact that the client has distributed an RFP, and all information of the client, its affiliated companies, customers, clients and partners, which is disclosed to or otherwise obtained by the supplier in whatever form in connection with the RFP process.

- Disclaimers. These include various statements intended to avoid any possible legal misinterpretation including, but not limited to:
    - The client retains all legal right, title and interest in the RFP and all responses to the RFP.
    - The RFP does not constitute a legal contract between the client and any respondents to whom it is sent.
    - The supplier's proposal response constitutes an offer to do business with the client.
    - The supplier's proposal must contain a statement that it is firm for a period of at least 180 days after the specified deadline for receipt of the proposal.
    - The client is not committed to pay any expenses incurred by the supplier in the preparation of a response, for discussions or negotiations related thereto, or any costs associated with component and service demonstrations.
    - The selected supplier must agree to observe and comply with all federal, state, and local laws and regulations relating to employment.
    - The supplier must disclose any plan or need to use subcontractors in order to perform under a final agreement with the client.

  - The client reserves the absolute right to withdraw the RFP by written notice or to reject any or all proposals submitted.

- Instructions to Respondents. This provision repeats and expands on the Submission Format and Deadline information previously stated in Section 1. It identifies how electronic and/or paper copies of proposals should be submitted and a date and time by which they must be received. For proposal content instructions, it is easiest to refer back to Section 4 of the RFP rather than repeating information and possibly introducing inconsistencies. Suppliers are told to direct any questions to the contact person identified in Section 1. To properly set expectations, I usually include a table of RFP process events and dates such as, for example:

Events	Dates
Release RFP	May 1, 20xx
Questions from suppliers for clarification	May 7, 20xx
Responses to questions distributed	May 15, 20xx
Proposals due at Client	**June 1, 20xx**
Notification of RFP status (short-list)	June 15, 20xx
Supplier site visits and presentations	June 20-25, 20xx
Award decision & supplier notifications	July 10, 20xx
Contract executed	TBD
Services commence	TBD

- Selection and Notification. This provision briefly describes the supplier evaluation process, the use of a short list, finalist presentations and site visits. It also includes statements specifying that after the successful bidder has been determined and an agreement executed, all other bidders will be notified and that specific reasons for acceptance and rejection will not be furnished to unsuccessful bidders.

- Contract Negotiation. This provision states that the client intends to enter, with the selected supplier, into the negotiation of an agreement containing the terms and conditions of the proposed service. The supplier should assume that all terms and conditions specified in the RFP, and all rates and pricing specified in the supplier's proposal, will be incorporated into the final agreement signed by the client and the selected supplier.
- Invoicing. This provision simply states the client's expectations regarding how the supplier will submit invoices and the payment terms for undisputed invoices.

Exhibits

The exhibits are variable for each RFP I've written and are specific to the client and the purpose of the RFP. For an example, see the list of exhibits included in the sample table of contents near the beginning of this chapter.

Summary

As mentioned previously, the key to a solid RFP is to have requirements properly documented. See Chapter 15 for a discussion of requirements. Writing the remainder of the RFP is fairly straightforward, as discussed in this chapter. I've found that a good RFP can significantly help in facilitating an eventual contract with the selected supplier. See Chapter 17 for discussions of contract negotiations and service level agreements.

Chapter 16 – RFPs

Chapter 17 – Contract Negotiation

> "Do not reveal your thoughts to everyone, lest you drive away your good luck."
>
> -- Apocrypha, Ecclesiasticus 8:19

The first time I was asked by a client to be a member of his contract negotiations team, I had previously been the project manager responsible for defining the requirements, writing the RFP and selecting the supplier with whom we were about to negotiate a contract. In spite of the fact that I did not have experience as a negotiator, my client assumed I should be part of the team because I knew better than anyone else every requirement (because I wrote them), every word contained in the RFP (because I wrote it), and the supplier selection decision process (because I orchestrated it). The purpose of the deal was to outsource computer infrastructure and operations, and the core negotiating team included:

- My client, who was the executive sponsoring the effort and who had authority to sign the eventual contract.
- A Director who reported to my client, who was assigned full time to the negotiating effort, and who represented my client when he was unable to participate due to his other conflicting responsibilities.
- Outside legal counsel, consisting of two attorneys from a firm with extensive experience with outsourcing contracts.
- Internal legal counsel, who eventually abdicated in favor of the more experienced outside counsel.
- A Human Resources representative because several hundred of my client's employees would be re-badged to become employees of the new supplier.
- Myself as a subject matter expert and as an authority on the documents and events leading up to the negotiations.

The core team was supplemented by a variety of subject matter experts who could answer technical computer operations questions for us and provide advice about the implications of specific options we were considering.

This first experience doing contract negotiations resulted in a signed contract with which my client and the supplier were both satisfied. I had thought when we started that we would be done in four to six weeks. After all, we had the written RFP and the supplier's written proposal, so how long could it take to hammer out a legal contract using those two documents as the basis? I was so naïve. As it turned out, it took almost four months of long hours and difficult work because our starting positions were quite far apart. The supplier wanted to use their "standard contract" as the foundation, but we felt it was completely one-sided and totally ignored our RFP as well as their proposal, which we insisted had to be attached to and made a part of the eventual contract. Too many members of both teams felt no urgency and were therefore unmotivated to compromise.

I learned a lot during this first contract negotiation engagement, and I was much less naïve after the experience. Since then, I've learned several additional valuable lessons.

Lessons Learned

Lesson 1: Understand basic contract terminology and language. This was initially more difficult for me than it needed to be because the first attorneys I worked with were poor educators and didn't care whether or not I understood their language. The following table is a terminology "cheat sheet" that I developed after my first few experiences. I arbitrarily grouped the contracting topics into general categories within the sheet.

Terminology	Description
Structure & Participants	
Number of Contracts	A single contract, or a MSA (Master Services Agreement) with addendums and/or work orders
Parties	Customer and (a) one supplier or (b) multiple suppliers or (c) a prime with sub-contractors
Timing	
Term Length	Number of years contract is in effect
Termination	Provisions addressing end of contract definitions and obligations of both parties upon termination (a) at end of term, (b) for default, (c) for convenience
Transition Period	Months after initial term expires that prices remain firm
Transition Assistance	Supplier services available and fees to effect a smooth transition after the contract expires
Options	Number of and length of extension option(s) at the end of the initial term
Scope	
Services Covered	Detail Statement of Work (SOW) defining supplier responsibilities
Proprietary Rights and Title	Supplier has the right to sell the products and services to Customer
Assignment	Agreement cannot be assigned to a third party without Customer approval
Quality	
Service Levels (SLAs)	Availability of support in days per week and hours per day; minimum percent of time service is available during supported hours; acceptable maximum response times
Performance Remedies	Root cause analysis for SLA failures; corrective measures; reporting and process improvement
Performance Incentives	Service level performance is tied to

	financial penalties and/or credits
Money	
Fees & Payments	Pricing and billing terms
Installation Costs	One time start-up fees
Signing Bonus	Credit or rebate received by Customer for signing
Prices Effective	Date prices go into effect
Total Commitment	Minimum dollars to be paid over the initial term
Annual Commitment	Minimum dollars per year, if any
Commitment Retirement	Other services Customer purchases will retire the commitment
Substitute Services	Total commitment is reduced if new services are offered by supplier that replace existing services
Additional Users	Selected users other than Customer (e.g. sister companies) may buy off the Agreement and will retire the commitment
Rate Reduction Leverage	Remaining commitment can be reduced in future years if prices are not competitive based on industry benchmarks
Benchmarking	Prices benchmarked by independent third-party
Miscellaneous	
Confidentiality	Both parties agree to keep each other's information confidential
Representations and Warrants	Both parties agree to non-infringement of any third party's rights; no viruses will be introduced by either party to the other party
Survival	Should client be acquired by another entity, all rights and privileges of the agreement accede to the acquiring entity. For software licenses, in the event of business termination by the supplier, continued possession, right to maintain, and right to modify the software accede

	to the Customer.
Indemnification	Hold harmless of other party for first party's wrongdoing
Limits of Liability	Maximum amount either party can recover from the other
Dispute Resolution	Arbitration and other methods to be used prior to legal proceedings
Notices	Address of each party where formal notices are to be sent
Insurance	Who has responsibility to insure products
Audit Rights	Supplier rights to inspect product usage and Customer rights to inspect billing practices

Lesson 2: Understand the big picture before starting. This requires a serious discussion with the executive sponsor to get his/her decisions regarding major themes including:

- Who has responsibility for the success of service delivery? If the service fails and the supplier gets paid anyway, then the responsibility for success belongs to the Customer, and negotiating focus should be to get a commitment for the best/most supplier resources into the contract. If the service fails and the supplier doesn't get paid, then the responsibility for success belongs to the supplier, and negotiating focus must be to get a commitment for specific RESULTS into the contract. Neither scenario is right or wrong, and both have pitfalls and risks. However, clearly understanding this issue is critical because the entire negotiating approach depends on it.
- What is the preferred deal structure, and what is our fallback position? In other words, are we negotiating a purchase, or a licensing arrangement, or an OEM deal, or a joint venture, or some other arrangement?

- What are we primarily negotiating overall? Do we want to obtain a lower price, or more/better products and services, or better value (optimal combination of price and service), or better contractual and business terms, or something else?

Lesson 3: The most important leverage for the Customer is COMPETITION. Every attempt should be made to convince suppliers that there are at least two suppliers being considered all the way through the process, right up to contract signing. Obviously, when there is more than one competitor being considered, there is more work for the Customer; however, the Customer needs to resist the desire to simplify the process and reduce workload. Adhere to the competitive environment to the end.

Lesson 4: Do not disclose your entire position early. Force suppliers to negotiate selected points to resolution before moving on to the next set of points. Maintain a position that the supplier doesn't yet need to hear the Customer's position on other points … "because if the current issues aren't resolved, the rest won't matter." This piecemeal approach puts additional pressure on suppliers to concede issues, and it provides Customer flexibility to add new issues without appearing to be dealing in bad faith.

Lesson 5: Time usually favors suppliers. Customers have deadlines, and suppliers don't. Suppliers can stall and delay until the Customer feels compelled to cave on issues just to meet a deadline. Avoid conveying a sense of urgency to suppliers. An exception to this lesson occurs near the end of the supplier's fiscal year because supplier sales representatives want to book business in the current year to achieve a quota or some bonus incentive, and this can work to the Customer's advantage.

Lesson 6: Do not use a standard supplier agreement as the basis for a contract. Instead, use a Customer created template, another previously negotiated contract, or a blank sheet of paper. Anything is better than the supplier's standard contract.

Lesson 7: Make document management a Customer responsibility. He, who controls the documents, controls the process. Do not accept "generous" offers by suppliers to take this responsibility.

Lesson 8: If it's not in the contract, then it's not part of the deal. If the Customer wants the supplier to comply with provisions contained in the Customer RFP, the supplier proposal or other documents, then those provisions need to be repeated in the contract, or the documents themselves need to be appended to and referenced in the contract.

Lesson 9: Avoid signing a letter of intent. Regardless of wording, a letter of intent can possibly be interpreted by a court as a commitment to sign a contract.

Lesson 10: Performance remedies are essential in the contract. Do not think of remedies as a means of punishment or as a means of Customer compensation for supplier shortcomings, but rather as a means of motivating positive supplier performance.

Lesson 11: The Customer must say, "No" during negotiations. Know the issues you are unwilling to compromise, and be clear in stating a firm position. Conversely, The Customer must hear, "No" during negotiations. If the supplier hasn't refused to move any further on an issue, then the Customer hasn't pushed hard enough.

Lesson 12: Silence is golden, and it can be one of the Customer's most effective negotiating tools. Rarely resist the opportunity to keep your mouth shut. During discussions, do not feel compelled to fill an awkward empty space when there appears to be an impasse … because usually, whoever speaks first is offering a compromise. Between negotiating sessions, be slow to respond to supplier inquiries, and when calling back, be sure to apologize with an excuse of being "tied up in discussions with one of your competitors."

Lesson 13: Walk away at the most critical or difficult point during negotiations. Stop the negotiations and send the supplier representatives home early. Then go completely silent, not responding to any messages for a few days. This can be a very effective technique, but it should only be used sparingly.

Lesson 14: Communicate internally, especially to senior leadership, that they should anticipate contact from one or more suppliers attempting to bypass formal negotiations by cutting a quick "gentlemen's agreement." Provide clear instructions that supplier attempts to circumvent the negotiating process should be responded to by stating, "All supplier communications, formal and informal, will be handled exclusively by our negotiating team who has our full confidence." Also, insist that any contacts from suppliers be reported back to the negotiating team. The team can use these incidents to put the supplier on the defensive and win concessions.

Lesson 15: Ideals such as "partnership" and "trust relationship" although admirable, will not be achieved. If they could, why bother with a contract? As Ronald Reagan said, "Trust, but verify."

Lesson 16: Keep logistics options open throughout the process. Most negotiations start by using a traditional back-and-forth process with teams working in their respective offices and sending documents to each other. If the process appears to be stalled, changing logistics can jump-start it. Some options include:

- A "lock-down" process where both sides stay in a hotel, and no one leaves until negotiations are complete. This requires multiple conference rooms in the hotel: one for the

supplier, one for the Customer, one for face-to-face negotiations, and possibly one for document management. When negotiating with two suppliers, this approach needs to be done during different weeks, one for each supplier.
- Internet web conferencing (using for example Google Docs or www.placeware.com) with concurrent telephone conferencing. This can be especially productive for document management.
- Any combination of these and other techniques. They are not mutually exclusive.

Valuable Experiences

I've helped negotiate contracts for several clients over the years, and each engagement has been both unique and educational. The above lessons were not all learned during my first experience, but they are the result of many contract negotiation engagements.

One of those engagements was for a client who needed to select an external technology-hosting provider for proprietary software that my client's organization had developed. My client engaged me to define requirements, write an RFP, lead the selection process and negotiate the contract. After completing the first few phases of work, we initiated negotiations with the two finalist suppliers, and we spent alternating weeks with each one. During the third week, we were back with supplier A, and we had reached what seemed like an impasse with them over service levels. Both sides had very different perspectives on the definition of availability, the metrics to measure it and appropriate remedies for not achieving targets. The supplier refused to discuss any SLAs other than their standard ones that they offered to all their Customers. We felt their standard availability targets wouldn't satisfy our specific business needs, and if the supplier's targets weren't achieved, their remedies wouldn't provide much of an incentive to improve. We had been negotiating all morning, and when we finally took a break, I needed to respond to nature's call. As I entered the rest room, I saw and heard the supplier VP of sales and his attorney standing next to each other at the urinals laughing and joking about how they were getting the best of us by pretending to not budge on the SLAs. I slipped quietly into a stall and waited patiently for them to finish their conversation and leave. I learned that they planned to "grudgingly" give in on the SLAs and use that as an excuse to raise the price significantly above their proposal bid. After I returned to the negotiating room, I gathered our team for a private discussion in a separate conference room and informed everyone about the supplier's tactics. When negotiations resumed, we took the position that our RFP clearly described our preferred SLAs, that their proposal stated they could and would comply with our SLAs, and that the pricing in their proposal did not mention any dependency on their standard SLAs. We eventually got what we wanted without a change in price. The lesson I learned was not that hanging out in the bathroom is a preferred negotiating tactic. The real lesson from this experience is to keep your mouth shut unless you're positive the other side can't hear you. The other members of our team didn't pass up the opportunity to tease me unmercifully for the next few weeks for being "the bathroom creeper."

Another of my clients asked me to step in for him and be the lead business representative during contract negotiations with the two finalist vendors. We formed a three person negotiating team consisting of the company's internal lead counsel, an external attorney and me. We unanimously agreed which vendor was the best choice, but unfortunately the vendor we preferred was the least flexible in compromising on the legal language we wanted in the contract. Therefore, I compiled a list of the known points of disagreement and asked our two attorneys to work with me to prioritize the points so we would know on which of them we could compromise and on which we wouldn't. During our priority setting discussion, the external attorney took a position of not wanting to compromise on any of the points. He and I debated point after point, but he refused to consider any of them as less than mandatory. I finally took a different tactic by addressing our timeline. I said we had a fixed deadline established by the VP I was representing (my client), we were not making progress, and in order to get the vendor negotiating team to compromise on the most important issues to us, we would need to give in on at least a few from our side. The external attorney became angry and started yelling about how important it was to not compromise on any points. I decided to stop talking. The company internal lead counsel and I waited silently, occasionally glancing at each other, until the external attorney finally ran out of steam. Then the lead counsel asked me to leave the room. About 30 minutes later, he informed me that he and I would finish the negotiations, and our external attorney had been excused from the engagement. The lesson I learned from this experience is that I was correct to not argue with an idiot; otherwise the other person in the room might have assumed I was equally crazy. I've considered this situation, and in hindsight it's possible that the uncompromising attorney may have been driven by a need to generate a high number of billable hours, and that need may have outweighed whatever motivation he might have had to do the right thing for our mutual client. My experience has taught me that it's important to be willing to compromise and to know on which points to be flexible and on which to hold firm. Without compromise, a negotiation ceases to be a negotiation.

One of my contract negotiating engagements was unusual because during the entire engagement, I never met the lead attorney from our side in person. I still have no idea what she looks like. She and I spoke a few times on the phone and exchanged several emails, so I learned very precisely what her priorities were as well as what terms she was willing to compromise and how far. In addition the business executive sponsoring the effort (my client) was tied up with several other unrelated matters, some of which required her to be out of town extensively, and she was able to personally attend only the initial negotiating session with the supplier finalist. In effect, this left me as both the business and the legal representative on our negotiating team. Yikes! Fortunately we had an astute person from Procurement on the team who understood the business issues, and we had a senior technologist on the team who had significant relevant knowledge from working with the supplier finalist previously. The lesson I learned from this experience was the importance of understanding the big picture, both from the business and from legal, before starting negotiations. See my comments regarding Lesson 2 from the Lessons Learned section earlier in this chapter. Another lesson was to take advantage when key team members are absent. Occasionally, while negotiating a particular term, I informed the other side that I had clear instructions from legal or the business on the issue in question and I was not authorized to compromise on it. Because the person with authority wasn't present, this left the supplier with no choice but to cave or to give us time to go back and regroup while we adjusted tactics. More often than not, they just caved. We turned what initially appeared to be a disadvantage (not having key executives physically present) into an advantage.

This next story has little to do with contract negotiations per se. It was my first experience working closely with a group of attorneys, and it gave me a deep appreciation for their skills and how they think. I was a fairly new consultant and got assigned to a litigation support engagement because the trial was in Minneapolis, and I happened to have a few hours available. We worked for five different legal firms who represented several drug companies that were being sued by the Federal government (and others) for "uniform pricing" practices related to a specific antibiotic. The government's damage claims were based on retail prices because they argued that manufacturer prices drove wholesale prices, which in turn drove retail prices. I was asked to analyze over 20 years of pricing data (including drugs in suit and other antibiotic drugs not in suit) previously compiled by a neutral third party to determine the validity of the government's damage claims. I designed and programmed a mini-system to do the statistical analysis, and I coerced Art C, a colleague and a CPA who had one of his degrees in statistics, to help me verify and interpret results. At first, our results appeared to support the government's position, but the attorneys kept pushing us to try different angles. Eventually, Art had an epiphany. He said our approach was based on how the manufacturers priced which was by dosage (per pill), but pharmacies don't sell by the dose; they sell prescriptions. So I re-programmed our system, and when we re-ran the analysis, our results showed with a 95% confidence level that retail prescription prices consisted of the manufacturer's price plus a fixed amount, and this held true for all drugs examined, both those in the suit and those not in the suit. In other words, retail prices were not driven by manufacturer prices. We were as excited as little children on Christmas morning when we told the attorneys what we found. They didn't quite share our enthusiasm, but asked us to explain our analysis, so we verbally described the statistical premises and methods we used. Their eyes glazed over, and they said the court would never understand or admit our findings as evidence. So we wrote down the details about how we arrived at our conclusions, but the attorneys still didn't understand or accept our results. Finally, on about our fourth attempt, Art produced a lengthy educational document that started with black and white balls in an urn to explain basic statistics, and he built up to inferential statistics, Bernoulli distributions, Chi-square probabilities and other more complex statistical methods. The attorneys finally got excited and packaged our document into a brief that they presented to the court. Three weeks later the government accepted the brief and reduced overall damage claims by half a billion dollars. I learned that litigating attorneys don't accept what consultants tell them on blind faith; they need to not only understand a concept but also to be able to explain it themselves and to the court as if it were their own idea. The successful relationships I've had with attorneys since then have been partially a result of my ability to educate and clarify details for them.

Attorneys are as human as other professionals. Most are good at what they do. Some of the outside counsel I've worked with were more interested in generating billable hours than doing what's right for their clients. Some of the internal counsel I've worked with were so focused on avoiding mistakes (or ensuring they couldn't be blamed for them) that they became roadblocks to progress. There are excellent attorneys though, and I've had the good fortune to work with and learn from some truly outstanding individuals like Steve P., Aaron O. and Candice C. They are representative of the best attorneys who are experienced, knowledgeable and who also care about schedules and what's in the best interests of our mutual clients.

Outsourcing Considerations

As I mentioned in Chapter 16, more than half of the RFPs I've written have been for outsourcing initiatives. As a result of the linkage with the RFP work I've conducted, many of the resulting contract negotiation efforts I've conducted have also been for outsourcing initiatives.

Prior to my first experience with an outsourcing project, I had thought that "outsourcing" generally meant going off shore for services, and that most of those awards went to India. Interestingly, my experiences have been the exact opposite. Almost all of the awards for the outsourcing projects I've done have gone to domestic suppliers. I only remember one time when the winning supplier was an off shore company.

When a client is first considering outsourcing for a particular function, I encourage looking at a variety of staffing options. Outsourcing is only one of several possible strategies along a spectrum of alternatives, and it's possible to use more than one. Obviously, staffing decisions should be carefully considered because each option comes with its own set of risks, as the following table shows.

Staffing Options and Risks

Option	Typical Aspects	Risks
Internal Employees	• Customer work site used • Customer manages • Customer equipment used • Customer may terminate at will • May include any Customer functions	• Data Security risk is "normal" • Data Confidentiality risk is "normal" • Risk to Intellectual Property rights is "normal" • Employment risk is N/A because staff are employees
Staff Augmentation	• Customer work site used • Customer manages • Customer equipment used • Customer may terminate at will • May include any Customer functions	• Data Security risk is "normal" • Data Confidentiality risk is "normal" • Risk to Intellectual Property rights is "normal" • High risk of "employment" based on: - IRS 20 factors applied in Microsoft trilogy of cases - Supreme Court's Darden case 12-factor rule

Partial Staff Augmentation	• Customer or Consultant work site used • Customer manages • Customer or Consultant equipment used • Customer may terminate early • Less likely to be Customer core functions	• Data Security risk is higher • Data Confidentiality risk is higher • Risk to Intellectual Property rights is higher • Customer loses some control • Customer still manages and controls, creating co-employment risk under IRS 20 and Darden case 12-factor rule
Partial Outsourcing	• Consultant work site used with Customer visits • Consultant manages and reports to Customer • Primarily Consultant equipment used • Customer's termination rights are set forth in contract. Early termination penalties may apply • Very unlikely to be Customer core functions	• Data Security risk is high • Data Confidentiality risk is high • Risk to Intellectual Property rights is high • Minimal Customer control outside of contract terms • Partial Outsourcing is unlikely to create co-employment risk

Outsourcing	• Consultant work site used • Consultant manages • Consultant equipment used • Customer termination for breach by Consultant • Should be no Customer core functions	• Data Security risk is highest • Data Confidentiality risk is highest • Risk to Intellectual Property rights is highest • No Customer control or management of individual Consultant agents • All work based on contract terms • No co-employment risks

Because outsourcing involves the transfer of responsibility from the customer to the supplier, how the arrangement is to be managed needs to be properly documented within the contract. One of the primary tools of outsourcing supplier governance is a Service Level Agreement (SLA), which is our next topic.

Service Level Considerations

A Service Level Agreement (SLA) is a negotiated agreement between a customer and a service provider, and it is typically created as part of the overall contract negotiation. The SLA documents an agreed understanding about services, priorities, responsibilities, guarantees, and warranties. The SLA may involve financial penalties and the right to terminate if the SLAs are consistently missed. Note that contracts between the service provider and other third parties are often (incorrectly) also called SLAs; these agreements are simply "contracts". Internal groups sometimes use OLAs (Operating Level Agreements) to support SLA(s).

The SLAs I helped create during my earliest contract negotiation engagements were lengthy documents that defined dozens of service levels. Each of these service levels was meticulously described along with measurement metrics, targets, reporting methods, and penalties. My participation was primarily to ensure technical relevance and accuracy. Some of these SLA documents were more than 100 pages long, and they were appended as separate Schedules to their associated contracts. The attorneys who crafted them typically started with an SLA schedule from a contract they had worked on previously for another client. The oldest SLA documents I've seen were from the late 1980s for contracts with telecom carriers (AT&T, Qwest, British Telecom, etc.). Each newly minted SLA document was a masterpiece of legal language merged with technical jargon, and the attorneys were quite proud of the results as well as the huge number of billable hours needed to complete them. I had the good fortune of continuing my client relationships and being engaged for additional unrelated projects with a few of those clients. This gave me the opportunity to go back and re-visit three SLA situations a year or more after they were each put in place. I was surprised and disappointed that all three organizations had abandoned the SLAs we'd negotiated. It turned out that the documents contained far too many service levels for which the metrics were either impossible to capture or so expensive to track that the organization stopped trying. As a result, the organizations also stopped tracking all the SLAs and shelved the entire concept. I suggested to one client that we pick the most important three or four SLAs and ignore the rest, but he said we'd need to re-negotiate everything with the supplier, and he had neither the appetite nor the funding to do that. Besides, opening up the contract for the SLAs carried the risk that we might lose advantages we had won previously in other areas.

Those disappointing client situations made me re-think the whole approach to SLAs I had previously learned from the various attorneys with whom I had worked. I decided brevity, simplicity, clarity and enforceability were much more important than being comprehensive. When I had my next opportunity to participate in a contract negotiation, which was for technology operations outsourcing, I told our team about the experiences of those prior three clients and strongly recommended we use a prioritization method I had conceived. I was surprised how quickly the entire team, including outside counsel, agreed. The following paragraphs describe the method we used for that project, and I've used it (or something like it) for almost every contract negotiating engagement since.

Establishing a Service Level Framework

1. Categorize service levels into two broad classifications:
   - Service Level Commitments. Each of these includes (1) a definition, (2) a single target metric for measuring whether or not the service level is achieved, (3) a reporting cycle that identifies the frequency with which supplier will inform the customer of performance results, and (4) a remedy calculation to determine financial service credits applicable when performance results do not meet the target metric.
   - Service Level Goals. Each of these includes a definition, a target metric and a reporting cycle, like a Service Level Commitment. However, there is no remedy for a Service Level Goal. Although there are no remedies (penalties) for missing a goal, they are measured and reported just as commitments are.

2. Determine to which environments each of the two above categories apply. My recommendation is usually that Service Level Commitments apply only to the production environment, and Service Level Goals apply to all environments: production, test, QA, development, etc.

3. Create a list of all service levels. Most of the usual suspects fall into one of four categories:
   - **System Availability.** These are typically defined uniquely for each environment. For example, System Availability for the production environment is usually defined as the

percent of scheduled operating hours when the production system is operating properly to allow users to process transactions in the normal course of their business.

- **Severity Level Incident Service Restoration.** These are each typically defined as the elapsed time from the time that a problem is detected until service is restored. Most companies use three tiers of severity levels, with Severity Level 1 being the most important or urgent.
- **Help Desk Service Levels.** These typically include items such as calls answered in less than 20 seconds, calls abandoned, calls blocked, and first-touch resolution rate.
- **Service Request and Change Request Completion.** These may include items such as incident reports or tickets re-opened, on time completion of service requests, on time completion of change requests, time to dispatch third-party support, and on time delivery of scheduled reports.

4. Categorize every service level as either a commitment or a goal. This activity provides simplicity and clarity to the entire effort. During a recent contract negotiation engagement at a financial institution, I convinced my client that we only needed two service levels to be categorized as commitments, and all the rest could be goals. The two we picked were System Availability in the production environment and Severity Level 1 Incident Service Restoration in the production environment. I initially proposed only one, System Availability. My most compelling argument was that if all service levels exceeded targets except for System Availability, the VP of Technology Operations (my client), would likely be fired. Conversely, if System Availability exceeded the target and all other service levels failed, my client would likely still get his bonus at year-end. There were a handful of my client's direct reports in the conference room when we had this discussion, and they were all initially aghast that I was suggesting we not classify all our service levels as mandatory commitments. For example, the director responsible for the Help Desk felt all his service level

metrics were absolutely essential. Fortunately my client is a person with perspective, and he believes in setting priorities. He said we would "compromise" by adding Severity Level 1 Incident Service Restoration as our second commitment, and he ended the discussion by saying he would not add any others. I feel that I persuaded him with facts, logic and a scenario that was personal to him. I like leaders who make decisions rather than taking a vote. The supplier negotiating team was delighted when we presented our approach to SLAs to them, and they agreed almost immediately. They were used to other clients insisting on 20 or more "critical" service levels, and they said working with only two was like a breath of fresh air to them.

5. Define the supporting processes. These may include:
   - Escalation procedures for incidents and service requests.
   - Customer notification procedures when the supplier discovers a problem.
   - Root Cause analysis procedures to avoid repeating an incident or problem.
   - Review schedules and procedures to discuss the current period's performance.

As an example of how a service level should be documented, following is a summary description of a System Availability service level:

Definition: System Availability is the percent of scheduled operating hours when the production system is operating properly to allow users to process transactions in the normal course of their business.

Target: 99.5%

Reporting: The supplier will provide to the customer a report of the total hours of System Availability for the month (measured to the closest second) divided by the total Scheduled Operational Hours for the month (expressed as a percentage, calculated to the closest 0.01%).

Remedy: Based on achieved Percent Availability, the remedy percentage from the following table shall be multiplied times the prior month's invoice total amount. The resulting calculated amount will be applied as a credit against the current month's invoice total amount due.

Percent Availability	Remedy
99.50 – 100.00	0%
99.00 – 99.49	2%
98.00 – 98.99	5%
95.00 – 97.99	10%
0.00 – 94.99	15%

If documented properly, the Service Level Framework, including each individual service level description similar to the one above, can become (or serve as the foundation for) the SLA exhibit to be attached to the contract.

Summary

The intent of this chapter is to provide enough information, including lessons learned, for a technology consultant to participate as part of a contract negotiation effort. I've included stories about selected specific negotiations that provided me with valuable experiences. Outsourcing situations and service levels deserve special consideration when negotiating a technology contract, and I've included separate sub-sections for each.

This chapter is definitely not intended to eliminate the need for legal counsel participation, which is essential.

Chapter 18 – Implementation

> "It is common sense to take a method and try it.
> If it fails, admit it frankly and try another.
> But above all, try something."
> -- Franklin D. Roosevelt

Including a chapter about implementation projects is a challenge because implementation methods are continuously evolving, and soon after I commit ideas on current methods to paper, those ideas are likely to be viewed as obsolete. I can avoid this pitfall by not discussing methodology and focusing instead on other elements of implementation projects. However, omitting such a significant aspect of the discussion leaves an obvious void. Rather than leaving it out, I'll address development and implementation methods first.

Methodologies

I've been developing and implementing technology solutions during my entire professional career, even before I became a consultant. I was hired out of college in 1971 as a programmer at a large company with $50 billion in annual revenue. In those days, developers were called programmers, and formal methodologies were just starting to emerge. Before I became a consultant in 1974, I learned several programming languages such as Cobol, Fortran, PL/1, RPG, Assembler, Neat-3 and others. Experience with multiple languages helped me get selected for a variety of project teams where I also had opportunities to become experienced with different development methodologies. Over the years, I've worked on projects that used:

- Top Down, a method of repetitive decomposition of a system design into sub-systems, functions, routines, steps, etc. down to individual executables. Elements of this method still survive today.

- Bottom Up, which created numerous detail base elements that were then linked together to form sub-systems. Mercifully, this method was euthanized by most organizations soon after they tried it.
- Structured Documentation methods, which were not development methodologies per se, but were primarily rigid prescriptions for creating detailed system documentation. Several Fortune 500 companies purchased one or more of these documentation methods in the 1970s. Many of those companies later abandoned their purchased documentation methodology because of the on-going significant cost to maintain the documentation. Even small maintenance changes required costly rewriting and republishing of manuals.
- Structured Design, which required development of independent modules of code within a program that could be called and executed by other modules in the program. Each module had a single entry point and a single exit point, which significantly simplified testing and debugging.
- Re-usable Code, which grew out of the structured design movement. The objective was to develop small, self-contained blocks of code, each of which could be maintained as a single version and could be used by many programs and systems, thus simplifying software maintenance.
- Super Programmers, which consisted of having a genius super programmer surrounded by a team of support staff who would finish blocks of code after the super programmer had done the heavy lifting. This approach ignored basic human nature. No one wanted to be the genius because the expectation of producing brilliant results every day was too much pressure, and no one wanted to be relegated to a support role because of the jealousy and resentment it engendered. And from a practical perspective, acknowledged geniuses were in short supply.

- SDLCs (System Development Life Cycles), which were well-organized waterfall processes that defined the phases, activities and steps of the system development process. Each of the large technology consulting companies developed and sold their own SDLC, and there were about a dozen competing products in the 1980s, some of which survive today. The SDLCs brought structure into the chaos; however, the authors continued to expand their methodologies, and some grew to several volumes that took up three to four feet of space on a bookshelf. Many large companies insisted on rigidly following whichever SDLC they had purchased, and adherence became the primary purpose, while achieving project objectives took on secondary importance. Project Offices sprang up to enforce compliance with the SDLCs, and the more successful project managers had to employ a variety of stealth techniques to give the appearance of adherence so they could actually focus on delivering results.
- Data Driven, which inverted the old software first approaches by requiring that the database be designed prior to the functional software processes. Previously, data structures were an afterthought.
- CASE (Computer-Aided Software Engineering), which employed the use of automated tools, such as database directories, as part of the development process.
- Prototyping, which promoted the rapid development of partially complete sub-systems with limited functionality. These samples or models were demonstrated to users early in the project in order to get feedback that would determine what additional functions to build during the next iteration of development.
- Object Oriented, which built systems consisting of blocks of data and function (components), which each can inherit attributes and behavior from other components and which communicate with other components using messages. This was similar to and built on the concepts of Structured

Design, but it also included data in the components and had more rules.

- Rapid Development, which expanded the use of prototyping and multiple development cycles in a project. This method allowed scope to be limited (and errors reduced) in each cycle. For example, cycle 2 would not be allowed to start until cycle 1 was clean, and the errors found in cycle 2 could usually be corrected by focusing on the new functionality that was introduced as part of cycle 2.
- Agile, which is based on incremental development using rapid iterative development cycles called sprints. Each cycle typically includes requirements definition through solution development. Testing is also an integral part of each sprint rather than left to be addressed as a separate phase, as with traditional waterfall SDLC projects. Agile projects have been successful with smaller scope efforts. I've observed mixed results with larger Agile projects because there is an incomplete understanding of requirements prior to starting development.

The above techniques are not mutually exclusive. In fact, a handful or more of the different techniques are often used within a single project. Many have real value, and while most have positive aspects, each one also has negatives. Unfortunately, every methodology has had a religious following of rabid zealots who have been unwilling to admit to the possibility of a downside to their chosen deity, at least until the next cure-all methodology comes into vogue.

Methodologies have come and gone for as long as I've been in the technology consulting business, and I predict that newer methodologies will emerge to supplement or replace those I've discussed here. The reason I'm confident in my prediction is that technology executives are desperate to find the elusive "silver bullet" that will improve their system development batting averages. Those batting averages are embarrassing at best, and they are frequently career limiting for technology executives. Various studies conducted over the past 20+ years report that more than half (one study says more than 70%) of all technology development efforts fail, and the larger the project, the higher the failure rate. My own anecdotal observations are consistent with those studies. Most of the system development projects I've witnessed within my client organizations have:

- Failed to deliver expected results, or
- Cost 150% to 300% of the planned budget, or
- Taken twice as long as planned, or
- Some combination of the above.

And the failures continue. A very public example is the failed October 2013 launch of the HealthCare.gov website as part of the Affordable Care Act implementation. Failures like this motivate technology executives to continue searching for the silver bullet by acquiring the newest technology or methodology in the hope of prolonging their careers.

Classic Mistakes

Following is an abbreviated version of a list of classic technology project mistakes that Steve McConnell included in his 1996 book, "Rapid Development."

People-Related Mistakes

1. Undermined motivation. Motivation probably has a larger effect on productivity and quality than any other factor.
2. Weak personnel. This includes adding team members who could be hired fastest instead of who would get the most work done over the life of the project.
3. Uncontrolled problem employees. Failure to take action to deal with a problem employee is the most common complaint that team members have about their leaders.

4. Heroics. This manifests itself as a pattern of scheduling brinkmanship in which impending schedule slips aren't detected, acknowledged or reported up the management chain until the last minute, which encourages extreme risk taking and discourages cooperation among the stakeholders.
5. Adding people to a late project. This is perhaps the most classic of the classic mistakes because adding people can take more productivity away from existing team members than it adds.
6. Noisy, crowded offices. Noisy, crowded work environments lengthen development schedules.
7. Friction between developers and customers. On most large projects, friction between customers and software developers becomes so severe that both parties consider canceling the project.
8. Unrealistic expectations. Customers establish deadlines with no understanding of the effort required.
9. Lack of effective project sponsorship. An effective executive sponsor can buffer the project from other executives who may undermine the project.
10. Lack of stakeholder buy-in. Without support from all those affected, the cooperation needed during difficult periods won't materialize.
11. Lack of user input. Early user involvement improves the quality of requirements.
12. Politics placed over substance. Keeping a steering committee happy by only telling them what they want to hear works temporarily, but is deadly in the long term.
13. Wishful thinking. This involves closing your eyes and hoping something will work when you have no reasonable basis for thinking it will.

Process-Related Mistakes

14. Overly optimistic schedules. This usually results in under-scoping the effort and not doing a thorough requirements definition.
15. Insufficient risk management. When risks are not anticipated and mitigated, it only takes one thing to go wrong to derail a project.
16. Contractor failure. Outsourcing pieces of a project almost always takes longer and costs more than keeping it in house, especially when the relationship is poorly managed.
17. Insufficient planning. If you don't know where you're going or how you're going to get there, you won't.
18. Abandoning planning under pressure. Discarding an unrealistic plan isn't a problem, but not replacing it with a better one is.
19. Wasted time during the fuzzy front end. Getting through the approval and funding processes quickly will leave more time for project work.
20. Shortchanged upstream activities. Projects that skimp on upstream activities, like requirements and design, typically have to do the same work downstream at anywhere from 10 to 100 times the cost of doing it properly in the first place.
21. Inadequate design. Rush projects undermine design by not allocating enough time for it and by creating a pressure-cooker environment that makes thoughtful consideration of design alternatives difficult.
22. Shortchanged quality assurance. Shortcutting one day of QA activity early in the project is likely to cost you from 3 to 10 days of activity downstream.
23. Insufficient management controls. Before you can keep a project on track, you have to be able to tell if it's on track in the first place.
24. Premature or overly frequent convergence. Convergence includes activities done to prepare a product for release, and spending time on these activities too early is a waste.

25. Omitting necessary tasks from estimates. Omitted effort often adds 20 – 30% to a development schedule.
26. Planning to catch up later. When a project schedule has slipped, not adjusting the overall timeline is naïve.
27. Code-like-hell programming. This assumes developers are super heroes who can meet any unrealistic deadlines.

Product Mistakes

28. Requirements gold-plating. Complex unnecessary features add disproportionately to a development schedule.
29. Feature creep. The average project experiences about a 25% change in requirements over its lifetime, but rarely do those changes result in extending the deadline, even though the deadline should be moved.
30. Developer gold-plating. Developers typically want to try out new features of their language or environment or to create their own implementation of a slick feature they saw in another product, whether or not it's required in the product being developed.
31. Push-me, pull-me negotiation. When a manager approves a schedule slip on a project that's progressing slower than expected and then adds completely new tasks after the schedule change.
32. Research-oriented development. If you have product goals that push the state of the art (such as algorithms, speed, memory usage, and so on), you should assume your schedule is highly speculative.

Technology Mistakes

33. Silver-bullet syndrome. This is too much reliance on a vendor's advertised benefits of previously unused technologies.
34. Overestimated savings from new tools or methods. Organizations seldom increase their productivity in giant leaps, no matter how many new tools or methods they adopt or how good those tools and methods are.

35. Switching tools in the middle of a project. The inevitable learning curve, mistakes and rework needed with a new tool cancel out any benefit.
36. Lack of automated source-code control. Without source-code control, the coordination necessary between all developers becomes a huge risk factor.

My experiences indicate that McConnell's list is as valid now as when he first published it. Most of the items on the list are applicable not only for projects that develop systems from scratch, but also for implementations of purchased software packages. I'm confident that a lot of veteran technologists could add their own items to this list. One addition I would make to the process-related mistakes is "Inadequate Requirements." Experience shows that large projects with poorly defined or incomplete requirements are destined to fail.

Salvaging Failed Projects

Many of the implementation projects I've been engaged to manage had been started prior to my arrival and were in the process of failing. In each of those situations, my client asked me to assume management because he/she was at risk of being held accountable for a major failure, and I have a reputation for delivering results. I've found that it's actually easier to take over a failing project than it is to start a new project because expectations are comparatively low for the failing effort. When no one expects me to succeed, then each day that I push the project in a positive direction, my efforts are greeted with high praise.

For example, a financial institution, with over 40% of the market in their home state, was implementing a new demand deposit (checking account) software package. The project was stalled, and John, a banking consultant, and I were asked to evaluate the situation. We conducted a half-day assessment and found that the project had been in process for over a year, but minimal progress had been achieved. The new package software had been loaded into the software library, but less than half the programs had been compiled and none had been tested. A new communications module that allowed checking transactions to be processed by their ATM machines was not working, and the software vendor refused to take responsibility. The Demand Deposit department had mailed out checks to over 20,000 customers, but the proof machines that would process written checks that had already started coming back into the bank were still wrapped in plastic shrink wrap, and the proofing section had not received a single minute of training. The new demand deposit software was built to run on the bank's mainframe, but no one knew if there was sufficient capacity to process the additional transaction load. The 50 people directly involved in the project, as well as many people who were not, were pointing fingers at each other, and morale was abysmal. By my quick estimate, over 8,000 hours of effort were still required (assuming all those hours would be productive), and the deadline was only three weeks away. After our half day assessment, John and I informed the president that he should mail an apology letter to his customers and start over with a target completion date about five or six months out. He turned green, mumbled something about reputational suicide and said the resulting loss of market share would cost him his job. He then asked us if we could save the project. I recited some platitude about ignoring the facts doesn't change the facts, and said getting everything up and running in three weeks was impossible. He asked us, "Are you at least willing to try?" We agreed and established some ground rules which the president communicated to his direct reports: (1) the project would be the bank's only priority (not just the number 1 priority) for the next 3 weeks, (2) I would take over as project manager with complete authority over all project-related matters, and (3) John would take over bank operations with complete authority over all non-project-related operational matters. By early the next morning, less than 24 hours after we'd arrived, John and I had developed a detailed plan and re-organized the entire 50-person project team. We all worked 20-

hour days, dealt with multiple uncooperative vendors, a flu epidemic, communications software bugs, an ice storm, and other unforeseen obstacles. We held 30-minute status meetings twice every day in our "war room" that focused exclusively on what we didn't accomplish that we wanted to since the last meeting and what we needed to do before the next meeting. One of the most important decisions we made was to defer several system capabilities into "Phase 2" to be addressed after the most urgent features were operational. For example, we decided that getting checking transactions to work on the ATMs was not a core function, so we placed signs on each ATM apologizing to customers for the inconvenience and explaining that checking transaction would need to be temporarily handled by a teller but other ATM transactions were fine. Since we had no clue whether or not the existing mainframe could handle the added volumes, I hedged our bet by ordering a second mainframe and negotiated a no-penalty cancellation clause. By establishing and adhering to priorities, we got the most critical system functions operational by the three-week deadline, and the bank retained market share. The entire team was exhausted, and the system we got up and running was clearly a bare-bones operation. It took us another three months to resolve outstanding issues and get the remaining system functionality operational. We did cancel the second mainframe. By the way, the three-week project timeline spanned Christmas and New Years, so we sacrificed the holidays with our families for this client, which I still regret even though it was one of my most intense and exhilarating consulting experiences.

I've been engaged to conduct other, similar turnaround efforts at insurance companies, health care providers and financial institutions. Most were not as bloody as the one described above, and none had such a short timeline, but each of those salvage projects was professionally rewarding for me and resulted in a highly satisfied client.

Keys to Success

Discussion thus far in this chapter has focused on mistakes to avoid and failed projects. To strike a more positive tone let's turn now to what can be done to improve the batting average for technology implementations. There are several tools and techniques that can help a project to succeed, and I've discussed many of them already in prior chapters. See especially Chapter 14 on Project Management. Of the various tools and techniques I've used, my experience is that the four most important ones are:

- **Team:** Assembling the right people is essential. This includes team members who know the relevant business process, the project methodology and the relevant technology. I don't require every team member to know all three topics, but everyone must be experienced in at least one. It takes courage to not accept a candidate whose primary qualification is availability. I always prefer a small team of experienced, knowledgeable veterans rather than a cast of thousands. One of the techniques I use to identify desirable team members (like Terri H., John M. and Gary G.) is the "who do you trust" method that I described in the Approach section of Chapter 11 on Assessments. I convinced one client to allow me to include only team members I wanted when I asked him, "Are you paying me to successfully complete the project or to run a day care center?" Knowledgeable team members provide valuable responses to simple questions like, "Will this work?" or "What might go wrong?"
- **Requirements:** A thorough and detailed definition of requirements is essential. See Chapter 15. I know that some of my colleagues who are proponents of Agile will disagree, but my experience is that requirements must be defined early and need to be referenced continuously throughout the remainder of the project. Requirements are methodology independent, and the team requires a smart, tenacious business analyst to get them properly defined. Waterfall, Agile and every other type of project will take

longer, cost more or fail outright unless solid requirements are defined at the beginning of the project.

- **Risk:** Don't wait for problems to occur. Look for risks every day, and when a risk is identified, figure out how to eliminate or mitigate it. Some examples:
    - Avoid "Big Bang" implementations. A Big Bang happens when a new system goes live with all features in all locations at the same time. A smarter play is to go live first at only one location, and then roll it out a few locations at a time, accelerating only when error rates begin to approach zero. This common sense approach was totally ignored by the team that launched HealthCare.gov in October 2013.
    - Pay attention to capacity constraints and scalability by identifying possible technical bottlenecks and choke points, and then employing proven techniques such as caching (keeping frequently used modules or data in active memory) to minimize those constraints. It surprises me how few projects pay attention to capacity issues.
    - Avoid single points of failure. If all transactions must pass through a single switch or router, then architect in a second device for redundancy.
    - Never schedule two changes at the same time. Make the first change; test it to ensure it works, and then make the second change.
- **Priorities:** In Chapter 14, I discussed high-level project priorities. In addition, the major system features should also be prioritized, and the project team should focus on the highest ones. It's surprisingly easy for team members to get side tracked into working on lower priority items, and they need to be continuously reminded of what the priorities are. This is commonly referred to as "herding the cats."

The above four success elements were particularly evident in a recent project. John H, a client executive in a financial services company, hired me to salvage an important initiative that had stopped making progress. The objective of the project was to implement technology tools and business processes to protect customers and meet regulatory requirements related to the capture, archive and supervision of electronic communications, such as email, text messages, instant messaging, etc. Scope included implementing package software and developing custom integration programs. The regulatory and technical issues made this a complex effort, and because of the numerous business functions affected, it was a political minefield. Our team included two brilliant BAs (business analysts), and one had implemented the predecessor system several years previously. Our BAs, together with the senior business user, meticulously defined 234 detail requirements and documented them in an Excel spreadsheet. The requirements spreadsheet was sorted, parsed, searched and referenced daily up until the final week of the project. The team aggressively identified risks, kept a running log of them, reported the status of risks weekly to John and our steering committee, and found creative ways to eliminate them. John was a stickler about focusing on priorities. During the first week after I was hired, John asked us to create a Top 10 list of critical project activities. After we developed the list, we then numbered them from 1 to 10 with 1 being the most important. Then during our next team meeting, John crossed off items 4 through 10 and told us that when we had completed 1 through 3, we'd create another Top 10 list and repeat the exercise. I really enjoy working with John H. The project was difficult, but thanks to the terrific team we assembled, our requirements spreadsheet, risk mitigation and continuous focus on priorities, we successfully completed the implementation on time and on budget.

My youngest son Rick, who is also a consultant, has a good story about one of his client organizations that chose to ignore scalability risks. Rick was the quality assurance lead for his client's largest system development project, and during his first week on the project, he raised the possibility that the system architecture might not support the expected several thousand concurrent Internet customer users. Rick was denied permission to conduct load testing to either verify or disprove the risk, and he therefore kept "scalability" on the risk log and raised the issue in every weekly status meeting throughout the remainder of the project. Each week, the overall project manager classified the risk as having no resolution and stated it was not to be addressed. Yikes! Finally, two weeks before the "go live" date, the team ran a test simulating about 250 users, consuming all the process threads, and they crashed the system. Rick showed enormous self-restraint by not saying, "I told you this might happen." He didn't have to because everyone knew he had kept scalability continuously on the risk log. The team was forced to push the launch date back several weeks while the entire system was re-architected. Ignoring the facts doesn't change the facts.

I always prefer a small team of individuals I trust. At one company, I accepted an assignment to lead a large re-engineering effort that affected the entire technology organization. I was given a team of individuals who were all complete strangers to me, and I therefore spent the first week getting to know them. With one exception, each appeared to have an appropriate role within the project based on their current and prior job responsibilities. Initially the exception, Mr. Jealous was a mystery to me. He was argumentative during meetings and refused to agree with any ideas he didn't author. Eventually other team members told me that he had requested to be given my position, but he was denied because the rest of the team had refused to work under him, and that's why I was hired. I decided to try charming him into being more cooperative while I figured out where he could add the most value. My efforts failed, and he continued to annoy everyone on the team, including me. After a month of frustration, I told my client, the project sponsor, I was going to release Mr. Jealous from the project. My client told me that Mr. Jealous had informed him several times that I was not doing a good job. My client wanted me to make peace and find an appropriate role for Mr. Jealous. I did try for another month, but during that time I had two other team members threaten to quit if they had to continue working with Mr. Jealous. I told my client that I had failed, that Mr. Jealous was undermining the effort and that I had no choice but to release him. My client informed me he had no other job for Mr. Jealous and I was stuck with him. My client's stand reminded me of Rule 9 from the Ten Pretty Good Rules, "Never have a philosophy which supports lack of courage." Mr. Jealous was damaging team morale, but I couldn't get rid of him. Therefore, I carved out a role for him that consisted of writing drafts of selected sections of our final report. I chose specific report sections that required no interactions with other team members, effectively isolating him. Before publishing our report, I heavily edited what Mr. Jealous produced, effectively rewriting most of it. It was a frustrating experience, and I did not accept further assignments from that particular client. Having the wrong people on a project team can make the effort significantly more difficult.

Here's another story to further emphasize the need to focus on those four success elements described above. A former client who had recently been hired as the IT director for a national health care provider was concerned because her new company's biggest I/T project appeared to be failing. She engaged me to do a two-week assessment, which when completed, confirmed her fears. We jointly presented the findings to the company's executive committee, and near the end of the presentation, the president asked me to assume project management responsibilities. I created a new plan and went to work assembling a new team. Initially I released all the prior project team members, who were a mix of internal and contract personnel, and informed them that they could each apply for a position on the new project. I rehired about half of the employees and none of the contractors, who frankly were all clueless about what we were doing and how it should be done. The new team wanted to start developing code, but I held them back because I wanted to have requirements thoroughly defined first. I hired a contractor BA, but she had no familiarity with the company, so my client, the IT director, volunteered to be a temporary BA and work alongside the contractor, and this approach worked extremely well. It was a bit strange because I reported to her as the project manager, and she reported to me as a BA on the project. Fortunately we both thought it was funny and didn't let our egos get in the way of getting the work done. Throughout the project I focused on risk management and communicating with users and the executive team. Despite an unavoidable project scope expansion because of the acquisition of another company, the team still achieved all our project goals and implemented the new system for each of the company's 30 locations on time and within budget.

Summary

Implementing technology systems is hard work. If it were easy, there wouldn't be such a high failure rate, and I wouldn't have had as many consulting opportunities as I've had. It should be noted that implementations are unique from other types of consulting projects because the team delivers a working product at the conclusion, while most other engagements only deliver a well-written document.

I've found that exclusive reliance on a new methodology or tool to make a project succeed is naive. Methodologies are clearly useful, but none of them is a silver bullet. The same is true for tools. I've met a number of project managers who believed that once their project plan was loaded into Microsoft Project, they could coast to the finish line. How silly.

I've also learned to trust my instincts. If a situation smells bad, it probably is bad. I cross check every project against Steve McConnell's Classic Mistakes list, and I always identify at least a couple of items from his list that need attention. The keys to success seem to always include assembling the right team, nailing down requirements, mitigating risks, and focusing on priorities. There are other useful techniques and tools as described in Chapter 14, but my experience indicates that those four are the most important.

Because implementation work isn't for the faint of heart, it makes a consultant more knowledgeable and more confident. Anecdotal evidence also suggests that when a consultant has successfully implemented technology systems, that consultant is better able to execute assessments, planning, architecture and most other types of consulting engagements.

Suggested Reading and References

Yourdon, Edward. *Techniques of Program Structure and Design.* Prentice-Hall, 1975

Humphrey, Watts. *Managing the Software Process.* Addison-Wesley, 1989

Yourdon, Edward. *Object-Oriented Systems Design.* Prentice Hall, 1994

McConnell, Steve. *Rapid Development.* Microsoft Press, 1996

Fellows of the Strategic Studies Group, Naval War College, Newport, Rhode Island, *Ten Pretty Good Rules*, 1982-83

Epilogue

As I mentioned in Chapter 1, there are many "how to" consulting books that are long on theory but short on specifics. My intention in writing this book was to provide something more useful: stories and examples of work products that other consultants will be able to apply to their own situations.

I've included various stories that describe how I created and used a variety of deliverables and solutions. I've also included several of the more useful charts, diagrams, tables and other work products that I've developed, refined, re-used myself, and shared with other consultants to help them help their clients.

Hopefully, you've found this book to be a simple, "See Spot Run" version of how to create and manage a small consulting practice.

I've truly enjoyed my consulting career. I've been able to learn about how a lot of businesses work, and I have found myself in many unexpected places learning interesting things. But the most rewarding aspect of being a consultant has been the opportunity to work with so many outstanding professionals, both clients as well as other consultants. I'm grateful to all of them for their wisdom and counsel. "I am still learning."

Dave Faulise

Bibliography

Brandt, Steven C. *Strategic Planning in Emerging Companies.* Addison-Wesley, 1981

Fellows of the Strategic Studies Group, Naval War College, Newport, Rhode Island, *Ten Pretty Good Rules*, 1982-83

Swedroe, Larry E. *The Only Guide To A Winning Investment Strategy You'll Ever Need.* Truman Talley Books/Dutton, 1998

Bogle, John C. *Common Sense on Mutual Funds*. John Wiley & Sons, Inc., 2010

Levitt, Theodore. *The Marketing Imagination.* The Free Press, 1983

High, Peter A. *World Class IT*. Jossey-Bass, 2009

Porter, Michael E. *Competitive Advantage: Creating and Sustaining Superior Performance*. New York: Free Press, 1985

Conner, Daryl R. *Managing at the Speed of Change*. Random House, 1992

Ross, Jeanne W.; Weill, Peter; Robertson, David C. *Enterprise Architecture As Strategy*. Harvard Business Press, 2006

Orr, Ken, *Structured Requirements Definition.* Ken Orr & Associates, Inc., 1981

Yourdon, Edward. *Techniques of Program Structure and Design.* Prentice-Hall, 1975

Humphrey, Watts. *Managing the Software Process.* Addison-Wesley, 1989

Yourdon, Edward. *Object-Oriented Systems Design.* Prentice Hall, 1994

McConnell, Steve. *Rapid Development*. Microsoft Press, 1996

www.ingramcontent.com/pod-product-compliance
Lightning Source LLC
Chambersburg PA
CBHW070239200326
41518CB00010B/1617

* 9 7 8 0 6 9 2 8 1 5 2 0 5 *